CHANGING PUBLIC/PRIVATE PARTNERSHIPS IN THE AFRICAN BOOK SECTOR

PERSPECTIVES ON AFRICAN BOOK DEVELOPMENT

Titles in the series

CHANGING PUBLIC/PRIVATE PARTNERSHIPS IN THE AFRICAN BOOK SECTOR

Paul Brickhill, Chris Chirwa, Bengt Lindahl

WORKING GROUP ON
BOOKS AND LEARNING MATERIALS
ASSOCIATION FOR THE DEVELOPMENT OF EDUCATION IN AFRICA

Published by the Working Group on Books and Learning Materials of the Association for the Development of Education in Africa (ADEA),
7-9 rue Eugène-Delacroix, 75016 Paris, France.

ISBN 92-9178-056-1

Distributed by ABC, African Books Collective Ltd.,
Unit 13 Kings Meadow, Ferry Hinksey Road, Oxford OX2 ODP.
Tel: +44.(0) 1865-726686
Fax: +44.(0) 1865-793298
Email: abc@africanbookscollective.com

DTP by Sub-Saharan Publishers
P.O. Box 358, Legon,
Accra, Ghana
Email: saharanp@africaonline.com.gh

Technical supervision: Sylvia Dorance
Pack 2 Agence éditoriale
Le Puy d'Auberge, 83560 La Verdière, France
Email: sylvia@pack2edition.com

Printed by Book Printing Services Ltd, Mauritius.

CONTENTS

ABBREVIATIONS

ADEA:	Association for the Development of Education in Africa
AFLAM:	Appui à la Filière du Livre [Mali]
APNET:	African Publishers Network
BAMVITA:	Tanzanian Book Development Council
BATA:	Booksellers' Association of Tanzania
BAZ:	Booksellers Association of Zimbabwe
BESSIP:	Basic Education Sub-Sector Investment Programme [Zambia]
BMU:	Book Management Unit [Tanzania]
BPAZ:	Booksellers and Publishers Association of Zambia
BSA:	Booksellers Association [Mauritius]
BSAT:	Booksellers Association of Tanzania
BSOA:	Booksellers and Stationery Owners Association [Mauritius]
CBP: .	Children's Book Project [Tanzania]
CDC:	Curriculum Development Center [Zambia]
CDU:	Curriculum Development Unit [Zimbabwe]
CEDA:	Center d'édition et distribution africaine [Côte d'Ivoire]
CIDA:	Canadian International Development Agency
CODE:	Canadian Organisation for Development through Education
CRDD:	Curriculum Research and Development Division [Ghana]
DBM:	Development Bank of Mauritius
DEO:	District Education Officer
DfID:	Department for International Development [United Kingdom]
DGIS:	Directorate General for International Co-operation [Netherlands]
DRC:	Democratic Republic of Congo
ECU:	Education Co-ordination Unit [Tanzania]
ELP:	Editions Le Printemps Limited [Mauritius]
EMAC:	Education Materials Approval Committee [Tanzania]
EMPDA:	Educational Materials Production and Distribution Agency [Ethiopia]
EMTC:	Educational Materials Technical Committee [Zambia]
EMU:	Educational Materials Unit [Zambia]
EOI:	Editions de l'Océan Indien [Mauritius]
FBLP:	Fundo Bibliografico da Lingua Portuguesa [Mozambique]

FPE:	Free Primary Education [Kenya]
GBDC:	Ghana Book Development Council
GBPA:	Ghana Book Publishers Association
GBS:	Ghana Book Supplies
GBSA:	Ghana Booksellers Association
GPC:	Ghana Publishing Corporation
ICB:	international competitive bidding
ICD:	Institute of Curriculum Development [Tanzania]
ICDR:	Institute of Curriculum Development and Research [Ethiopia]
IMU:	Instructional Materials Unit [Uganda]
INDE:	National Institute of Educational Development [Mozambique]
INLD:	National Institute for Books and Records (Instituto Nacional do Livro e do Disco) [Mozambique]
INRAP:	National Institute of Education (Institut Nationale de Recherche d'Action Pédagogique) [Guinea]
JKF:	Jomo Kenyatta Foundation [Kenya]
KIE:	Kenya Institute of Education
KKF:	Kenneth Kaunda Foundation [Zambia]
KLB:	Kenya Literature Bureau
KPA:	Kenya Publishers Association
KSES:	Kenya School Equipment Scheme
MEPSU:	Ministry of Education Procurement and Supplies Unit [Zambia]
MOEC:	Ministry of Education and Culture
MPA:	Mauritius Publishers Association
MRALG:	Ministry of Rural Administration and Local Government [Tanzania]
NABOTU:	National Book Trust of Uganda
NBA:	Nigerian Booksellers Association
NBF:	Nigerian Book Foundation
NCCRD:	National Curriculum Center for Research and Development [Mauritius]
NCDC:	National Curriculum Development Center [Uganda]
NEA:	Nouvelles Editions Africaines [Côte d'Ivoire, Senegal, Togo]
NEAS:	Nouvelles Editions Africaines du Sénégal
NEI:	Nouvelles Éditions Ivoiriennes [Côte d'Ivoire]
NGO:	Non-Governmental Organisation
NPA:	national publishers' association
OUP:	Oxford University Press
PABA:	Pan-African Booksellers Association
PASA:	Publishers' Association of South Africa
PATA:	Publishers' Association of Tanzania
PEDP:	Primary Education Development Plan [Tanzania]
PO-RALG:	President's Office – Regional Administration and Local Government [Tanzania]
PPP:	Pilot Project for Publishing [Tanzania]
PTA:	Parent–Teachers' Association

SALIBA:	Salon du Livre de Bamako (Bamako Book Fair) [Mali]
Sida:	Swedish International Development Agency
TEPUSA:	Network of Technical Publications in Africa [Tanzania]
TES:	Tanzania Elimu Supplies
TIE:	Tanzania Institute of Education
TPH:	Tanzania Publishing House
UNDP:	United Nations Development Programme
UNESCO:	United Nations Educational, Scientific and Cultural Organisation
UNICEF:	United Nations Children's Fund
UPABA:	Ugandan Publishers and Booksellers Association
USAID:	United States Agency for International Development
UWAVITA:	Tanzania Writers Association
WAEC:	West African Examination Council
ZBPA:	Zimbabwe Book Publishers Association
ZEMP:	Zambian Educational Materials Project
ZEPH:	Zambia Educational Publishing House
ZIBF:	Zimbabwe International Book Fair

EXECUTIVE SUMMARY

The majority of African countries embarked on state monopoly publishing of textbooks for schools in the early years after Independence. In consequence,   local commercial publishers and booksellers were excluded from the most lucrative part of the book sector in Africa – the school market. The absence of competition in state publishing monopoly led to inefficiency, low quality, pedagogical stagnation and, in some cases, corruption.

However, during the 1990s there has been a decisive shift towards greater liberalisation of textbook provision. New partnerships between the state and the local private sector in book publishing for primary level have been emerging, but the differentiation of roles and responsibilities between the Ministry of Education and the private sector varies enormously. Textbook liberalisation appears to be the most advanced among the Anglophone countries in this study, in relation to the withdrawal of the state from textbook publishing, the establishment of textbook approval mechanisms and the development of strong national publishers' associations.

This study shows that interaction at all levels between ministry officials and the commercial book sector is growing, and differences in attitudes are narrowing, despite tensions arising at every stage of liberalisation. However, decentralised procurement continues to be problematic in that it places new demands on Ministries of Education in terms of financial planning, management and accountability.

The study concludes that a triangular relationship, taking in government, development agencies and the private sector can be the basis for the balancing of interests that is needed to overcome the distortions that can undermine diversity of textbook supply and choice for the consumer. One of the major findings is that multiple textbook systems, founded on Ministry of Education textbook approval mechanisms, can be pivotal in achieving an appropriate balance of interests in textbook provision. Multiple textbook systems lead naturally to decentralised selection, thereby providing the basis for the engagement of booksellers in the supply chain.

The study identifies the key challenge in emerging public/private partnerships in textbook provision as being how to increase the capacity, resources and diversity of the private sector in such a way that schools are the direct and long term beneficiary. The conclusion is that the correct balancing of these interests should be seen as the basis for an effective public/private partnership.

INTRODUCTION

This study, commissioned by the ADEA Working Group on Books and Learning Materials updates their earlier study, *The Economics of Publishing Educational Materials in Africa*. (Bgoya *et al.*, 1997). However, it also incorporates new research and perspectives on the emergence of public–private sector relations and the increasing engagement of the local private sector in African textbook provision.

The study is not intended to be a descriptive overview but is an analytical study to identify problems, contradictions and key issues. The aim is to stimulate and provoke discussion, and to explore diverse interpretations, innovation and opposing perspectives. It is not the intention of the authors to provide modules, checklists and 'blueprints' for Ministry of Education officials and book-industry leaders: that task has been admirably accomplished in many other textbook-provision manuals.

The data for this study came from field research in Ethiopia, Ghana, Guinea, Mali, Mauritius, Mozambique, Nigeria, Senegal, Tanzania, Uganda, Zambia and Zimbabwe. Information collected on Kenya by Janet Njoroge was incorporated in the country reports. A large amount of data was collected from published and unpublished literature, details of which can be found in the bibliography. The study is presented in two sections:

An eight-chapter review:
1. The State and Textbook Provision
2. The Liberalisation of Textbook Provision
3. The Emergence of the Indigenous Commercial Sector
4. The role of the Ministry in a liberalised system
5. Some African challenges in Liberalised systems
6. An example of liberalisation: The case of Tanzania
7. National book policy in Africa
8. Conclusion

Country Studies

A Country Report for each of the thirteen countries listed above. The country reports do not follow a uniform format, since the issues and priorities discussed differ widely.

Definitions have proved difficult. 'Public/private partnership' is a broad term, conceivably covering every aspect of textbook provision from language and curriculum to publishing, printing and distribution – indeed, the entire book chain. Definition of words has also proved a problem. Terms such as 'liberalisation', 'privatisation', 'commercial', and 'free-market', on the one hand, and 'state monopoly', 'centralised', and 'state-owned', on the other, can be vague and frequently interchangeable.

In this study, the term 'liberalisation' is used to refer to a broad transformation away from state-monopoly textbook-procurement systems and also to the specific liberalisation of single-textbook, state-publishing models. The term 'decentralisation' is used to refer specifically to the devolution of centralised authority over procurement (selection, ordering, payment) and distribution (consolidation, delivery) of books, usually combined with single-textbook monopoly approaches, towards a multi-textbook system in which schools and/or districts have responsibility for procurement decisions and in which booksellers, or other commercial partners, have responsibility for supply. Decentralised procurement is commonly combined with a multi-textbook system in which there is no single-textbook monopoly and the consumer (school and/or district) has a choice from several textbooks.

Box 1: Liberalisation and Decentralisation

LIBERALISATION = Broad transformation away from state monopoly, single textbook publishing.

DECENTRALISATION = Local procurement and distribution, typically through booksellers.

The names and acronyms of the ministries responsible for education are not always the same in the different countries studied. For ease of use, they are referred to generally throughout the text simply as the 'Ministry of Education'.

Attempts to categorize countries and systems by 'type', or as sharing certain characteristics, are not a feature of this study: the circumstances, history and problems of African book industries and textbook systems are too diverse. However, we recognize that there are currently four broad, overlapping, approaches to textbook provision (see box 2).

Box 2: Four overlapping approaches to textbook provision

- Moving from state monopoly, centralised provision to a variety of liberalised, market=based decentralised systems (eg Kenya, Uganda, Tanzania, Zambia).

- Long term, liberalised, free market provision (eg Nigeria, Zimbabwe).

- Countries with background of centralised socialist state ownership (eg Ethiopia, Mozambique).

- Francophone countries moving from dependence on imported books from France to using curriculum institutes for developing manuscripts, often printed and published in France(eg Guinea, Mali, Senegal).

The role of multinational publishers in African textbook markets cannot be avoided in a study on relations between government and the private sector. The historical dominance of multinationals over African textbook supply has influenced every aspect of policy towards the provision of school books in Africa.

Much of the study is focused towards emerging 'public/private partnerships' between ministries of education and local, indigenous publishing and bookselling companies. The emergence of African book enterprises, owned and managed by African nationals, and their efforts to gain a foothold in textbook markets form a pivotal trend in much of Africa.

Given the pervasive extent of state textbook provision in Africa, and the weakness of the local private sector, attention is directed towards the different ways in which a commercial book sector, at a formative stage in most of Africa, has come about under different and frequently contradictory conditions. Many examples are provided, often with some historical references, illustrating the diversity of issues.

Box 3: Towards greater liberalisation of choice

- Movement away from a single textbook (per grade, per subject) system

- towards a multi-textbook system

- with some degree of competition among commercial publishers and consumer choice.

Accurate, up-to-date information relating to the size, turnover, output, staff, financing and even the number of companies active in African book industries is critically weak. A perusal of UNESCO statistical yearbooks relating to publishing will attest to this.

The study concerns itself largely with provision of core primary school and other basic-education textbooks. Secondary, tertiary and vocational education in much of Africa has a large component of imported books, involving many different factors. It is, potentially, the subject of a separate study.

Special thanks are due to the African booksellers, publishers and education officials who gave freely of their time and expertise. In large measure, their perspective, founded in day-to-day problems in building an African book industry to provide textbooks to schools, is the core of this work.

BACKGROUND: THE STATE AND TEXTBOOK PROVISION

Public/private partnership in African textbook provision is an emerging process that began to take shape in much of Africa from the 1990s. With few exceptions, provision of textbooks, especially at primary school level, has been undertaken through overwhelming centralised state intervention in authorship, publishing, printing and distribution, leading to a state monopoly in most African countries. A liberalisation of textbook provision, allowing space for commercial participation and therefore for a new vision of public/private partnership, is taking place. This study concerns the problems and complexities of this transition, its successes and setbacks, and the many new issues it has thrown up, for this is the reality of 'public/private partnership' in African textbooks.

It is not our intention to delve into a detailed history of state textbook systems. Throughout the text there are many references to the previous 'state' era since the pervasive legacy of state-monopoly determines today's transitional phase towards public/private partnership. In this chapter, we consider just a few salient aspects in state textbook provision that are a necessary background to the chapters that follow, and we investigate the only two cases in this study where state monopoly has been entirely absent – Nigeria and Zimbabwe.

The decision to embark on state-monopoly textbook publishing was most frequently taken against a background of dependence on imported books in the early years of the country's independence. Missionary presses aside, local publishing barely existed in most African countries at the time when decisions were reached to impose a state monopoly over textbook production. Countries such as Mozambique, Sierra Leone, Ghana, Zambia, Tanzania, Guinea, Senegal, Mali, Mauritius and Uganda were either massively dependent on book imports or on the local agencies of multinational publishers.

The government-monopoly systems were initially established to fulfil the textbook needs of the rapidly expanding education systems of Africa's young nations. For new governments with many urgent issues to tackle, the single textbook per subject/grade was a rational way of providing subject matter for the education system. The single-state-textbook system was also a way of providing a common ideological platform, of unifying the new nation. For developing countries with an active social agenda in the 1960s and 1970s it was natural to see the state as provider of books.

The essential feature of all state-controlled systems was monopoly over textbook development, production and distribution. Centralised state textbook systems have generally taken two different forms, frequently in combination (see box 4).

Box 4: Two forms of centralised state textbook systems

• Cooperation with one or more multi-national publishers to supply textbooks.

• Ministry of Education and national curriculum institute, responsible for development, production and distribution (often with government printers and parastatal organisations).

The common element in both forms of state textbook-provision systems lies in their monopolistic approach – both in sources of supply and in pedagogical and ideological content. However, state systems have also usurped the dominant position of multinationals (especially as regards the importation of books) in Mauritius, Ghana, Zambia, Tanzania and Kenya (after 1985) through the creation of state-monopoly textbook-publishing and -procurement parastatals.

Much of Africa today is moving towards a market economy, and in this context the monopoly textbook system is seen as an anomaly. Governments are also realising that the absence of competition in the monopoly has led to inefficiency, low quality, pedagogical stagnation, and often corruption. Moreover, African publishers and booksellers have themselves created many new autonomous, private-sector enterprises, and in doing so have created a voice and platform for alternatives to state monopoly. The fact that the monopoly systems have excluded local commercial publishers and booksellers from the school market, the only lucrative book market in Africa, previously prevented the growth of a vital domestic publishing industry and a functioning distribution network for books.

Apart from the absence of local capacity, there is a further factor to consider. The adoption of state-monopoly textbook provision in Africa was not based solely on the need to rectify, and replace, dependence on book imports, but also on a political culture that saw a need for the state to exercise control over an important aspect of national development. In Kenya, for example, multinationals were dominant in the supply of books and publishing in the years following independence, but there was a significant development in local commercial capacity: multinationals localised their operations. A few small publishing firms had also been started by enterprising employees of multinationals (so often the case throughout Africa), but Kenya imposed a state-publishing system in primary education in 1985 despite significant local commercial capacity. Zimbabwe nearly took the same path at around the same time, soon after its independence, after the government had purchased the major bookselling chain in the country. Even in South Africa, the most developed private book sector in Africa, proposals in education circles to adopt a state-publishing system, with a fundamentally political rationale, were fended off as recently as 1998.

In education circles, a deep mistrust had developed of local commercial publishing, which in so many ways represents diversity – the opposite of control through monopoly. As a result, emergent indigenous publishers were considerably marginalized by a confluence of state-monopoly and multinational publishing – each representing an alternative perspective of monopoly in textbook provision but, at times, working in direct collaboration.

'Competitive' international tenders – which grew dramatically in World Bank-supported textbook programmes after the mid-1980s, and may superficially have appeared to be a form of 'liberalisation' – did not change the basic character of this state monopoly. Nor did they fundamentally alter the nature of the partnership between the state monopoly and the small number of multinationals active in African textbook provision. In numerous cases where African governments, dependent on external financial resources, have procured textbooks by international tender, typically under World Bank lending procedures, multinational publishers have been the *de facto* partner/supplier in single-title per grade/subject centralised textbook provision. Virtually every African country provides numerous examples, and this is currently the situation in much of francophone Africa.

Multinational publishers have had a massive impact on every aspect of textbook provision in Africa, since at independence every African country except South Africa depended on imported books for its education system. We shall return to this theme throughout the text, but it is important to recognize from the start the essential difference between dependence on imports from overseas multinationals, exemplified throughout francophone Africa, and the many instances where multinationals have established, and invested in, African subsidiaries to produce African textbooks in Africa.

The question of multinational versus indigenous interests in textbook publishing is patently not the same as that of imported books versus local production. There are benefits to be gained through the localisation of multinationals that are not at all evident when the same multinational elects to simply export its books. The point may be put another way: most localised multinationals are members of the national publishers' association, and in many respects their immediate concerns *vis à vis* textbook publishing are identical to those of indigenous commercial interests. With reference to their international experience they may be able to introduce standards for the book trade and to argue with the government on behalf of the industry with more authority than newly established local publishers, e.g. over policy issues. On the other hand, foreign ownership does mean that major decisions related to investment in and the development of books are taken outside the country, and against a background of remittance of bottom-line profit.

Nigeria and Zimbabwe: Exceptions to state textbook publishing

Zimbabwe and Nigeria have had fully liberalised textbook systems in place throughout, and their experiences, in widely contrasting environments, highlight the challenges and opportunities provided by local private-sector publishing.

From the viewpoint of continuity, Nigeria and Zimbabwe stand out as comparable case studies where (albeit under the considerable influence of multinationals at independence) textbook provision has remained a private-sector activity. The state has not sought any direct role in textbook publishing, and neither have these countries adopted any written textbook policy. Both countries have pursued a multi-textbook per subject/grade strategy that has allowed both for continuity and for the emergence and development of a commercial book market, even within the constraints of developing African economies. In Nigeria, in contrast to Zimbabwe, there is a far greater element of parental financing of textbooks, but in both cases textbooks are selected by the consumer (schools and other educational institutions) from a wide choice – sometimes as many as six or seven prescribed texts.

By way of caution, we must note the vast differences in scale. Nigeria has well over a hundred daily newspapers (Zimbabwe has two or three) and dozens of television stations (Zimbabwe, one). Nigeria's population is around 120 million, Zimbabwe's is around 12 million. Nigeria is a massive book market in African terms – over 60,000 educational institutions of all kinds with an estimated enrolment of 30 million. In such a large, diverse, multi-ethnic (250 language groups) and densely populated country, the magnitude of the task involved in producing sufficient books, and the myriad problems of book distribution, are almost unique in Africa. Nigeria's federal structure is quite different from Zimbabwe's unified state structure, and has allowed for slightly different textbook-provision systems in its thirty-six states. Anecdotally, we may also note the relatively lower input of foreign aid into the book sector in Nigeria, as compared to the generous aid that poured into Zimbabwe in the decade following independence and that provided significant capital for development and scholarly publishing.

Both countries have a history of direct involvement by British publishers prior to independence that shaped textbook-provision policies. In both cases post-independence growth in enrolments in education provided the impetus for foreign investment in textbook publishing. Multinationals rapidly localised and invested in local publishing operations after independence, in tandem with a localisation of the curriculum, providing for stability, transfer of skills, and development of local authorship, with substantial benefits for their book industries over the first decade of independence.

However, in contrast to Zimbabwe, Nigeria in 1977 introduced its 'indigenization policy', and all foreign publishing companies were forced to relinquish 60% of their equity to Nigerian interests. In Zimbabwe, there has been no corresponding policy, and the market share (around 70%–75%) of the two major British publishers active in Zimbabwe has been maintained, while the proportion of foreign investment has actually increased.

The Fourth National Development Plan (1981–1985) in Nigeria stipulated 100% local production of all textbooks at primary and secondary level and 50% at tertiary levels. Such levels of production remain a massive undertaking for key providers – writers, publishers, printers and booksellers. Nigeria's pursuit of solutions to the problems of book scarcity could be considered the genesis of public/private partnership in the book sector.

A series of major conventions have followed – with the active, vocal participation of the commercial book sector, writers, educationists and government stakeholders – which sought to review and recommend policies towards the fulfilment of book needs. There have been differences of opinion between commercial interests and state and federal decision-makers – for example, over some methods of supply and tender (particularly where international tenders marginalized local publishers), over taxes and allegations of corruption. But the main divergence has emerged over the perceived failure of federal authorities to accord the book industry 'strategic national industry' status with an integrated, national book policy. On the whole, however, there has been extensive dialogue, mutual sharing of perspectives, and – in principle – a common determination that Nigeria's book needs require Nigerian solutions, on the basis of public–private consensus, in which all textbooks are commercially published.

Fundamentally, the same can be said of Zimbabwe. A five-fold increase in school enrolment within the first five years of independence provided the springboard for public/private partnership and, in common with Nigeria, a search for innovative, home-grown solutions in which the commercial sector was integral. In Zimbabwe's case, a Ministry of Education and Culture directive in the mid-1980s stipulated that all books imported in quantities of 1000 would henceforth be required to be published locally, as this threshold was a viable print-run. The result, within two years, was that all previously imported secondary school books were licensed from British publishers and printed locally. With a number of other mutually agreed policy decisions adapted to Zimbabwean needs, Zimbabwe was by 1990 self-sufficient in 95% of primary school books and in secondary school books to Form IV level. In Nigeria all primary school books and 80% of secondary school books are locally authored and published. In both countries, textbooks comprise about 90% of formal-sector publishing output.

In Zimbabwe's case, and without precedence in Africa, the bedrock of its textbook-provision policies has been the role of its booksellers. Shortly after independence, the Ministry of Education and Culture and trade associations concluded an agreement stipulating that all textbooks would be ordered from strictly-registered booksellers, without exception, that booksellers would deliver to districts and schools free of charge, and that retail prices would be standardized nationally. Within a few years, every town had a conventional bookseller, close to educational consumers in rural districts, and the terms of trade (credit facilities, discounts and deliveries) between publishers and booksellers became highly efficient.

In Nigeria, there was no equivalent arrangement. During the Second Republic (1979–1983) the five populous southern states purchased books at bulk discount directly from publishers, setting a ruinous precedent of excluding booksellers. Many publishers have continued to supply educational institutions directly at discounted prices (at the same or a lower price than that offered to booksellers), through a network of local agents in the case of the larger publishers, and they provide little or no credit to many booksellers. Spirited efforts by the Nigerian Booksellers' Association since 1997 have revitalized bookselling somewhat, and a new generation of noticeably professional and enterprising booksellers has developed in the past five to ten years.

On the other hand, Nigeria has developed the most sophisticated network of street-vendor, market-stall booksellers in Africa, so much so that this informal sector has given rise to a market in cheap, popular reading materials and has also pioneered cross-border trade in books – for example, into Ghana. On the down side, given the problems of regulating a large informal sector, Nigeria has been plagued by problems of piracy. The Nigerian Publishers' Association claims that between 30% and 40% of its textbook market is lost on account of piracy, an astounding figure.

As a norm, NGO and 'professional' activity in books develops at a faster rate against a background of commercial activity in publishing and bookselling. Such is the case in Nigeria and Zimbabwe. The Zimbabwe International Book Fair (ZIBF), Africa's book showcase, was an initiative of professionals within the commercial book sector, critically from 1991 when the Ministry of Information relinquished control to an independent trust. The cumulative benefits to book industry development have been immense. Founded in 1991, the Nigerian Book Foundation is an umbrella organisation bringing together all sectors of the book industry and government representatives in education and culture. It is among the most effective and innovative book-promotion bodies in Africa and has a distinguished record. Nigeria and Zimbabwe each have active writers' associations, representing 'established', 'budding' and women writers, and textbook and national-language writers, for example, providing training and dialogue to promote authorship. Although book and reading campaigns in both countries are sometimes criticized as 'unco-ordinated and sporadic', the fact remains that dozens of book-related NGOs and professional associations are active, in stark contrast to those countries where state-monopoly textbook publishing has been imposed, stifling private initiative even in the NGO sector.

The issue of free textbooks

State monopoly systems have usually been based on a single textbook per grade and subject, produced and distributed by the state for free to schools. 'Free textbooks' is the *de facto* policy of many multilateral and bilateral funding agencies. Their principal concern, shared by education ministries, is inequity in the provision of education as a result of rural poverty in many parts of Africa. It is an understandable predicament. As we have noted elsewhere, poverty itself lies at the epicentre of the many problems in developing national book industries in Africa. Yet free textbooks pose a major dilemma for the industry.

In countries that adopted complete state-monopoly textbook provision, funded by international partners (Zambia, Tanzania,

Ethiopia and Ghana being the prime examples), free textbooks provided over decades entrenched attitudes and systems. It has been very noticeable in all these countries that schools, parents and communities developed a passive attitude towards textbook provision, even when faced with dire shortages. There was neither encouragement nor incentive for schools (except private schools) or parents to consider purchasing any textbooks.

Many studies have shown that schools would wait patiently for months, even years, for books to be provided. In Tanzania, schools developed a pervasive attitude of storing any new textbooks in order to keep them in perfect condition, away from the classrooms. It never occurred to them that textbooks could be bought – and for all practical purposes they could not be bought: they were state property and not for resale. This situation still exists in Ethiopia (for state textbooks), as it did for many years in Tanzania, Zambia and Ghana.

Despite this, state textbooks began appearing in the markets in Tanzania, since there were always a few parents who were concerned that their children had very few or no textbooks, and the government could not finance a textbook–pupil ratio of 1:2. A similar pattern has been reported in Mali, and this has been a fairly common occurrence throughout Africa.

Even where state publishing has been partially liberalised, the free-textbook policies of funding agencies, in their response to poverty and inequality, is often combined with international or local competitive bidding and central procurement. The logic seems to be presented thus: if books are to be free, they must be purchased by the state and sent to the recipient schools, also for free. The adverse consequences of the free-textbook syndrome – inadequate awareness about books or any notion of developing a book-buying culture – have largely been ignored. Alternatives to the central purchase of books, such as the Zimbabwe and Kenya models, have also mostly been ignored.

Zimbabwe got around 'free textbooks', as Kenya has done after 1998, by providing 'per capita' finance to districts and/or schools so that the money was in or close to the hands of the consumer, even where the funds were provided through the state – the prerequisite for this, of course, being decentralised procurement through a network of commercial booksellers and the related financing systems. Their textbook provision was structured such that booksellers were incorporated into the ordering system. In Zimbabwe, the process has deepened considerably in that schools retain school fees in their own bank account. School Development Committees oversee the use of the funds, and it is the ministry's policy that these committees develop strategies for parental contributions towards school textbook purchases, through, for example, levies. Interestingly, in the early 1990s, Zimbabwe failed to reach agreement with the World Bank over aid to textbook provision precisely because the procurement regulations and policies of the Bank could not encompass the Zimbabwe model.

Thus while free-textbook policies could embrace the liberalisation of state textbook publishing (because central procurement was involved), they could not sit side by side with decentralised procurement systems. Uganda's novel decision to decentralise selection while maintaining central purchase is a direct outcome of the dilemma. Ghana will adopt a variation on the Uganda model, selection by schools with some form of central purchase, as Tanzania has done in its liberalisation model and as is the current practice in Botswana.

Textbooks as a procurement issue

It is not unusual for educationists and funding agencies, even in the context of national policy, to see textbooks almost exclusively as a procurement issue – getting books into classrooms – typically in project terms. From this standpoint, many state-monopoly textbook-provision systems received considerable support, in an effort to boost falling supply, long after it had become apparent that the state-monopoly system was not able to respond to the need for diversity and growth in textbook provision.

The Zambian Educational Materials Project (ZEMP) from 1986 underlines this point. From 1966 to the beginning of the liberalisation phase in 1991, the government established a monopoly over textbook writing through the Curriculum Development Center (CDC) and over publishing and distribution through the Kenneth Kaunda Foundation (KKF) and its subsidiary companies. After initial successes through the mid-1970s, a relatively buoyant period of Zambia's economy, textbook provision began a downward spiral. KKF and its subsidiaries, with the sole mandate for publishing and distributing all textbooks, consistently failed to meet Zambia's textbook needs. The commercial sector had been considerably weakened without any central role in textbooks. The multinational and most local commercial publishers and booksellers had ceased operation.

The response of the education ministry and funding agencies, through ZEMP, was to rehabilitate textbook provision by investing in material and technical assistance through KKF (renamed Zambia Educational Publishing House, ZEPH, in 1991) and CDC, and providing free textbooks to schools. In effect, the problem was not approached in recognition that the book chain could not function because the state monopoly itself was at fault, but rather in the belief that a lack of financial and technical capacity was hindering the 'procurement' of textbooks through the existing state system, a common feature during the era of state textbook provision in Africa.

Large investments into the system ameliorated textbook scarcity for a time, but dependency on external aid increased, and the core problem – the inefficiency of state publishing – was not tackled. The alternative of a role for the commercial sector was not even considered until 1991, when a policy of liberalisation was announced by a new government, and as a result a few new indigenous publishers emerged and multinational publishers returned to Zambia.[1]

The reality of developing a commercial book infrastructure, with the capital and technical means to engage in long-term textbook-publishing programmes, can hardly be envisaged in 'project' terms. Yet there is not a single country in this study – with the partial exception of Zimbabwe between 1980 and 1995 and Nigeria – that has not experienced textbook provision being approached, conceptually, as a series of funded projects in textbook procurement. Since the education ministry is essentially a consumer of textbooks, and since funding agencies are financing this consumption to a considerable degree, it is natural that they should see textbook provision as a series of procurement exercises.

For the commercial sector, however, success in textbook provision depends on the holistic development of 'standards and conventions' that, in effect, regulate trade and private business investment and competition throughout the book industry. The commercial sector approaches the same problem from the perspective of a 'book chain', meaning a system of linkages from authorship through production to marketing that underpins the development of profitable business.

Thus, the procurement of textbooks, including issues of quality and relevance, is an educational issue, but developing commercial book industries and infrastructure is an industrial issue, since books are like any other manufactured commodities. One may liken this to the 'downstream, supply-driven' component of the industry – procurement, distribution, consumption (the direct concerns of educational system) – and its 'upstream, demand-driven' component – capital investment, technical inputs and skills, production and marketing (the direct concerns of commercial book industry).

These issues of procurement and allowing pupils access to 'free' textbooks have often remained unresolved in governments' attempts to liberalise textbook provision in Africa. As a result, contradictory, anomalous situations frequently occur in which 'hangovers' from monopolistic state systems exist within apparently liberalised systems. These will be discussed in the next chapters that look more closely at the involvement of the private sector in textbook provision and its relations with the state.

Chapter 2

THE LIBERALISATION OF TEXTBOOK PROVISION

Decades of centralised state textbook provision are giving way to a liberalisation of textbook authorship and publishing and a decentralisation of procurement, incorporating a locally based private sector and sections of society (regions and districts, language groups, communities, schools, parents) outside the central state bureaucracy. Liberalisation has led to a huge diversity of home-grown textbook-provision solutions, and has required the active, local participation of commercial publishing and, at a later stage, bookselling. This, in turn, has given a major impetus to the emergence of indigenous publishing and the localisation of multinationals through joint ventures or subsidiaries. Thus, liberalisation of textbook provision, decentralisation of procurement, selection and purchase, and the emergence of indigenous and local commercial publishing are the major features of African book development in the current era.

This new reality provides the framework for a new public/private partnership in the African book sector. It is distinct from old forms of dependence on multinational publishers in that it involves strategic partnerships between the state and locally based publishers, which is typically followed by decentralisation in the procurement process. The differentiation of roles and responsibilities between the state and, in many cases, a new generation of commercial publishers and booksellers has become a critical process all over Africa. It is an incomplete process and cannot be said to have 'matured' at this stage; there are some common general features in this process, but no universal agreement about the specific characteristics of the new roles of the private and public sectors. One strikingly common feature, however, is that the Ministry of Education is the effective authority over the *modus operandi* of the emerging public/private partnerships.

In broad terms, the liberalisation of state textbook systems away from monopoly approaches has developed in three ways (see box 5). There are many variants of these general principles, but an understanding of the overall pattern in the break-up of state monopoly systems is important.

The liberalisation process, which has involved changing the entire network of economic relations by which textbooks are provided, has proved far more problematic than was expected. Complex issues arise because of two factors: the initial weakness of commercial systems that could not develop 'organically' because state textbook provision had negated their growth, and the need for textbooks to continue to be produced and distributed throughout a period of transition, which takes years to complete.

The permutations in public–private relations, with fragile, new and untried government policies subject to influences from new funding arrangements and new ministry appointees, and a mass of undeveloped book-industry systems have at times suggested an impenetrable tangle because of the *ad hoc* nature of decisions. Systems in place are reversed or not allowed to develop because procurement takes precedence over the development of the book chain and the commercial interests inherent in it.

With few exceptions, the idea of a partnership between the state and the local private sector in the publishing and distribution of primary school textbooks has taken shape within a little over a decade after 1990. The pace of change has been dramatic and the shift of emphasis throughout the continent towards public/private partnership is considerable.

The focus has been on the large primary school markets, where textbooks are financed by the government. Secondary education, although not insignificant in terms of overall volumes, presents a complex patchwork of supply in comparison: there is greater diversity, and private education and parental purchases have a significant influence. Textbooks are often imported, and far more titles are purchased in smaller quantities from many publishers and, increasingly, from different countries. There has been considerably less government activity in secondary-level textbook publishing, although the large-scale centralised importation of secondary school books has featured in donor-funded programmes.

Liberalisation of textbook publishing since 1990

Among the anglophone countries, Tanzania took the decision to open the primary school market to commercial publishing in 1991, as did Zambia, although the direction of Zambia's textbook liberalisation drive was not fully articulated until a policy statement was issued in May 1996. Uganda adopted a competitive system involving private publishers, and decentralised the selection of textbooks to schools from 1993/94. Kenya's textbook liberalisation emerged virtually fully functional in 1998, thirteen years after the state monopoly had been established, with a strong sense of partnership between the responsible ministry and a vibrant local commercial book sector. Ghana's wide-ranging basic-education textbook liberalisation policy was adopted in 2002, four years after its formulation had started, on the basis of extensive consultations spanning almost a decade.

The former socialist-orientated countries, where state ownership of the economy has been dominant, have also moved cautiously towards liberalisation. Mozambique, totally dependent on book imports at independence, followed a socialist-orientated development model, with centralised state textbook provision. Ethiopia adopted a similar pattern, based on the public ownership of major economic sectors after the change of government in 1974, although there had been a prior history of state involvement in textbook publishing dating back to 1957.[2] Mozambique began to consider its options in 1997 in the context of the privatisation of its state-run economy. By 2001 a new policy encompassing liberalisation was in place, due for implementation from 2003/04. Ethiopia had a draft textbook-liberalisation policy in 1998, but had given initial priority to the devolution of the language of instruction towards the eleven major local languages and the strengthening of regional identity.

The francophone countries are also following the liberalisation route. Mauritius, Senegal, Guinea and Mali imported all their primary school books from France until in each case the Ministry of Education's curriculum institute took over the preparation of all textbook manuscripts in a single-title system – Mauritius, 1977, Senegal, 1987, Guinea, 1989, and Mali, 1995. The use of external printing services often continued, however, and in Senegal, for example, all textbooks from the 6th Grade are still imported from France. In Mauritius, a haven of free-market enterprise in the printing sector, the curriculum institute centrally prepares and publishes core primary texts in a single-textbook system. Printing is generally put out to tender, and two main publishers (one parastatal and one private) compete over rights for reprints for the open market.

Liberalisation in these countries is taking the form of international competitive bidding (ICB) tenders for existing state-owned texts, and does not necessarily involve the full participation of the local commercial sector, which finds it extremely difficult to compete with multinationals under ICB rules. However, there are signs that a more vigorous local commercial sector is beginning to compete with French publishers, particularly over local-language books. Mauritius adopted limited liberalisation of primary school textbook provision in 1994, which essentially involved issuing tenders for prepared state texts. Guinea involved private publishers (through ICB tenders) and booksellers in textbook provision from the early 1990s, but then strengthened centralised procurement in 1997 under a World Bank-funded programme, removing the role of booksellers. A textbook policy under consideration will pilot-test the first competitive multi-title system in coming years. The government of Mali transferred the publishing rights of its state primary school textbooks to four local publishers in 2001 as part of a long-term textbook-liberalisation plan. In Senegal, the government decided in 2002 that private publishers would develop and publish local-language books for the new curriculum in a pilot phase, but only through ICB arrangements.

Box 6: The state and foreign multinationals in Francophone Africa

Publishing in Côte d'Ivoire provides an excellent example of the extent of foreign multinational partnerships in centralised state-textbook systems in francophone Africa. At independence in 1960, the government of Côte d'Ivoire created the Center d'édition et distribution africaine (CEDA) in partnership with a French private company, primarily to sell and distribute books from France. In 1972 the government joined those of Senegal and Togo to create Nouvelles éditions africaines (NEA), in which the governments were the majority shareholders and a consortium of French publishers the other shareholders. By the 1980s, both CEDA and NEA were actively publishing (as opposed to merely importing from France). In 1982 the two companies assumed a monopoly over the publishing of school textbooks, in agreement with the Côte d'Ivoire government. Until 1994, when the CFA franc lost half its value, almost all the textbooks published were nevertheless still printed in France.

In 1992 the government divested itself of majority ownership in NEA, and a new publisher was created in the process, Nouvelles éditions ivoiriennes (NEI), with the French publisher Hachette as the majority shareholder. In 1996 the government sold 31% of its equity in CEDA to the public, so that the company emerged with a shareholding of 40% (French publisher), 9% (Canadian publisher), 20% (government) and 31% (public), effectively making the French and Canadian interests the major shareholders in a textbook monopoly. While the Côte d'Ivoire case is somewhat special, its principal feature – partnership between the state and French commercial interests in a textbook monopoly – resonates in various forms throughout the francophone region.

In Cameroon, a private monopoly has emerged. In 1998, the Ministry of Education, in agreement with l'Agence de la Francophonie (which provided substantial subsidies), granted a monopoly over the publishing and distribution of primary school books to a newly privatised parastatal company run by the parent/teacher association in that country. In addition to granting ownership of copyright to the new monopoly for all the books, the agreement exempted the monopoly from all taxes related to print inputs. This decision was taken despite the existence of one well-established commercial indigenous publisher, Editions CLE, which by the 1980s was the largest publishing house in sub-Saharan francophone Africa, with some 250 titles on its backlist.

The case of Uganda

Uganda provides an example that is typical of the how the liberalisation process has taken place and illustrates how inherent weaknesses and anomalies still remain. The decision to liberalise textbook provision in Uganda from 1992 was taken against a background of dependence on aid and an inability to sustain textbook provision locally.

Significant aid for the rehabilitation of textbook provision from 1986 improved textbook supply in a centralised procurement model using international competitive bidding, but all the textbooks were procured direct from British publishers: booksellers had no role whatsoever. It was a necessary crisis measure at the time, with the country emerging from years of strife, but it generated heated controversy.

The previous state textbook system, in which books were authored at the National Curriculum Development Center (NCDC) and frequently published in association with UK- or Nairobi-based British multinationals, had undermined efforts to establish local publishing and bookselling industries.

So it was that, by 1992, Uganda was locked into a spiral of dependency, with only superficial local publishing capacity and the few remaining booksellers (about a dozen) concentrated in the capital. James Tumusiime reflected ruefully in 1995:

'Uganda has no viable publishing houses. The few printing firms which exist operate at about 10 percent capacity and bookshops are only active in the capital Kampala. This is in spite of massive expenditure by the government on providing books to schools. ... Nearly all these books are provided by British publishers based in London. ... The monopoly has equally killed the bookselling industry because all books purchased by the Ministry of Education are centrally procured and distributed to schools.' (Tumusiime, 1995)

In 1993/94 the new system was launched. Underlying this was the founding in 1992 of UPABA, the Ugandan Publishers and Booksellers Association. UPABA unified the small, nascent local book interests and put forward compelling arguments that the sustainability of textbook provision could be realised only on the basis of local commercial publishing, which required the dismantling of monopoly approaches to textbook provision.

Book selection was decentralised to schools, under the guidance of district selection committees. A textbook-approval mechanism was set up, allowing for selection from multiple textbooks, and was administered by the newly established Instructional Materials Unit (IMU) of the Ministry of Education. The impact was felt within a few years. Multinational publishers found it necessary to relocate their operations to Uganda to supply the Ugandan market; indigenous commercial publishing emerged. Although the books were still centrally procured (orders were collated at the IMU and placed with publishers for central consolidation and delivery by tender), bookselling grew on the back of an initial upsurge in publishing and a growth in secondary school funding where books were still largely imported.

Ten years into liberalisation, Uganda has recorded impressive achievements. All primary and junior-secondary textbooks are authored locally and published by around nine or ten locally based commercial publishers. The quality is high. The textbook–pupil ratio has improved dramatically to a national average of about 1:2 or 1:3 in primary schools, and there is a choice from at least three core textbooks per grade/subject. Bookselling has grown dramatically, with around 200 booksellers in the country, although the decentralisation of procurement is still in a pilot phase. A national book trust (NABOTU) has been formed, largely at the initiative of the book industry, to foster book-development efforts such as training, workshops and library supply.

However, Uganda still exhibits weaknesses in the development of a commercial book industry. A decade after liberalisation was adopted, indigenous publishers account for no more than 15 per cent of the market, with the balance coming mainly from multinational subsidiaries active in Uganda. Textbook procurement combines decentralised selection from a maximum of three approved core textbooks, with a tender-based pre-qualification system (since books are still purchased centrally) that sets strict production, quality and price parameters and requires significant initial investment – in effect, a high entry level. Indigenous publishers have found it difficult to enter the system and compete effectively. Bookselling remains marginal in the area of core textbook provision for primary schools. The bulk of textbooks are printed outside Uganda (in Kenya and South Africa), and local print capacity remains weak.

Thus Uganda, in common with many African textbook-provision systems that have embraced liberalisation, finds itself at a new crossroads. Within a decade, encouraging foundations have been laid, but the new system has not yet matured and the indigenous book industry retains weaknesses from its legacy of former dependency and monopoly approaches.

The example of Ghana

Ghana's long journey from state monopoly to liberalisation is important, given its role as the first African country to gain independence from Britain (in 1957) and its influential voice among newly independent countries in subsequent years.

Writing on state publishing in Ghana in 1975, A. K. Brown commented, 'the picture in Ghana before 1965 showed an entire absence of foreign or indigenous publishing firms, and a heavy dependence on the importation of books and educational materials' (Brown, 1975). Major UK multinationals active in Africa had established agencies in Ghana, and Ghana had little publishing capacity, other than missionary presses, at independence. The Accelerated Development Plan for Education of 1961 championed the cause of making books appropriate (using Ghanaian authors), but books were still published and printed outside Ghana, and Ghana was effectively dependent on multinationals for its books. The government initiated and then accelerated a series of decisions that provided for state monopoly over textbook procurement that has persisted until 2002 (Crabbe, 1996).

In 1963, the government introduced the Free Textbooks Scheme for Basic Education. This well-intentioned policy had singularly disastrous effects on the development of commercial publishing, since it practically prevented any purchase of books on the open market or through bookshops to supplement the state-provided free textbooks, even where no books were available. In the same year Ghana Book Supplies (GBS) was set up to take charge of the procurement and distribution of textbooks to schools. In 1965 the state-owned Ghana Publishing Corporation (GPC) was established to produce and later distribute educational and scholarly works. Where local authors were not available, GPC was mandated to license or commission books published elsewhere (typically from the UK). In the years following, the state maintained an effective monopoly over the provision of core educational textbooks in Ghana.

Richard Crabbe notes that, 'between 1961 and 1974, textbooks for primary schools were written by Ghanaians and published by British multinational publishing houses' (Crabbe, 1996).

After 1974, the Ministry of Education decided to publish its own materials. All books were authored by the Curriculum Research and Development Division (CRDD), which was formally responsible for 'developing, producing and supplying textbooks to government basic and secondary schools' alongside the GBS and GPC parastatals.

As Crabbe observes, 'Ghanaian publishers could hardly penetrate the market at pre-university level with the few textbooks and supplementary readers they published. Ironically, during this same period, the government was contracting foreign [multinational] companies to publish for the educational market, virtually shutting out local publishers.'

The activities of multinationals were sharply curtailed in 1976, when the Ghana Investment Policy forced many foreign publishers to withdraw or conduct business through local representatives, although multinationals continued to bid for and win a number of World Bank and other ICB tenders for books. In 1980 a single textbook per grade/subject was adopted, completing the process of state-monopoly supply. The effectiveness of state textbook provision deteriorated steadily. GPC activities were reduced by massive operational problems. Few new textbooks were being developed. Funding from co-operating partners fell. The national economy was in decline. The state system could not sustain itself.

In 1984, the government entered into an agreement with five local publishers to co-publish certain textbooks for primary schools. The Co-publishing Project, as it was called, was intended to combine state, parastatal and private publishing resources to publish core materials for formal education. It also permitted private partner publishers to reprint extra copies for the open market. It was a notable early form of public/private partnership and a unique model in Africa at the time. However, Crabbe notes, 'although the agreement was signed in 1984, implementation began in 1990 – six years later! Taken in perspective, this move ... had little positive impact on the Ghanaian publishing industry as a whole. The agreement covered only selected textbooks – thirty titles for primary schools. By 1991, not more than 14 registered publishers were active.' (Crabbe, 1996).

Commercial publishing in Ghana, at its lowest ebb by this time, persisted under duress, seeking partnership with the state where possible in co-publishing ventures, and publishing in niche, but marginal, areas of tertiary and scholarly books, supplementary textbooks, children's books, and religious and general books.

The Ghana Book Publishers Association (GBPA) was revived in 1993, with notable institutional assistance from the Canadian NGO, CODE (the Canadian Organisation for Development through Education). It established a secretariat and started to organise a series of training workshops. By 1996, its membership had grown to 52; today, it numbers around 60.

Throughout the period from the early 1990s, publishing

professionals sought dialogue with the Ministry of Education with a view to developing a cohesive textbook-policy framework and partnership between indigenous publishing and the state that focused on the sustainability of textbook provision. A crucial meeting took place between publishers and the Minister of Education in September 1993, the first such meeting in the history of Ghana. Contacts between the GBPA and the Ministry increased markedly thereafter. However, decades of mistrust and apprehension could not be dispelled quickly, especially misunderstandings in government about the functioning of a commercial book industry and the all-too-common suspicions that private enterprises would be 'profiteering from the education of children'.

Very slowly all the efforts towards dialogue have succeeded in developing a spirit and reality of partnership between the state and the indigenous commercial publishers. In 1996, GBPA won approval for Ghanaian publishers to reprint required textbooks up to secondary level. In the same year, government waived the 15% tax on inputs for book publishing by GBPA members only, a recognition of GBPA's growing professionalism. Also, in 1996/97, twelve members of GBPA were afforded the opportunity to participate in a Non-Formal Education Division programme (funded by the World Bank) to publish post-literacy materials in fifteen Ghanaian languages. In 1998, the Ministry of Education announced an invitation for publishers to submit titles as supplementary readers for selection and purchase for primary schools. Some four million books were purchased, including one million local-language books; 60% of the books bought were from British publishers and 40% from Ghanaian publishers.

In February 2002 (after a four-year review period) the Ministry approved a new textbook policy for basic education. It provides for the writing and publishing of all core textbooks to be undertaken by commercial publishers, while the curriculum authority (CRDD) undertakes textbook approval, and selection (of up to five approved core textbooks) is devolved to school level. It represents the dismantling of state monopoly of textbook provision and its replacement by a partnership between the state and the commercial sector.

The importance of indigenous commercial publishers

It has been difficult for ministry policy-makers to change internal perceptions of state procurement, especially after a history of functional and sometimes necessary state procurement in the absence of a developed local commercial book chain. However, these difficulties may be alleviated if an indigenous commercial publishing sector is able to participate in the process of change.

Even if local commercial publishers have been marginalized by a state-monopoly publishing system, their depth of publishing experience and commitment can provide crucial impetus. The experiences of Kenya and Ghana, in particular, provide considerable evidence for this.

Kenyan commercial publishing had a distinguished record of achievement, so when, in 1985, the Ministry of Education introduced state-monopoly textbook publishing, it threw the local publishers into disarray. A number of multinationals left Kenya in the wake of this, though a few remained, and local publishers set up a number of new enterprises, sometimes buying British companies. Commercial publishing survived by publishing 'supplementary' educational materials that famously exceeded the quality of core state-published textbooks. In addition, they entered into innovative publishing initiatives, licensing important works from overseas publishers, developing children's folklore and Kiswahili texts, academic books, some works of fiction and general publishing, and books of 'export quality' in efforts to create and find viable markets. Indigenization of the formerly British-dominated industry was of crucial importance to Kenyan publishers and this, too, influenced attitudes in developing a national publishing industry.

So it was that by 1995/6, when the Ministry of Education began considering methods of textbook liberalisation, the Kenya Publishers Association (KPA), which had an active and increasing membership and had established a full-time secretariat, was an active participant in the process, and played an important role in the construction of the textbook policy adopted in 1998.

Not only did this allow successful textbook liberalisation in terms of commercial capacity to replace the state monopoly but it was inconceivable by then that liberalisation could be realised without policy input from the local commercial publishers. Thus the ministry had a ready partner, with expertise and capacity, in the form of the indigenous commercial sector, that made their decisions effective.

A similar situation occurred in Ghana. Much like the Kenyan publishers, Ghana's publishing houses had established a reputation from the 1960s for scholarly and general publishing, even under the most difficult circumstances. The 'culture of publishing', and its contribution to national intellectual development, was severely tested in Ghana during the period of state-monopoly textbook publishing, but somehow its demise was never total. Ghana's publishers found niche markets in areas such as children's books, religious and scholarly books and 'development' publishing, and consistently attempted to enter into supplementary educational publishing.

The Ghana Book Development Council (formed in 1975, under the Ministry of Education) remained active throughout the period of state textbook monopoly and the Department of Book Industry at Kwame Nkrumah University in Kumasi trained many book professionals. After the GBPA obtained institutional support in the early 1990s, its membership virtually quadrupled within a few years, and effective development efforts were started, culminating in the breakthrough tax exemption for paper imports agreed with the ministry in the mid-1990s.

As Ghana inched towards a policy of textbook liberalisation from the mid-1990s, commercial Ghanaian publishers were active participants, providing ideas and solutions to problems. Success in two large-scale procurement exercises (the 1998 primary reading programme and World Bank-funded non-formal education post-literacy materials) involving GBPA members cemented some measure of trust between the ministry and commercial publishers. In 1997, the GBPA even set up a think-tank on its own initiative to provide publishers' input into the Free Compulsory Universal Basic Education law. It was not asked to do this, nor was it invited to ministry deliberations, but the publishers understood that their input was essential in the long term for sustaining the output of textbooks needed to make the law a success; they acted in the national interest. The efforts of Ghana's small commercial publishing sector over more than a decade, with a handful of dedicated professionals, became the critical catalyst in the formulation of a fully liberalised textbook policy agreed in 2002.

Indigenous publishers in Mali have also recently played their part in the transition from state publishing. In 2001, when the government decided that the four major local publishing houses should take over the copyright of existing primary school titles, the decision was taken with an awareness of the importance of an active national book sector – Mr Konare, the previous state President, had once been director of Editions Jamana, a prominent indigenous publishing house. The small but energetic Malian commercial publishing houses had emerged from very modest origins, but their output of books representing Malian culture and their contribution to national debates about a Malian book culture provided telling influence.

It is a central thesis of this study that the activities and relative strength of local, indigenous publishing is a critical catalyst for both textbook liberalisation and the development of public/private partnerships in textbook provision, in the most practical sense. Conversely, therefore, where local or indigenous publishing capacity has been exceptionally weak, constructing public/private partnerships in educational publishing has been more complex, and presented greater challenges.

Many countries find themselves with an undeveloped indigenous publishing sector, and therefore having to deal with these complexities. In Guinea, for example, the first commercial publisher began its operations only in 1990, and the second in 1992; these two remain the major commercial publishing ventures, although a few others have started. In Ethiopia, the first private publisher began in 1975, and remained more or less the sole commercial indigenous publisher for over a decade; today there are just four commercial publishers in Ethiopia, a country of 65 million people. In Mozambique (as in Sierra Leone) state publishing has been so pervasive, necessary, and relatively successful from the 1970s that no significant indigenous commercial textbook publishers have emerged. In Angola, the writers' union provided a quasi-commercial (and particularly successful) outlet for non-state publishing. In Benin there is one commercial publisher of substance, in Cameroon perhaps three. The particular problem with francophone countries, as has been noted, has been the overwhelming dominance until recent years of imports from French publishers and the continued influence of French companies in the textbook market, which has been exacerbated by ICB regulations.

Earlier a figure of 15 per cent was given as the estimated share of the textbook market enjoyed by indigenous Ugandan companies, the balance being in favour of multinationals. The situation in Zambia is roughly similar, although there are no figures to confirm this. In general, however, indigenous interests in Zambian textbook publishing are somewhat weaker than they are in Uganda, and the book chain as a whole is weaker still. The formation of the Uganda Publishers and Booksellers Association in 1992, and the energy and vibrancy associated with a new vision in local publishing, was a massive factor in later developments towards textbook liberalisation. In Zambia, on the other hand, the relatively more depressed state of the commercial book industry, which in recent years has grown up around a central tender procurement system, is a major hindrance to the Ministry of Education's policy towards deepening textbook liberalisation.

It is clear that, while local publishing has propelled textbook liberalisation in countries like Kenya, Tanzania, Ghana and Uganda, its weakness elsewhere has undermined the scope and pace of change: Mozambique, Ethiopia, Benin, Angola, Sierra Leone, Cameroon and much of francophone Africa have seen a slower and more ponderous development of public/private partnerships in textbook provision. This is a practical, not theoretical, scenario that manifests itself in the capacity of the local book industry to provide solutions to problems posed by full textbook liberalisation in an open market.

Successful state publishing initiatives and infrastructures

It must be remembered that state publishing systems were not always uniformly failures. Between 1973 and 1993/94 Ethiopia's EMPDA had produced 972 separate titles, the majority in indigenous language, in an environment in which Ethiopia lacked private publishing capacity. Mozambique – another of Africa's poorest countries – produced more than 700 non-textbook titles between 1976 and 1989. It is hard to see how this could have been matched by the private sector, even if one had existed. Mozambique's state-owned textbook publisher, Editora Escolar, trained a large proportion of that country's textbook authors, editors and designers.

Zimbabwe's Literature Bureau, a state-owned publisher under the Ministry of Education, almost single-handedly pioneered the publishing of books in national languages, creating some 900 titles by the time it was dismantled in 1999. In many cases these books, having been developed by the Literature Bureau, were licensed to commercial publishers and their commercial publication was effectively subsidized. Zimbabwean publishers agree that there is no possibility that this output could have been matched by the private sector in an area that is considered commercially risky, and the publishing of indigenous-language books was fallen dramatically since the demise of the Bureau. This provides a compelling example of public/private partnership, for broad language-development purposes, in an area where full commercial publication was not viable.

Tanzania reached unprecedented levels of literacy (over 90%) during the era of state monopoly. The zenith of Zambia's literary output in terms of national languages was similarly reached through the state-run Zambia Publications Bureau. The effect on Zambia's literary history is indelible, and in many cases the books produced by the Zambia Publications Bureau are regarded as national treasures.

A question arising from the Mozambique scenario, and one that applies to all former state monopolies, is why the former state monopolies have failed to apply their infrastructure, experience and skills to the development of indigenous, commercial publishing. To all intents and purposes, Mozambique has fashioned its textbook-liberalisation process around a drive to attract foreign investment, so that not even the former state textbook publisher, Editora Escolar, was pre-qualified to publish the new generation of textbooks. Yet Editora Escolar has not only trained almost all textbook writers, editors and illustrators in Mozambique but has built up an enviable infrastructure in the process, with virtually all the equipment necessary for textbook development. The majority of former Editora Escolar staff are to be found in the private sector today, in media houses of various kinds, but virtually no private-sector textbook publishing has emerged.

In Tanzania, Tanzania Elimu Supplies (TES) developed a network of warehouses and retail outlets throughout the country to house and store textbooks under the state-monopoly system. Today TES is insignificant in terms of textbook deliveries to districts, which remains a huge problem in textbook distribution. In Ethiopia, the parastatal EMPDA today competes with a few private companies over the few tenders available for textbooks, but it has refashioned itself largely around printing, rather than providing some basis for commercial publishing. Zambia's ZEPH has survived, much in the same way as EMPDA has, in competition with new private-sector players and, like Tanzania's TES, has a book retail network that extends to most parts of Zambia. While ZEPH's publishing programme remains fairly active, the distribution network is in poor shape: the salient issue is that it has not been able to provide capacity and partnership in a such a way that the commercial book industry could benefit.

In Uganda, the textbook writers and publishing capacity developed in the curriculum institute (NCDC) in collaboration with multinationals have hardly been used in the textbook-liberalisation process. The NCDC is currently attempting to reposition itself to compete with private publishers in the open market for supplementary books – and bemoans the fact that so much of the expertise they had developed has been lost. Likewise, Ghana and Kenya's former parastatal publishers are hardly mentioned today, in the era of liberalisation.

The pattern is quite clear. The state and parastatal infrastructures developed in the heyday of state monopoly have seldom proved capable of privatising in such a way that their considerable assets can play a part in solving the lack of capacity in commercial publishing development.

Conclusion

Policy formulation is guided in many instances by consultants provided and paid for by funding agencies. It is worth remembering that such consultants have exercised considerable influence over the decisions of education ministries, often providing the data and analysis that have led to ministry policy, and thereafter frequently providing the technical assistance to implement the same policy.

These policy instruments and *ad hoc* decisions have one immediate aim: to lay the foundation for the relations between commercial publishing and the education system during the transition towards liberalisation. As an overall pattern, this is typically by imposing price and quality control over commercially produced textbooks, either through tender specifications or through book textbook-approval mechanisms.

The character of such interventions is not stable, the process of change not yet organic; it might rather be described as mechanical, responding to shortcomings and challenges as each new decision in the overall implementation of liberalisation is made. However, in recent years, there have been indications that the early difficulties experienced in the transformation from state to free-market-based textbook-provision systems have to a degree been resolved.

Patterns have emerged among the diverse paths taken in different countries. In contrast to the depressingly numerous examples of failed state textbook-provision systems in the early 1990s, often marked by infrastructural decay and wastage, just ten years later successful models of newly developed commercial systems exist, exemplified by efficiency and quality. Such examples can be seen in the quality of textbooks in the first generation produced by commercial publishers in Zambia and Tanzania compared with their state-published counterparts.

In the case of Tanzania, many of these books are being produced by the first generation of indigenous commercial textbook publishers, most of which did not even exist in the 1980s. There were serious concerns at the beginning of liberalisation in Ghana, Uganda, Tanzania and Zambia about whether publishers had the capacity to finance the volumes (frequently in hundreds of thousands) needed for primary school orders. Notwithstanding the difficulties encountered by publishers in financing these print-runs, at times involving considerable financial risk, it is hard to find a single case where a commercial publisher failed to meet delivery on time.

In Kenya, the rapid development of commercial book-distribution mechanisms based on trade relations between publishers and booksellers has proved to be a model of efficiency in its first distribution exercise to primary schools. In Zimbabwe, the decentralisation of selection, purchase and payment to School Development Committees, even in the most remote schools, has taken almost everybody by surprise in the quality and care in selection of textbooks, and in the interest of parents. The pilot decentralised procurement models in Uganda in four rural districts, and in Tanzania through the Tusome Vitabu project in far-flung Western districts, have similarly exceeded expectations and resulted in the rapid emergence of new booksellers to serve the 'new market'.[3] In Ghana, local publishers captured 40% of the massive 1998 DfID-funded Ministry of Education programme (comprising four million copies of books) to supply supplementary readers to all primary schools. Not only did they produce and deliver according to contract, but they played an active role in the entire process. There are difficulties, setbacks and challenges everywhere, but the broad tide of liberalisation and its results are overwhelmingly positive.

While these general features hold true, Africa is hardly one entity. In regard to books, as much as anything else, it presents a fantastic kaleidoscope of ideas and paths, which, if anything, are increasing in diversity. Grandiose development blueprints have seldom worked and a central point emerging from this study is that African countries are increasingly seeking home-grown solutions that sit comfortably in their own history, culture, language, and social and economic systems. New forms of public/private partnership in the African book sector, and the divergent, often unique, models and development paths being pioneered, illustrate the many different factors at work, not least in the economic and political terrain. In this process, the real experts are the local practitioners – publishers, booksellers and educationists grappling with day-to-day problems.

Chapter 3

THE EMERGENCE OF THE INDIGENOUS COMMERCIAL SECTOR

The African Publishers' Network (APNET), the Pan-African Booksellers' Association (PABA) and their national trade association members have, since the 1990s, placed the creation of a national, indigenous book industry at the center of textbook provision. This has reflected the previous marginalization of local, commercial interests. It is a vital theme in emerging 'public/private partnerships' because centralised state textbook provision has been a form of monopoly, in exactly the same way as dependence on multinationals has tended towards monopoly.

In November 1993, APNET presented the argument as follows, in a submission to the World Bank (APNET delegation to World Bank, 1993):

'Monopoly or centralised approaches of any sort to book supply have proved to be the downfall of book development in many African countries. They initially appeared attractive because indigenous publishing was weak, and by concentrating production prices were theoretically lower. The cost to the book industry and to book provision in general is great. Small specialized publishers and publishing lists cannot develop. Quality deteriorates through lack of competition. Corruption emerges because the user is not in control of buying, which is handled by officials who are not directly affected by the results. Book industries stagnate and fall into a downward spiral of crisis management. African countries provide a rich learning experience in this regard.'

In 1991, at the Manchester Conference referred to above that set the scene for coming liberalisation as far as funding partners were concerned, APNET's Chairman, the late Victor Nwankwo, expounded the views of indigenous African publishers with bold irony: 'The development of a publishing industry is a major building block in book provision. But for some reason this has only been realised recently; in Africa it has traditionally been assumed that a publishing industry would somehow emerge simply because there is a need for books.'

Henry Chakava put the necessary conclusion to the same argument in June 1993 when he addressed a seminar of the Uganda Publishers and Booksellers Association:

'Since independence African governments have pursued policies aimed at book provision but have not paid attention to the more critical question of book creation and the critical role played by local publishers in this process. In sum, approximately 30 years after independence, there is no African country that can claim to have indigenized its publishing industry. Nothing short of a new beginning can make this possible' (Chakava, 1996).

Ten years ago, many African states barely had an indigenous commercial book sector, more than half had no publishers' or booksellers' association, APNET had only just been founded and PABA was a dream. A decade later, the landscape has changed significantly. In early 2004 APNET represented thirty-seven African countries, of which thirty-five had national publishers' associations; it had a further nine prospective country members. Together, APNET's constituent national members represent at least a thousand publishers, and APNET has developed the capacity and experience to respond to a host of training, trade and information needs in Africa's book industry. From a strategic viewpoint, APNET has proved most effective at bringing African publishers together in such a way that book-industry developments are rapidly communicated from one member country to another. PABA, still at an early stage of institutional development, has largely succeeded in placing, for the first time, the beleaguered African bookseller within major African book debates.

African indigenous commercial publishers and African-based multinational publishers, faced with the challenge to manage the authorship and production of primary school and some secondary school textbooks, to comply with standards, pricing and delivery on time, are effectively engaged in establishing the components of newly-emerging book industries. From their standpoint this is no simple procurement exercise. Working with market research, pedagogical issues, analysing new curricula, commissioning authors and illustrators (and often training them in the process), editing and designing new series of books, obtaining paper and print services (often from outside the country) – all entail developing the technical and financial capacity of the industry, and forging the many linkages required for their businesses to function. Simultaneously, a working relationship must be established with the Ministry of Education, itself engaged in restructuring new relationships with the private sector – for example, in setting up an approvals mechanism for textbooks, and working out financing for textbook purchases.

A commercial book infrastructure barely functioned in some

countries when they adopted liberalisation in the first half of the 1990s. It would be no exaggeration to say that commercial publishing had almost ceased to exist in Zambia and Uganda by the mid-1980s, apart from a few small 'niche' or academic and university publishers. The situation in Tanzania in the 1980s was a little better, owing mainly to the stronger NGO support in that country, particularly the innovative Children's Book Project. Bookselling was at its lowest ebb, with few viable bookshops remaining.

With the opening up of the primary school textbook market, publishers had to begin to develop their own business, train new textbook authors, editors, illustrators, photographers (a particular problem in Tanzania), set up their own computer-based (desktop publishing) systems, gear their concerns financially and organisationally to textbook writing and publishing, and deal with the acute problem of printing. They found that local print capacity was either inadequate or too expensive to enable them to compete for textbook tenders. They therefore moved rapidly towards importing printing, which meant establishing foreign-currency payment systems, and shipping and import procedures for large quantities of books.

The publishers also had to seek capital and the means to finance the new textbook tenders; they had to develop, often from scratch, trade relations and distribution arrangements with booksellers, including credit-control systems and suitable accounting practices. Catalogues and promotional materials had to be produced. Every dimension of the book publishing business had to be attended to simultaneously.

Capacity in commercial publishing

Countries can achieve the liberalisation of textbook provision only to the extent that the commercial sector has sufficient capacity to replace state textbook systems. But what exactly is meant by 'capacity' in commercial publishing? Some dated views are still prevalent. Since most state textbook publishing companies have been large operations, housed in huge premises with a large staff and bureaucracy, it is sometimes assumed that the emerging African commercial publishers must operate on a similar scale to undertake textbook publishing.

However, most indigenous African publishers are small to medium-sized enterprises. This is partly the result of digital technology, but at the same time publishing has been organisationally re-structured. The editor, as well as copy-editing and liaising with authors, will co-ordinate other core book-development tasks such as page design and illustration, which are increasingly sub-contracted. Typesetting and page make-up have been simplified with computer software. Printing can take place in any country, as long as shipping and the import of the finished books is not cost-prohibitive or bureaucratically complicated, and if foreign currency is available to pay.

Sub-contracting gives a publisher choice in recruiting short-term skills for highly specialized tasks and the opportunity to cut overheads associated with permanent staff. As a result, African publishers have always out-performed former state-enterprises through the relative advantages of flexibility. They are streamlined businesses, operated by buying-in expertise and minimizing overheads, typically owner-managed, and the more successful are run along exacting cost-efficiency business principles. Most of them are less than ten years old.

Box 7: Costs and commercial publishers

The authors of this report are convinced that commercial publishers have, in real terms, significantly reduced all indirect and direct costs in producing textbooks in Africa, as compared to the more bureaucratic state-publishing enterprises (despite no figures to prove this). This is a critical point because, to this day, adherents of state textbook provision base their main argument on the notion that commercially produced books (with a margin of profit embedded in the price) are more expensive. In reality, it is more likely that this misconception arises from the fact that the actual costs of producing textbooks, their direct costs and all the overheads, are, for the first time, being accurately reflected in publishers' prices. The cover price of a commercially produced book is calculated to cover all costs of that copy (e.g. royalties to authors, editorial, printing and distribution costs, and overheads), but it was virtually impossible to know the real cost of a copy produced by the state monopoly system. Books were written and edited by public employees, printed on donated paper by heavily subsidized, and often grossly inefficient, government printers, and distributed through government transport.

Multiple-textbook systems adopted by the state profoundly influence the way in which publishers work, which is quite different from their work in a single-textbook system. The adaptation, rewriting, re-design and publishing of an existing single textbook to pre-set specifications, as in a tender process, are largely mechanical, rather than creative, processes. The terms of the tender tightly define these processes, whether in content, production specification, or cost. The risks are limited to the costs of tendering, manuscript development and the financial and technical conditions imposed. Thereafter, the winner of the tender entertains little or no risk. A book produced to specification is purchased in a definite quantity. In such arrangements, publishers are protected from competition and from the vagaries of the market. Observers have noted this situation in both Zambia and Tanzania, where some development of liberalised publishing has taken place but with a distinct weakness in marketing.

As soon as multiple textbook selection and use comes into effect, publishers entertain risk. In many publishing training manuals one will read a statement to the effect that the business of publishing is fundamentally an exercise in risk management. Publishers invest in the costs of publishing a book because they believe that they can secure a return on that investment. This is as much a marketing decision (will the market respond to a product, in competition with others?) as it is a product-development decision (exactly what type of product, at what cost, and with what physical attributes is needed?). It is a highly creative and challenging process, and it is equally a long-term process. Mistakes bring failure, and failure means commercial loss, perhaps even the loss of livelihood. It may be argued that this is precisely the driving force behind Nigerian, Kenyan and Zimbabwean textbook publishers, who have adopted strenuous marketing and market-research measures to ensure successful publishing decisions and minimize the risk.

Every effort must be made to minimize risk, and this is precisely how publishing matures into new, higher forms of institutional and creative development. To minimize risk, a book must not only be of a desired quality, it must match the price of competition, and if it does not there must be very sound reasons why a consumer would pay more. But even if these decisions are made correctly, failure can occur because the product may be unknown in the market, or does not reach the market at precisely the time orders are being made, which is essential because of the seasonal nature of the educational textbook business.

Access to capital and financial-support schemes

Because of the innovations in publishing, issues of capacity (especially in the sense of large print-runs for primary school books) are more related to access to technology, production facilities and relevant editorial and business skills than to the 'size' of a business. Over and above this, it is access to capital that dictates commercial capacity in the modern publishing world, and this remains the most crucial issue for African publishers, as only scattered efforts have been made to confront it.

The Dag Hammarskjöld loan-guarantee scheme in Kenya, initiated in 1988 with funding from the Ford Foundation, provided a useful model for access to capital from commercial banks for publishing projects. The programme, with guarantees against the repayment of bank loans, was conceived to enable Kenyan publishers to develop relations with commercial banks so that the banks would later have the confidence to extend further loans unilaterally on commercially viable projects. It had a notable impact ·on Kenyan publishing at the time: several publishers increased their output, and a few succeeded in establishing independent bilateral relations with banks without further loan guarantees. The programme foundered after a few years as a result of high interest rates, which made bank loans almost unserviceable with or without a guarantee.

In Tanzania, the Children's Book Project initiated a buy-back scheme. Children's books proposed by publishers – in the form of manuscripts with illustrations – would be selected through the Project. After rigorous training and assistance towards developing the book, finished copies would be purchased by the project for free distribution to schools and libraries, in quantities (of about 1,000) at a price that would help offset the production costs. Profit could, however, be attained only if the publisher sold the remaining stock (typically 2,000–3,000 copies) on the open market, and it was therefore a form of what might be termed 'incentive' or 'lead' funding. It remains in operation and is one of the most innovative publishing-support projects in Africa. To date, some 150 titles have been published through this scheme, and within Africa Tanzania has achieved an enviable publishing output in children's literature as a result.

Although these examples might be regarded as peripheral to textbook publishing, with the large volumes involved, there are very few other projects in Africa that have sought to provide capital (rather than training or other assistance) for publishing in any form. From time to time, African publishers have been able to attract funding, on a book-by-book basis, from NGOs and other agencies for publishing projects that are 'developmental' in some way, but this has excluded textbooks, which are perceived as a commercial activity.

It is no surprise that publishers throughout Africa, in a formative stage of development and lacking access to loan and venture capital, have vociferously complained about the 'prohibitive' costs of tender pre-qualification, especially in international competitive bidding procedures, and about the regulations relating to the proof of their existing turnover and size of business. The interplay of public/private partnership is taking place against a background of many new small or medium-sized African publishers striving to achieve and maintain viability, to enter the textbook market that alone assures their business future, and to attain a measure of competitiveness against multinational publishers with long-established African markets.

In the main, African publishers have sought capital from private investment or from commercial bank financing arrangements. Success in these efforts has been patchy. When tenders have been involved, those publishers that have won a tender have, in some cases, secured bridging loans from banks to enable them to pay the printer and repay the bank from the sale of the books. In Ghana and Nigeria, there are several cases where capital has been raised from the local stock exchange, with shares floated on the open market. This in itself is an interesting, recent development in African publishing. Book publishing and bookselling, throughout Africa, are regarded with scepticism in banking and financial sectors. Unsecured bank loans to start a book business or develop a publishing project are virtually unheard of. Therefore, private capital in some form (e.g. personal savings, property) has been a prerequisite for new enterprises. However, there are almost no data available and no studies have been identified on the micro-economics and financing of newly emerging African publishing industries. Indeed, it is hardly accorded 'industry' status, even in comparison to smaller manufacturing sectors.

Data on African publishing

Reliable annual published data relating to turnover, output (by category or title), staff, financing, and even number of companies active in books, are either non-existent or unreliable, whether at national or company level, throughout Africa. The oft-quoted percentage of textbooks in the overall book market in African countries, usually placed somewhere between 80% and 90%, is guesswork. The number of employees working in books and publishing in any African country is unknown; growth or decline in turnover or output relies on almost anecdotal evidence.

Because of the almost complete absence of detailed data on African publishing output and book provision, including imports, generalizations are common. Despite this, it is important to appreciate the immense scale of the operations of the multinational publishers that have been active, indeed dominant, in African textbook markets. The annual turnover of the largest multinational publisher easily exceeds the annual exports (of all commodities) of many African countries, for example. Africa's book market, of which 80–90 per cent concerns educational books, generates considerable turnover, but there is no possibility of even guessing the gross value of the 'African' book market by region or language group: such figures do not exist. Nevertheless, one can get some idea from the following statistic: according to European Union trade statistics, EU countries (predominantly France and UK) export printed matter worth not less than US$600 million annually to Africa. (International Trade Center UNCTAD/WTO of Harare, 1999). Obviously this does not include trade carried out by

European publishers within their African operations, which extends to almost every country in Sub-Saharan Africa, and, one would surmise, is certainly higher than the volumes of imports into Africa.

Non-textbook educational publishing

Textbook publishing by its nature, given the capital investment required and the volume of production, leads to concentration, regardless of whether multinational publishers or ICB tenders are involved. However, this rather narrow perspective is true only if one sees educational publishing solely in terms of core textbooks at primary school and junior secondary school levels, with high volumes. In its broader scope, educational publishing offers opportunities for, and requires, 'specialist' publishing in small quantities – supplementary books, library books, early-reading materials, national-language books, study guides, teachers' resource books, and books in non-core subject areas such as music and sports.

These are the risky areas for publishers to invest in. Moreover, these non-core-textbook-publishing efforts require considerable local cultural input, national-language and early-reading books being useful examples. Indigenous publishers, or locally based multinationals with flexibility over publishing decisions, are in a good position to develop such materials, and to create the market for them.

Examples of this abound in Nigeria and Zimbabwe. Individual publishers have frequently been able to cross-subsidize 'risky' publishing decisions from the profits obtained from core-textbook sales. The industry as a whole, freed to some extent from the restrictive over-concentration imposed by tender procurement, has allowed enterprising publishers to develop lists of readers and supplementary textbooks of all kinds. Niche publishing has developed as a direct outcome of decentralised procurement systems and decisions.

Kenya's publishers have developed in a comparable way from the 1970s on the strength of a well-established and vibrant commercial sector. Thereafter, the efforts of many small publishers were hampered by the return to centralised primary school textbook supply between 1985 and 1998. That they survived this period was the result of innovation – by placing on the market 'supplementary' books which were much better than the 'core' texts hurriedly written and published by the parastatal publishers. In Uganda, the development of such niche lists in local publishing can be traced exactly to the era of the decentralisation of book selection from 1992, though this was limited to some degree by the effect of restrictive tender-based supply.

Ethiopia presents similar evidence, although it does not yet boast depth in commercial publishing: the state-monopoly publishing system, under EMPDA until the 1990s, was comparatively effective, even in the area of general and supplementary publishing. Since the move towards limited tender-based primary school textbook publishing, in a single-textbook system, there has been a noticeable upswing in author-published texts, and the fact that authors (who are often teachers) are managing to publish informally and sell supplementary educational books points to significant market potential.

Tanzania's approach of emphasizing indigenous publishing is important in that it was largely successful: the results can be seen in the efforts by smaller Tanzanian publishers to gain a foothold in the educational market with non-core educational materials as well as with core textbook series. Tanzania's pioneers in indigenous publishing – unlike those in Zimbabwe or Kenya, where more developed markets have created a conducive environment, by African standards, for this type of publishing – have had to struggle harder to get markets and buyers. Thus, it is all the more impressive to see indigenous publishers in Tanzania investing, and taking no small risk, in publishing, for example, music tutorials for primary school, science encyclopaedias, classic Kiswahili readers, biographies, classroom wall-charts, study guides, and similar materials.

Box 8: The importance of local readership

Everywhere in Africa (there are no exceptions) publishing development in the broad sense of cultural and intellectual output and local readership – even, or especially, where local economic constraints have been significant – has been the preserve and the strength of indigenous publishers. Perhaps nowhere is this better illustrated than in the Democratic Republic of Congo (DRC) during the years of unrelenting hardship and civil war between 1990 and 2000. Not only were multinational textbook publishers not in evidence during these years, but the country was rapidly deserted by aid workers and the many Westerners who used to occupy all areas of civilian life.

The number of titles submitted to the national library in Kinshasa (virtually cut off from parts of the east for long periods) in this turbulent period was 1492. The rate of published works does not show a significant decline. In 1995, 179 titles were registered (a record year); in 1992, there were 99 titles (the least productive year). Titles supported by funded projects are insignificant: most titles were published or co-published with local resources. The market for these books is mainly the Kinshasa public. There are very few bookshops in the DRC (five in Kinshasa, two in Lubumbashi, and one in Matadi), which derive more income from stationery than from books. Ninety per cent of the books are in French, the rest mainly religious works in Lingala. The majority of these books were published by small (then) Zaïrean publishers with between one and five titles on their list, and about a third are religious in nature. The remaining titles largely concern law, literature, social sciences, applied sciences, agriculture and human rights.

Notwithstanding the many disparities that disguise an element of 'false' publishing (such as public figures having a 'published work' for career purposes), the fact remains that publishing in the DRC, in the complete absence of multinational publishers, survived because of the depth of indigenous interest and commitment during a period of immense upheaval.

The disadvantaged printers

Textbook liberalisation, which is strengthening local publishing in Africa, has seldom been matched by a corresponding policy to strengthen the local print industry. Thus printers often have to pay import duties on paper, ink, film, etc. for book production, although the same country may have long ago removed duties on finished books. Thus, for example, Uganda, Tanzania and Zambia are dependent on imported printing services for the new generation of primary textbooks.

The situation is particularly acute in Guinea, where local printers have to pay 20%–22% import duty on paper and up to 32% on other inputs. As a result, it is impossible for them to compete with foreign printers for the production of Guinea's textbooks. It is actually cheaper for Guinean publishers to have their books printed as far away as Mauritius, in spite of the transport costs, than by a printer next door. In contrast, Ghana has taken the almost unprecedented step of removing duties on paper imports specifically for book publishing purposes by GBPA members. This has proved to be a massive boost for local publishing and printing.

While there are many arguments in favour of purchasing print services internationally – at the best price and quality available, especially for specialized printing services – it is debatable whether countries should import primary school textbooks that represent both a basic need and relatively simple print technology. It is hardly a wise policy by a country to starve its printers, missing openings for work, technological development and taxable revenue from a healthy industry to get Customs receipts on raw material. Countries with a stronger print industry, such as Kenya, Mauritius, South Africa and Zimbabwe, have therefore become net exporters of printing in Africa, while African textbooks are also being increasingly printed in Asia, in addition to France and Canada (used by most francophone African countries). In addition to the unfavourable treatment of printers by their own governments, funding agencies sometimes offer the government free printing of its textbooks overseas: this is what CIDA is doing in Mozambique at present, but other agencies have done the same and this is not an isolated case.

Decentralised procurement and distribution

Liberalisation of publishing *per se*, in single-textbook 'procurement' systems, creates conditions in which some commercial textbook publishers can expand the scope of their activities as well as their technical and financial capacity. In publishing primary school textbooks, the huge quantities involved bring profit and reward to a few publishers. The effects can be profound, but are necessarily limited. The decision to publish and the risk involved is out of the hands of the publisher and in the hands of the ministry as a procurement exercise.

The liberalisation of publishing without the decentralisation of procurement usually implies that the distribution chain itself can remain static, and the considerable problems of creating a commercial distribution network will remain unresolved. Central purchase means central distribution in one form or another, but even when it is designed to incorporate local 'distributors', as has been the practice in Mozambique, it is usually simply a haulage and delivery operation. The distribution mechanism has little or no bearing on the development of a book-buying and book-provision culture, in the sense of developing a market, a consumer culture, and the availability of books through booksellers.

Guinea's experience within francophone Africa provides a good example of the problems involved in establishing commercial distribution. When the curriculum authority (INRAP) started developing primary school books from 1990 in collaboration with private publishers, the ministry engaged private booksellers to distribute the books. The cost of the books was heavily subsidized, booksellers received a discount in the normal way, and parents purchased them. According to the booksellers in that country, the system functioned well, particularly because the parental contribution to the cost of books inculcated a culture of buying books: it was said that pupils appreciated the books when the family had paid for them. Booksellers also observed that 'with totally free textbooks, the government becomes dependent on donors for financing, which is not sustainable' (Comment made during field visit). Ultimately, the system was done away with because many poor rural families simply could not afford even the subsidized book prices.

Bookselling

The effects of 'free textbooks' provided through central purchasing mechanisms and other systems that effectively bypass the bookseller to reach the consumer have hit the bookselling sector hard, as borne out by the figures.

In Zambia, bookselling companies with accounts with major publishers appeared to number five or six by 2003, according to our estimates during the field trip. The total number of bookshops (including outlets of the parastatal ZEPH) numbered twenty, which are concentrated mainly in urban areas, far from rural textbook consumers. In Tanzania, a geographically huge country of some 35 million people, estimates on the number of booksellers are vague, with '40 to 50' usually quoted. Of these, perhaps a dozen are sufficiently well established to have accounts with major publishers. Ethiopia has 58 established bookshops (36 belonging to one chain) and around 110 informal book retailers in a country of 65 million people. Nigeria's booksellers' association has around 300 members in a country of 120 million people. Ghana has around twenty established booksellers remaining (compared to 60 members of the book publishers' association). Mali has practically no bookshops outside the capital Bamako, and Guinea and Senegal each have around four or five established booksellers. In the case of Guinea, three of the established booksellers are retail chains with perhaps thirty point-of-sale outlets in total. Mozambique has seven well-stocked bookshops in Maputo, but has very few booksellers in the rest of the country.

Kenya, on the other hand, has an estimated 1,500 booksellers, of which around 300 have accounts with major publishers. The number of booksellers has been rising rapidly because the new system allows booksellers to consolidate orders from schools. Bookselling in both Uganda and Tanzania has also experienced growth in recent years because of the piloting of decentralised procurement and the rapid expansion of private schools in both countries. Uganda today has an estimated 200 booksellers; around 75 per cent are either local agencies of booksellers in Kampala or recently established district booksellers.

Zimbabwe's 105 remaining booksellers (a sharply reduced number as a result of the recent economic downturn), all of which have credit facilities with major publishers, comprise a network covering every major town in the country. Booksellers are no longer only concentrated in the capital and large urban centers as they were in the early 1980s. Small towns and growth points have been the springboard for growth in bookselling as a result of fully decentralised procurement or selection to districts and schools, requiring the sales functions of the book industry to be decentralised. It is worth noting that the pyramid shape of Kenya's and Zimbabwe's book industries mirror the shape of book industries globally – a publisher–bookseller ratio of somewhere between 1:5 (Zimbabwe) and 1:25 (Kenya).

An important role for an educational bookseller, where purchasing authority has been decentralised, is that of 'consolidation'. In contrast to a system in which every district education authority or school places a separate order with every publisher, the bookseller will 'consolidate' orders from a number of districts/schools and place orders with various suppliers. In this way, the bookseller acts as an intermediary in locally processing orders from many consumers to many suppliers, this simplifying the process.

In Uganda, Tanzania, Botswana, and probably in Ghana in the coming phase of decentralisation, the bookseller's 'consolidator' role has been circumvented by the state itself. Selection has been decentralised (to schools) and the state procurement mechanism, either centrally or at district level, has undertaken the role of consolidation. Orders are compiled by the procurement arm after school-based selection and then placed with publishers, following a process very similar to that which a bookseller would undertake.

Physical distribution problems

The physical difficulties of book distribution have rarely been addressed in textbook studies in Africa, and where they have, they are often the raison d'être for central haulage and delivery systems. In Zimbabwe, where booksellers deliver to every school in the country, the major problem is the cost associated with maintaining a transport fleet to accomplish this. There is no possibility of success in bookselling in Zimbabwe without transport to deliver to schools. Zimbabwe has an excellent road network but, even so, the majority of schools are far from tarred roads and educational bookselling is necessarily a seasonal activity – it cannot be accomplished in the height of the rainy season; and the final leg of a school delivery will, in many cases, be accomplished by rural bus, by donkey-drawn cart, or by school children themselves physically hauling the books the last few kilometres.

Zimbabwe is a compact country with a developed road network. In Tanzania, Zambia and Ethiopia, the physical transportation of books to remote areas is a study in overcoming physical terrain, flooded rivers, impassable roads (dusty in the dry season, muddy in the rains), reaching islands and coastal areas, or mountains with practically no road access. The ingenuity required at district education offices to administer such schools, pay teachers' salaries and carry out inspections is seldom mentioned in studies, but it is an exceptionally important part of their job. In most cases the district education offices bear the responsibility for delivering textbooks to these schools. Mozambique's novel system of local tenders for the delivery of textbooks has, where it entails delivery direct to schools, enhanced efficiency in that locally based haulage is more effective in overcoming the local physical problems of delivery. Zimbabwe has a similar experience, in that local booksellers have far greater ability to manage delivery in difficult situations than booksellers based in the capital do.

Tanzania's Pilot Project for Publishing, that successfully

liberalised the state-publishing monopoly between 1993 and 2000 and resulted in a multi-textbook system by 2001/02, found it difficult to decentralise procurement to districts and schools, not least because of the problems posed by rural transport. A road trip between the capital Dar es Salaam on the coast and the commercial hub of Mwanza on Lake Victoria is a two-day (some would say three) ordeal, which hardly compares with the problems of reaching the southern provinces during the rainy season. It is no surprise that building a network for marketing and book-distribution, from publishers in the capital through booksellers in the towns to all outlying districts, has proved complex and will take time and effort to develop. Mali is one of West Africa's biggest countries, nearly twice the size of France. More than half of the sparsely populated country is Saharan desert or semi-desert and there are practically no bookshops outside Bamako. Textbook distribution in that massive country is accomplished using a caravan of military lorries once a year.

The example of Zimbabwe

At independence in 1980, Zimbabwe had the infrastructure but not the capacity to supply the massive number of new textbooks required by thousands of new rural schools. The Ministry of Education and Culture was tempted on more than one occasion to establish a tender-based supply mechanism and simply obtain huge quantities of books from local and multinational publishers and deliver them directly to the new schools. At the time, there were only twenty bookselling firms, all located in urban centers, and less than a dozen publishers, only two of which were primarily engaged in textbook publishing. Fortunately, there was already a decentralised supply model in operation for the approximately 700 (mainly urban) government schools. The commercial book trade had an established *modus operandi* whereby publishers sold textbooks strictly through booksellers, who consolidated and supplied all government-school textbook orders.

Thus, when the Ministry was faced with the challenge of supplying textbooks to new rural schools, it could turn to the existing model of decentralised, commercial supply for answers. Nevertheless, furious lobbying and negotiation took place, as the booksellers were aware that the Ministry could be swayed towards tender-based, centralised supply, particularly as this was the principle that the World Bank textbook-provision system applied to its loans and grants at that time.

The result was the Government Contract for Supply to Government and District Council Schools, as it was called, that established a decentralised supply system to all types of schools and formed the basis of Zimbabwe's then fledgling book industry. This system was devised by publishers, booksellers and Ministry officials working in close co-operation.

There were three critical points of discussion. For the publishers, multi-textbook choice was paramount, and since this was already in operation in government schools and publishers pointed to the advantages in quality, it was agreed to. For the booksellers, supply through booksellers was the main issue, and since booksellers offered free delivery (after heated negotiation) to districts and schools, this relieved the Ministry from the financial and logistical problems that it would have entailed, and was also agreed to. For the Ministry, educational issues were paramount – particularly getting quality books to classrooms on time when there was a massive growth in the number of schools, and their worry, as always, was the potential for abuse by 'commercial interests seeking profit'.

The answer was a strict entry level and code of conduct applied to all booksellers wanting to join the new system. Since the agreement was devised as a binding legal agreement between the Booksellers' Association of Zimbabwe and the (then) Ministry of National Supplies (as a form of tender) that could be abrogated at any time as a result of non-compliance, booksellers' adherence to the standards set in the code of conduct was enforced. In effect, a bookseller that abused the system in any way could be struck off the register, and the agreement as a whole could be cancelled if the Association failed to fulfil its role. Compliance was also enforced by a requirement that booksellers pay a 'performance bond', equivalent to some US$1000 at that time, which the bookseller would lose if struck off the register. Booksellers were strictly inspected and monitored. Interestingly, the system functioned well in terms of self-regulation. Booksellers were obviously also in competition, and any bookseller that sought unfair advantage was quickly identified by others.

Equally important was that publishers had the confidence to extend credit facilities to most booksellers registered under the Government Contract, satisfied that 'briefcase booksellers' had all but been eliminated from the system. Typically, this was 60- to 90-day credit that, in practice, gave booksellers two months to receive payment and pay the publishers. The removal of credit facilities to booksellers by major educational publishers became another form of control over booksellers' behaviour and professionalism, simply because, without this credit, no bookseller could survive commercially.

The result is was that the entire chain in textbook industry functioned well and grew at a tremendous rate. Publishers concentrated on publishing and competing for the market. Exemplary standards were recorded in new textbooks, especially as consumer awareness grew, and publishers found it necessary to test many new textbooks directly with teachers in workshops as part of their marketing. Publishers' output soared. The number of booksellers grew nearly seven-fold in the next ten years, and Zimbabwe established a country-wide bookselling network, since it became advantageous for booksellers to be located in the rural towns for access and sales to districts.

Trade relations between publishers and booksellers, particularly in the areas of credit systems, delivery, marketing and promotional materials, became finely tuned. Importantly, booksellers' access to credit meant that the speed of supply was improved to such an extent that a bookseller could frequently phone an order through to a publisher and have it dispatched within 24 hours. It became immediately apparent to publishers that booksellers, being in contact with the purchasers, could influence which textbook might be selected. Districts and schools were visited continuously by sales representatives and to make deliveries; often these visits took the form of book displays. Deliveries to districts and schools were free. The Ministry concentrated its core (textbook) functions around budgeting and financing the system, curriculum reform, the approval of textbooks in a multi-textbook system, and monitoring the supply chain.

The initial system for procurement by districts that was tested in the 1980s proved very vulnerable to abuse. The large sums handled by education officers made this potentially a very serious problem, but the present system, where purchase decisions are taken close to the end users, is said to function very well. Now, the head teacher places the textbook orders following recommendations by a purchasing committee consisting of teachers, which is closely monitored by the school's parent–teacher organisation, whose members are naturally very anxious that the money is put to proper use. After delivery, the bookseller's invoice is duly signed and stamped by the receiving head teacher, whereupon it is sent to the Regional Education Office for payment. But first it goes to the District Education Officer, who countersigns the invoice and, on a visit to the school, checks that the books have actually been supplied.

Publisher–bookseller relations

The trade relations between publishers and booksellers are the foundation for the entire book chain. Trade relations between publishers and booksellers in Africa have generally been poor.

They cannot be developed in any environment in which publishers are obliged to bypass booksellers in order to reach the purchaser; in such conditions, publishers do not develop marketing strategies as part of their publishing activities. In Zimbabwe and Kenya, however, the practice of publishers holding workshops, directly with teachers and education officers in many cases, to 'test' new textbooks has been common.

The importance of 'standards and conventions' that underpin the development of the book chain is referred to elsewhere. Apart from discounts (i.e. booksellers' operational margin of profit, without which there is no possibility of retailing books), credit is the vital cog in relations between publishers and booksellers. Typically, textbook provision, from the viewpoint of ministries of education, is unconcerned with the issue of credit facilities between bookseller and publisher since it is an internal business relationship. They are, however, a critical factor in the liberalisation of textbook provision and in public/private partnerships.

From a bookseller's viewpoint, credit is the life-blood of educational supply. It is the principal way in which booksellers capitalize their business in terms of stock (inventory) and working capital to service educational consumers. Publishers, on the other hand, must guard their credit facilities strictly or they face a real risk of total business failure if booksellers do not pay. It is a sensitive issue at the heart of trade relations between publisher and bookseller.

In decentralised procurement systems, payment in advance by schools or districts to booksellers is unheard of, as is cash settlement on delivery. The bureaucracy of public funds requires adherence to accounting procedures, verification of delivery, and so on. Decentralised procurement hinges around the thorny issue of credit. Delayed payment by educational consumers (districts and schools) means delayed payment from bookseller to publisher, and this has a severe knock-on effect that reverberates throughout the system.

Naturally, publishers do not give a credit facility to every bookseller that knocks on their door. They are selective and cautious for good reason, more so with new booksellers. It takes a considerable time for credit relations to develop in the book industry because they are based on booksellers' track records. The predicament is obvious: growth in bookselling depends on the ability to service orders, or on stock, that in turn depends on obtaining credit from publishers. Publishers cannot risk giving credit to booksellers without a strong record. In centralised procurement, or any variant that bypasses the bookseller to the consumer, there is no foundation on which booksellers can develop either the financial capacity or the track record required.

Conversely, decentralised procurement, in particular where multi-textbook choice has been implemented, has a profound influence on the trade relations between booksellers and publishers and on the way in which these two sectors are able to work with the ministry in problem-solving innovation.

In Nigeria, publishers have developed a direct-supply relationship with most state educational authorities that has bypassed booksellers. The larger publishers have established local agencies (or retail outlets) at state level to simulate the kind of supply network (requiring local points of supply and representation) that would normally be accomplished through booksellers. More recently, a small group of well-established booksellers and some newly established booksellers offering professional services have vigorously questioned these out-dated patterns of supply. Publishers are beginning to respond. The process of change is gradual, but the benefits of a professional bookselling service are becoming increasingly important in the further development of Nigeria's book industry. Trade relations between booksellers and publishers have dominated recent debates surrounding a national book policy and its desired impact on the efficiency of supply and on readership generally. There is every sign in Nigeria that new thinking and a new generation of booksellers have started to close the rift in trade relations between publishers and booksellers. The Nigerian booksellers themselves frankly admit that their association, which has been ineffective in regulating trade relations, must now play a more active leadership role.

A parallel process is taking place in Tanzania, where publishers and booksellers are actively exploring ways of incorporating booksellers into textbook supply, solving problems of credit facilities, and empowering booksellers to take over the problematic deliveries in districts. About three quarters of the districts in Tanzania and Uganda have no bookshop and therefore no point-of-supply that could easily be incorporated into marketing and deliveries to schools. On the other hand, in both countries, where decentralised procurement has been piloted, booksellers have appeared almost immediately to handle the orders. In Tanzania's case, this was a remarkable development because the Tusome Vitabu project took place in one of the provinces most distant from the capital, Dar es Salaam, almost as far from publishers as one can get in Tanzania. Expected problems arose from the booksellers' lack of experience and track record, but both publishers and booksellers have expressed satisfaction with the results, and some new booksellers appeared as a direct result of the project.

Underlying new understandings in trade relationships between publishers and booksellers has been the historic Memorandum of Understanding signed between APNET and PABA in 2001 at the

Zimbabwe International Book Fair (African Publishing Review, 2000). This attempted to define the principles behind trade relations between publishers and booksellers throughout Africa, and specifically to illustrate that publishing and bookselling are so closely related that one cannot develop without the other. At the very least this agreement has stimulated renewed interest in solving the problem of trade relations.

Box 9: Booksellers in Uganda

The case of Uganda is instructive in that it provides a model of gradual but effective bookseller participation in general and educational book supply, from a background where there was virtually no role, except in retailing, for booksellers in the supply chain.

The East African Book Development Association (EABDA), in association with the Uganda Public Libraries Board, recently established a project to support school libraries in Uganda. It was projected to provide 8,000 books to 36 school libraries annually. Initially, procurement was managed by the Ugandan Publishers Association and books were procured directly from publishers; in a further phase, as a result of lobbying from the Ugandan Booksellers Association, procurement was routed through booksellers.[4] After initial reservations, the procurement worked well. It was specifically in their consolidation role, in addition to their marketing function, that booksellers were able to contribute and make the procurement process more efficient.

The importance of this example is that it has taken place against the gradual recognition of the role of Ugandan booksellers in educational textbook supply. When Ugandan textbook procurement was liberalised through tenders to publishers, and delivery was undertaken centrally by the ministry (1993/4), booksellers had no role and little recognition in textbook distribution since the IMU in the Ministry of Education consolidated, packed and delivered consignments of books to individual schools. After a limited and phased pilot decentralisation of procurement to districts in 2001, publishers realised that they could not manage the procurement to all rural districts. Significantly, this understanding emerged from a workshop in 2000, when all stakeholders were brought together under the auspices of the National Book Trust of Uganda (NABOTU) with assistance from PABA and the ADEA *Books* Working Group.

This train of processes illustrates the pattern in the commercialisation of book procurement and the development of capacity in the private sector. From the booksellers' point of view, it was formation of their association that led to an independent role in which they could engage both publishers and decision-makers in procurement at policy level. As a direct result, when the liberalisation of textbook publishing developed into the decentralisation of procurement under the management of the Ministry of Education, booksellers began to be included. Behind the scenes, performing a co-ordinating role and bringing stakeholders into one forum, was the book development body, NABOTU, set up at the initiative of the commercial sector. From this standpoint, the booksellers were able to successfully lobby for an NGO-led library acquisitions initiative, one example of many ways in which Ugandan booksellers have become an important component of the book chain in Uganda.

There are now some 200 booksellers operating in Uganda. The Ministry of Education can work reliably with a network of booksellers, not yet national but at least covering a quarter of the districts in the country; a decade ago there were less than thirty booksellers, all concentrated in Kampala and major urban centers.

Educational bookselling outside the primary school sector

In those countries where booksellers have not engaged in the supply of textbooks for basic education, most booksellers have derived a large proportion of their income from secondary and tertiary textbook supply, and from the massive growth in private education at all levels.

While textbook procurement for secondary schools is much less regimented than for basic education, and the spread of titles and sources of titles is far greater, in private education (from stet to commercial colleges) it is almost totally unregulated. To a large degree, upper-secondary and all levels of private education feature imported books. At junior secondary level in anglophone African countries, many books are published locally, and the provision of most secondary and tertiary level books has effectively been deregulated to the extent that booksellers supply most needs, often directly to parents or to schools with funds raised by parent–teacher associations.

Booksellers' fortunes in recent years in large parts of Africa have mirrored the growth in private education, which has provided a completely new and increasingly lucrative market. Mauritius, India and Dubai have become important new sources of imported books in several eastern and southern African countries.

There is an important principle behind these developments. Booksellers everywhere in Africa have illustrated skill and innovation in supplying effectively decentralised markets such as private schools and upper-secondary and tertiary institutions. The greater the funds available in these decentralised markets, the more booksellers have responded with supply. This is evident in Mauritius, where fifteen well-established booksellers and a further forty-five 'seasonal' booksellers exist in a population of just over one million, and in a system where books for basic education are provided free up to junior-secondary level. It is equally evident in the completely different environment of Ethiopia, one of Africa's poorest countries, where one of Africa's largest bookselling chains operates with 36 branches.

Booksellers' skills and training and infrastructure problems

There is little or no formal training for booksellers, and virtually all booksellers have learned their trade on the job. Professional standards are low among new booksellers. Publishers have complained that booksellers do little to generate markets or sales, and this is often true. It is equally true, however, that, with low profit margins, exclusion from parts of the educational market and problems of distance from suppliers, booksellers cannot afford or attract quality staff.

Where bookselling has collapsed, its rehabilitation poses great problems, especially as bookselling is learned on the job in existing established booksellers. It is not an attractive investment option. To open even a modest bookshop requires a shop, shelving, fittings, staff and some stock. Capital is needed from the start, and emergent booksellers typically lack the working capital to maintain a service throughout the year in their formative period, given the seasonal nature of educational supply. Overheads are difficult to reduce no matter how market conditions fluctuate. Publishers' discounts hardly go above 25% and are often well below that (in contrast to a standard 33% on stationery). Few booksellers obtain credit from publishers. Booksellers frequently complain of late payment by government customers. Booksellers in turn cannot pay publishers, and this creates mistrust between publishers and booksellers.

From a purely economic viewpoint, bookselling in much of Africa makes insufficient surplus to finance its own growth. Empowerment of local commercial publishing has been most effective when the ministry has collaborated closely with the industry, aware of the opportunities presented by the commercial sector, with a vision of fulfilling the potential national resources in book development. Future trends in bookselling will follow the same pattern, as the state looks more towards a holistic book industry.

Book trade associations

Strengthening trade associations of publishers has been a major emphasis of APNET throughout the 1990s. By 1999, APNET had twenty-seven national publishers' association (NPA) members under its umbrella (by 2004 this was thirty-five). Of these, nineteen had formal constitutions and elected executives guiding all aspects of their internal relations. Very few had independent offices, most being reliant on a benefactor or on one of its members to house a secretariat. About half had telephones and about a fifth had computers. Less than half had any form of annual budget. The majority financed some proportion of secretariat costs from members' subscriptions, but all were dependent on funding partners for any meaningful institutional or project activities.

NPAs throughout Africa remain institutionally weak, particularly in the absence of reliable and consistent communications to members, and between members and education ministries, on matters affecting them and the industry in general. They lack the resources and systems to achieve the efficiency required. The impetus towards professional standards therefore tends to derive from the activities of the leading publishers.

Nigeria, South Africa, Zimbabwe and Kenya all have self-supporting NPAs, at least at a minimal level of resources and administrative capacity. This directly reflects a relatively buoyant or established commercial publishing environment. Ethiopia and Mozambique do not have an active publishers' association, but irregular *ad hoc* meetings are held. Where NPAs have received institutional support, as in Ghana in the 1990s, they have, in most cases, made remarkable progress as long as they have had a clear plan and vision. When publishers' associations have, for example, secured resources, they have rapidly organised national book fairs, as in Tanzania, Uganda and Zambia.

The situation regarding booksellers' associations is weaker still. About ten African countries have active booksellers' associations, reflecting the relative organisational weakness of bookselling in relation to publishing. In contrast to APNET, established in 1992 and a major recipient of funding by 1994, PABA is still at the formative stage of developing its own institutional capacity and has not been able to provide any significant support to member associations.

Of the countries considered in this study, Zimbabwe, Kenya and Uganda have relatively well-organised booksellers' associations. The 300-member Nigerian association is emerging from a period of stagnation in the 1990s, and signs are that it will in future fulfil its considerable potential. Zambia has a newly formed booksellers' association that, while well organised, is still small and finding its feet. Tanzania's association has struggled for recognition over many years – at times all but folding up, lacking both administrative capacity and a constitution – but it has survived and grown in recent years, and with support will become an important element of Tanzania's book industry. Ghana's association has been in the doldrums for some years, its active membership dwindling as a result of marginalization from the educational market. In the last year, there have been encouraging moves among members to strengthen the association to play a more active role. Mauritius has a relatively inactive booksellers' association, despite its vigorous bookselling sector. Mali, Guinea, Senegal, Ethiopia and Mozambique lack active booksellers' associations.

The overall weakness evident in most national publishers' and booksellers' associations in Africa is a major inhibiting factor in the development of public/private partnerships in the book sector. As well as their training and project activities, trade associations perform critical functions. They are the most effective forum for efficient communication between the education ministry and the industry, for members to set development priorities, and to upgrade trade relations and 'standards and conventions' between publishers and booksellers that underpin a functional industry. This can be achieved with only a minimum of administrative capacity – a small secretariat, communications and computer – allowing for effective transmission of information.

THE ROLE OF THE MINISTRY OF EDUCATION IN A LIBERALISED SYSTEM

A particular problem inherent to the liberalisation of state monopolies relates to how to manage the process. Commercial publishing and textbook provision require, above all, continuity of policy, a stable environment and long-term 'standards and conventions' that guide the book trade. However, the nature of the changes taking place requires a fundamental overhaul of the entire textbook-supply system, although the long-term goal remains one of stability and continuity.

In developed commercial book industries in Europe, relations between the government and private-sector interests in book provision have taken shape 'organically', one could say, over a century or more in the context of a free market. Responsibilities are regulated, but not by anything approximating a single 'book policy', or encapsulated in any document, let alone under the singular 'authority' of one ministry. They are far too complex. They are the sum total of what constitutes 'conventions and standards' in the book industry, shaped over decades and providing for continuity. The function of each component in the book chain and the responsibilities of the private sector cannot be altered without extensive consultation. There is almost universal recognition that the private sector has a responsibility to pioneer innovations in textbook development, frequently leading to changes in systems and new expectations on the part of the textbook users, rather than innovation being the sole preserve of the curriculum authorities.

Conversely, in some parts of the developing world that have seen rapid growth in their book industries (Latin America and Asia being prime examples), state–private relations in books have been framed within extensive policy instruments, in some instances meticulously codified in law. This has provided the necessary continuity of policy that has allowed private investment and expansion in the book industry. Some experts view this as the reason for the extraordinary growth in scope and volume of Latin American book output in the last twenty years.

Book policies

In general terms, one can trace two distinctive patterns shaping textbook provision in Africa from the independence era in the 1960s to the new millennium. In the first, Africa was perceived by multinational publishers as an overseas market; in some instances, African states instituted centralised state textbook provision that either partnered or replaced the multinationals, or both. In any event, the result in these cases has been a *de facto* central monopoly over textbook provision. In other cases, such as those of Zimbabwe and Kenya, multinationals continue to dominate local commercially based textbook provision. This trend represented mainstream educational wisdom by the principal actors in textbook provision through to the 1990s.

In the second pattern, nascent African book industries pose the argument in terms of 'sustainable textbook provision' by overcoming dependence on imports, breaking up previous monopoly approaches, and building indigenous African book industries with local resources. The result is the kind of diversity and liberalisation of which Nigeria is such a striking example. This thinking forms the background to 'public/private partnership' in African book provision today. Because of the uncertainties in the transitional phase – from state monopoly to free market – which are inimical to private-sector investment and growth, African publishers and booksellers propose that transition be underpinned by policy. Education ministries, aware that liberalisation presents such a kaleidoscope of new actors in the system and options over roles, gradually but definitively adopts a textbook policy or national book policy as the foundation for the transition (A more detailed discussion of book policies appears in Chapter Six).

In Africa, the need for continuity within the new systems that are gradually taking shape is keenly felt. There is a growing tide of opinion that a 'national book policy' that regulates and codifies relations between the state and the private sector in book provision must provide the framework for future development. The catalyst for this has arisen from within indigenous book circles that perceive their needs in terms of a long-term stable policy that both defines the role of the commercial sector and reinforces the 'national character' of books, publishing and the publishing industry. Examples of this are the persistent efforts of Zambian, Kenyan and Ghanaian publishers throughout the 1990s to initiate dialogue with their ministries of education to develop a national book policy that will provide the framework for continuity of policy and sustainability of textbook provision.

A number of education ministries, recognizing that the transition to liberalisation cannot be achieved with purely *ad hoc* decisions, have responded and led the way in formulating policy. This has often been accomplished through extensive dialogue between the ministry and book-trade associations, with input from other stakeholders (such as library and writers' associations). In Ghana's case, for instance, a wide cross-section of 128 stakeholders (representing all aspects of book writing, publishing and distribution, plus the Ministry of Education) attended the 2001 policy review that led to the final basic education textbook policy in 2002. Similarly, in Kenya's case, the Kenya Publishers' Association was seen as a full partner of the Ministry of Education in its textbook policy of 1998. The textbook-provision policy – as part of a comprehensive national book policy covering all book issues – has been pivotal because textbooks comprise not less than 80 per cent of the book market. That 'textbook' policy in Africa invariably determines national 'book' policy is a simple enough concept, but it is often forgotten.

Thus, in virtually every instance, the liberalisation of textbook provision has been accompanied by a long process of policy formulation, eventually leading to a new textbook policy, to regulate change. Among countries adopting them are Tanzania (in 1991), Uganda (1992), Zambia (1996), Kenya (1998), Ghana (2002), and Mozambique (2003). Ethiopia's 1998 draft policy is still at discussion stage. Senegal, Guinea and Mali are all in the final stages of developing national textbook policies to guide textbook liberalisation.

Box 10: Liberalisation in Anglophone countries since 1990	
Tanzania	1991
Uganda	1992
Zambia	1996
Kenya	1998
Ethiopia	1998
Ghana	2002
Mozambique	2003

It was argued in some quarters in the 1980s and 1990s that the creation of a book policy is far too complex and drawn-out, and, in any event, free-market book industries (citing Zimbabwe and Nigeria, for example) do not have such policies. This was a popular view among some major multinational suppliers towards the supply of textbooks to their African markets, exemplified in the verbal contributions of some multinational publishers at the 1991

Manchester Conference on 'Textbook Provision and Library Development in Africa' (The British Council, 1992). The logical conclusion was presented thus: If you are moving towards a free-market system, do away with such grandiose policy instruments because they represent yet another form of state intervention. Simply let the private sector take over.

This train of thought ignored a single underlying concept in developing national book industries. It is that continuity of systems and policies is vital for indigenous growth and investment in national book industries. Providing there is a market, this is the main condition for the development of a commercial sector in publishing and bookselling – or, in other words, a national book industry.

The concerns of educationists

The APNET submission to the World Bank mentioned in the previous chapter refers to the conflict in attitudes and perspectives between educationists and the book industry:

'Educational development and development of book industries are different elements, however closely bound up in book provision. Decisions for educational development, as in textbook supply, must be fully cognizant of industrial considerations if they are to be productive. *One cannot crudely apply an identical rationale for both and expect reasonable results* [my emphasis].' (African Publishers Network, 1993)

African education professionals have to confront many critical issues, such as school infrastructure, financing, sufficient teachers, quality, gender, curriculum reform, AIDS awareness and language policy. In many countries in Africa, education ministries are simultaneously undergoing structural reform and decentralisation. Provision of learning materials, as vital as it is, is just one essential input among many. The intricacies of a newly emergent indigenous commercial book industry, with its own material and equipment requirements and skills and development needs, is not the prime focus of attention of ministries of education according to the findings in field visits from this study in thirteen African countries.

On the contrary, a widespread view exists that as long as syllabus-based books reach pupils' desks by the simplest and most effective means the education ministry is fulfilling its mission. And yet, throughout Africa, this ministry, concerned with 80 per cent of the book market, is the *de facto* authority over the development of a national book industry. This industry also needs its 'standards and conventions', policies, continuity and rapid and detailed decisions, responding to its own needs, in order to take shape.

A further reason for the state of flux in the transition period is that problems of poverty and a lack of resources complicate the development of a free market. An open commercial textbook market has the inevitable result of increasing retail book prices, since commercial publishers have no choice but to build all costs (direct and indirect, including overhead costs) into the retail price of the textbook and recover these costs through sales. The element of a margin of profit is necessary, since profit provides capital for further growth. A rapid transition to free-market system is not perceived as the sole route to vibrant textbook provision regardless of circumstances. In poor countries, poor people, the majority, cannot afford books, whether as direct purchases by parents or through some form of textbook levy.

As Zimbabwe illustrates, the changing structure of poverty has placed massive new demands on the system in all African countries affected by the HIV/AIDS pandemic. At Zimbabwe's independence, poverty conformed to a concept of 'historical disadvantage'. This assumed that poverty was 'social' and can be expressed in terms of infrastructure, capital stock and investment, and that, by these standards, rural communities were by definition the poorest social group. While this remains true in most senses, the situation on the ground concerning school children presents a different picture, as a direct result of HIV/AIDS. A study conducted in 1997 found that destitute pupils are found in virtually every school in the country (except private schools), including all urban schools (Ministry of Education and Culture of Zimbabwe, 1997). Of huge concern for future educational planners is that some 35% of adults in the 20–45-year age group are HIV positive and that around one third of children under 15 are expected to be orphans by 2010, with staggering implications for educational provision. While Southern Africa has a higher HIV prevalence than many parts of Africa, this pattern is evident in all African countries.

Mozambique, in the aftermath of its bitterly destructive counter-terrorism war, developed an interesting model of poverty alleviation in regard to textbooks. The circumstances were unique, with millions of displaced people and large numbers of war orphans and rural destitute. The School Welfare Fund (Caixa Escolar) was established in 1989 to provide textbooks to the most vulnerable pupils (e.g. orphans and displaced persons). Between 1991 and 1995, Caixa Escolar provided a fund for the purchase of textbooks directly for needy students. In 1996, with an injection of World Bank funding, Caixa Escolar was extended to all primary school pupils, through the free provision of books for Grades 1 and 2, and a textbook-loan system for Grades 3 to 7. From an original vision of a social fund to counter exceptional poverty, Caixa Escolar has become *de facto* the principal system and a means for the provision of all primary school textbooks.

The language issue

The book chain faces a fragmented market because so many languages are used. In Uganda, to cite one typical example, there are three major language groups, with dozens of dialects, and English and Swahili – the official and national languages, respectively – are in fact minority languages used by only 10% of the population. There is an illiteracy rate of over 40 per cent, mainly among rural dwellers. In Ethiopia, Amharic is both a minority language and the second language of 85 per cent of the population; English is a third language; the illiteracy rate is around 67 per cent. Twenty separate language groups exist in that country, several with different alphabets. Senegal is trying to develop the use of local languages as the medium of instruction in lower grades, but with more than twenty languages in use, deciding which six to use in schools has been a sensitive issue. To complicate matters, the orthography for some Senegalese languages has not yet been standardized.

Over the years, during the state-monopoly period, Ghana made impressive strides both in promoting local-language usage and in developing standard orthography. Tanzania's adoption of Swahili as its official language, as the medium of instruction in basic education, and as a *de facto* lingua franca has given massive impetus to overcoming the problems of fragmentation, from a publishing, reading and literacy standpoint. Amongst the writers' bodies in Tanzania there are strong sentiments to further deepen the use of Swahili and the 'mother-tongue' languages (since Swahili is a second language for the majority of Tanzanians). From a completely different perspective, the widespread use of English in Zimbabwe and Nigeria has achieved comparable results in overcoming fragmentation in publishing, although national-language publishing is weak in Zimbabwe, and this is a major concern.

Adoption of the mother tongue as the language of instruction in the first three grades of education is almost universally understood as an enhancement of quality of education from a learning retention viewpoint. It also stimulates and creates space for indigenous publishing and writing, and is positive for the cultural and reading environment. Its use (as the medium of instruction) in higher grades necessarily depends on the development of orthography and vocabulary. As the example of Ethiopia shows, there are also issues of identity and important social and political implications to language in African education, in addition to complex educational concerns.

From a publishing standpoint, however, the main dilemma is the technical and practical aspect of writing and publishing for many language groups. In so far as textbooks are concerned, this entails increased investment in manuscript development and quality control and increased risk in publishing smaller print-runs for smaller, less developed markets. This affects the price. One way or another publishers would have to confront viability problems concerns for multi-language publishing projects.

Issues surrounding national-language instruction in education and publishing present immense challenges. It is difficult to conceive how these will be overcome without common purpose between publishers (producers) and ministries of education (consumers). It is an excellent example of how public/private partnership in textbook provision is a pre-requisite for national development.

It is interesting to note that where language of instruction has involved local languages there has been a positive impact on the competitiveness of local publishing, specifically in international tendering for textbooks, but the use of local languages in schools has also had positive effects on general publishing development. This has been the case in both Tanzania and Ethiopia, in completely contrasting environments, and developments in francophone Africa seem to echo this. Primary school instruction in Tanzania is carried out in Swahili, and all textbooks are in Swahili, including those in the sciences. Tanzanian publishers have confidence in their ability to commission writers and to edit Swahili texts to a high level. In Ethiopia, the change of the medium of instruction at primary school to eleven regional languages has meant a *de facto* devolution of textbook authorship to regional writers. Unlike in Tanzania, however, this has not involved the commercialisation of the system.

In Mali, many believe that the low rate of literacy (39% for men, 23% for women, in 1995) is the result of French being previously used as the medium of instruction. The new basic-education curriculum being pilot-tested in a number of schools provides for mother-tongue instruction in lower grades, and there is already substantial evidence that the use of the children's first language improves retention and learning. In Senegal, a new basic-education curriculum is also on the way, and it has been decided that private publishers will develop and publish the books in local languages, initially in a pilot phase. While the publishers will be selected through ICB, the use of local languages gives a significant advantage to local publishers, working in direct collaboration with local writers. In an interesting move, comparable to the Tanzanian PPP capacity-building experiences, the Nordic Development Fund in collaboration with the curriculum institute is planning to offer technical assistance to the local publishers during the book-development process.

As in Mali and Senegal, French is still the medium of instruction in Guinea, but the introduction of local languages as the medium of instruction in primary schools is being discussed. Significantly, however, for the next phase of the World Bank textbook project in Guinea, the Ministry of Education will pilot-test the first multi-textbook system in selected subjects at Grade 6. The curriculum institute will develop syllabuses, from which private publishers will commission textbooks. An approval mechanism for textbooks will be established and schools and districts will select books of their choice. If the pilot test is successful, it will be extended in selected subjects throughout primary school, marking a watershed in Guinean textbook provision. It would be one of the first francophone countries to adopt decentralised selection in a multi-textbook system, and therefore be of immense significance to the region.

Mali, Senegal and Guinea have all made progress towards a textbook policy, embracing gradual forms of liberalisation which mark the beginning of new, and in many cases unprecedented, opportunities for local publishing, including local-language publishing. There is a strong feeling throughout the region that the future sustainability of textbook provision must be based on a flourishing local book industry, and education officials are increasingly adopting these views. There has been a significant increase in co-operation, information flow and sharing of perspectives between local publishers and the education ministries.

Procurement, tenders and consumer choice

In a state publishing bureaucracy (either within a curriculum department or through a state publishing company), a single-textbook system invariably exists. The books are written to curriculum standards within the system (usually by curriculum developers), and no approval mechanism is necessary. In Tanzania, Zambia and Ghana in the 1970s, and in Kenya a decade later, the establishment of state monopoly publishing came in tandem with the introduction of a centralised monopoly over textbook procurement. The Ministry of Education centrally ordered and procured textbooks for all (government) schools.

The movement away from state production of textbooks typically goes via a period of centralised direct procurement of textbooks through to some form of tender system. The education ministry remain's in direct control, and systems and attitudes within the ministry do not change much. The system still operates from a basis of large-volume centralised supply, meaning that procurement, financing and delivery methods hardly change.

On the other hand, development of a multi-textbook market system with decentralised selection and purchase brings profound and fundamental changes. Previous roles and responsibilities regarding textbooks disappear, new skills are needed and old attitudes have to change. From the standpoint of the ministry, this can be overwhelming.

From a situation in which the ministry dealt with one textbook per subject/grade – a total of perhaps 30 or 40 core textbooks in primary schools – it now has to deal with many times that number. Every major publisher will try to have its own textbook approved for each subject and grade. The ministry feels a loss of control, and with good reason – an entire level of decision-making has been devolved to the commercial sector.

Internal accounting systems must change to reflect the new methods of purchase. While a single-title central tender will have one payment for one textbook supplied, a decentralised system will have one payment per supplier for every point of purchase – every district, every school, depending on the extent of decentralisation. Budgeting itself must change, since every purchasing authority (at district or school level) must have its own budget ceiling.

At the core of the change is the replacing of 'direct control of procurement' with 'management of a system'. There is almost universal fear that it will be impossible to control all the new elements brought into play. Moreover, it is one challenge to effect these changes at head office, which is complicated enough, and quite another to ensure that district education offices, thousands of schools, and many new authors, publishers and booksellers are capable of playing their part. The transformation has to be effected throughout the system.

Liberalised textbook publishing, then, literally creating room for commercial publishing activity to replace the state monopoly, has often started with a centralised tender procedure whereby existing textbooks, created by the curriculum department, are published by a small number of pre-selected commercial publishers. This was the case in Tanzania, through the Pilot Project for Publishing (PPP), and in Zambia, through its early tender-based procurement models. In Uganda, a new generation of textbooks was developed by publishers, and a tender system applied at the point of submitting books, with a limit of three prescribed texts for grade/subject. Various tender systems are is use in Mozambique and throughout the francophone region as an integral part of 'commercialisation'.

The World Bank and some other funding agencies have a history of regulating textbook aid by imposing international competitive bidding, and this, too, has been applied widely throughout Africa in many 'one-off' textbook-provision programmes, Ghana being a prime example.

Systems of central purchasing define the responsibilities and attitudes of all actors in the process, including the Ministry of Education. Central purchasing is a major exercise, carried out periodically – commonly according to the life-span of a book, every three to four years – and is usually, but not always (as in Uganda), based on a single textbook per grade/subject. Even when the liberalisation of publishing has transformed one core function of the state (and in particular of the curriculum authority) from creating to approving textbooks, the Ministry of Education has to take on the role of central purchasing authority and requires a bureaucracy for that responsibility.

It is a direct management function: arranging funding, deciding on and imposing tender conditions, selecting the product for all schools, determining quantities, deciding on cost, placing orders, receiving the books, warehousing and delivering – all these are state functions in a 'central procurement by tender' system. Even when some of these tasks are carried out by a third party rather than within the ministry – or, as has often happened, when a funding agency undertakes them on behalf of the ministry – the character of central purchasing defines the role and attitudes of the ministry.

Every Education Ministry in Africa that procures books centrally has a procurement department established for this purpose. In Zambia, the Ministry of Education Procurement and Supplies Unit (MEPSU) has arranged the procurement of textbooks since the monopoly of the Kenneth Kaunda Foundation (later Zambia Educational Publishing House, ZEPH) was ended.

In both the Zambian and Ugandan tender models, where cost has been the justification for central procurement, the bottom-line costs of tender documents are, of course, lower than they would be if publishers applied a normal retail price, incorporating distribution costs and a bookseller's discount. The tender system distorts conventional publishing costing, reducing it to manuscript development, tender costs, production costs and the publisher's gross profit, on a given print-run, without risk.

What has been apparent in the Zambian tender model, as has been the case in virtually all central tender models, are the hidden costs of tender-based supply. These include storage at central and transit warehouses, separate haulage tenders and costs of central delivery, and overhead costs in the administration of the tenders.

Of even greater concern are the bottlenecks in supply from

districts to schools, since no provision had been made for district councils to deliver to schools. It is clear from various studies that these hidden costs have never been quantified. The Ministry of Education and stakeholders agree that the central tender system has not resulted in books reaching classrooms in their correct quantities and according to examination timetables. In fact, the tender system has proved cumbersome. Large amounts of funds earmarked for textbooks have not been spent. Of five major tenders floated for school requirements between 1999 and 2002 in Zambia, the results of three were still awaited by September 2002. Over-riding all this has been the difficulty in changing all the systems in the Ministry, since the whole edifice of textbook provision, from financing to choice, has been constructed around state procurement. The Zambian experience is not unique – identical problems have occurred in Kenya, Uganda, Ghana, Mozambique, Tanzania, Senegal, Guinea, Mali and Ethiopia.

In addition, where textbooks are government property as in most central procurement models, (such as Ethiopia, Mali, Ghana throughout the 1970s and 1980s and Tanzania), booksellers are not allowed to sell them on the open market, and there are no mechanisms for booksellers to purchase copies from the government. Yet many parents are interested in buying books for their children as governments are almost never able to finance one book per pupil. This has led, in Mali, to a parallel market for stolen books. Parallel examples can be found in Ghana, Zambia and Tanzania.

A host of factors influenced Zambia's decision to continue centralised supply long after 'policy' had dictated otherwise, including constant pressure to get textbooks to schools regularly since the book–pupil ratio was falling, a lack of booksellers, and publishers' hesitancy to enter into distribution (preferring to deliver centrally in Lusaka). Nevertheless, in Zambia (as elsewhere) the principal argument in favour of continued centralised procurement and supply was that it resulted in books being priced lower than could have been achieved in a decentralised purchase system. In Zambia's case this was because publishers could reduce their costs with one bulk print-run and maximize cost-efficiencies on production. In addition, publishers delivered only to a central point in the capital, and all costs related to sales, marketing and warehousing could be eliminated.

The winner-takes-all tender system puts publishers under considerable pressure to keep the prices they quote on tender low, since the tender represents such a major proportion of their overall sales that the loss of a tender could affect their continued existence. A similar scenario has been reported in Uganda in 1998/99 with the introduction of an ICB tender system that raised the financial entry level for publishers who submitted textbook tenders, and, more recently, with a limitation on the number of approved titles.

Against this background, publishers have been compelled into aggressive competition, sometimes setting unrealistically low tender prices. This has led to unhealthy competition between publishers and, in some cases, alleged attempts to influence tender procedures in an all-out effort to win. Indeed, there are frequent allegations in many African countries that publishers have submitted tenders at a loss in order to become the sole publisher in a winner-takes-all (effectively single-textbook) tender procurement system. Such allegations are difficult to verify, but the adverse effects of tender systems on the development of relations within the commercial book sector must be noted.

Whether it is local or international, central tender procurement invariably favours publishers with capital and resources: pre-qualification and security bids are designed to ensure this. Without some form of indigenization policy – as in Ghana, Nigeria and Tanzania – this system has strengthened the concentration of multinational publishers and restricted the emergence of more diverse indigenous publishing, which has been the case in Botswana, Lesotho, Swaziland, Zambia, Malawi, Uganda, Guinea and Senegal, for example. It was the situation in Ghana throughout the 1980s, and will become so in Mozambique under the current liberalisation plans, in which two British, one Portuguese and one local subsidiary of a Portuguese publisher pre-qualified to publish textbooks. Malian publishers are hoping to maintain their position in the forthcoming procurement tender, since these books will be in indigenous languages.

Tanzania, on the other hand, placed such a premium on indigenous publishing, with the relative advantages of publishing books in Kiswahili, that local publishers found space to compete. Kenya (when under centralised procurement) and Ghana had similarly strong internal drives towards indigenization. Kenyan indigenization has been particularly motivated by the commercial sector in that country. Heinemann's and Longman's interests in Kenya were bought out by Kenyans, a development almost without precedent in Africa but one that captures the depth of sentiment in that country on the issue of indigenization. In Ghana, indigenization became government policy with the 1976 Investment Policy Decree. While multinational publishers continued to dominate the arena of international tenders, local publishing has become a Ghanaian affair, 95 per cent of the members of the Ghana Book Publishers' Association being Ghanaian companies. Even so, in the Ministry of Education's 1998 primary reading programme tender (encompassing four million copies of books), British publishers won 60 per cent of the orders; significantly, Ghanaian publishers counted their 40 per cent as a stunning and unprecedented success.

In summary, winner-takes-all central tender models, usually but not always based on a single title per grade/subject, have a marked tendency to concentrate commercial publishing around fewer publishers with stronger financial resources. For this reason, multinationals have been the main beneficiary, and the newer, weaker African counter-parts have found difficulty in competing in tender procurement systems, unless some indigenization policy is prevalent. 'Central purchase' through tenders has a tendency to define attitudes and systems in ministries of education that are difficult to change, because ministries build a 'procurement bureaucracy' around this activity.

Consumer Choice: The Core of Public/Private Partnership

At the very heart of public/private partnership lies consumer choice, because it is choice that defines the ways in which the state works with the commercial sector. Choice of procurement method defines the activities of booksellers, their place in the system; choice of textbooks defines the activities of publishers, their roles and the scope of publishing activity in the system. Choices in textbook publishing have three main elements, involving quantity, supplier and product.

> **Box 11: The core of public/private partnerships**
>
> CHOICE of procurement method defines the role of the bookseller.
>
> CHOICE of textbook defines the role of the publisher.

Quantitative choice

There is choice about how to spend a budget in terms of the quantity of books required per grade and subject, according to actual school enrolments. Experience has shown that such choice, when made by a central authority, does not accurately respond to the diverse needs in thousands of schools. Over time, schools end up with different stocks of books, even though their needs as initially specified would have been similar. Reasons for this include student intakes, wear and tear, wastage and loss, previous shortfalls. This is borne out in Zambia and Tanzania, where numerous studies have shown wide disparities in textbook–pupil ratios for certain subject/grades and in the availability of particular textbooks even between neighbouring schools and districts.

Decentralising orders to schools or districts is a logical improvement in efficiency. Virtually every independent study concludes that the majority of schools make the right decisions when they are given the authority to decide their own priorities. A 2002 textbook study in Zambia confirmed the point (Ministry of Education of Zambia, 2002). Schools in remote areas were able to elucidate their needs accurately, and to justify them on the basis of their knowledge of their own priorities. They were able to do this despite being a considerable distance from the local district education office, let alone from Lusaka, with its well-stocked bookshops and access to book information generally. This was because, as the 'end-users', they have their requirements at their fingertips.

Box 12: Choices in textbook publishing

QUANTITY: *Budget expenditure.*
The quantity of books required per grade and subject according to school enrolment.

CHOICE OF SUPPLIER: *Where to order and from whom?*
• Bookseller?
• Direct from publisher?
• Distribution company?

CHOICE OF PRODUCT: *Per grade, per subject*
• Multiple textbook choice?
• Single textbook?

Rural school textbook supply in Zimbabwe began at district council level in 1983, and remained there for six to seven years prior to full decentralisation to the schools. During this period, schools in perhaps one third of the districts complained that their orders had frequently been altered to reflect influences at district level. More worrying for the ministry were growing occurrences of booksellers seeking to gain lucrative district orders by means that were unprofessional. One effect of full decentralisation to schools was that booksellers with a reputation for unethical practice disappeared. This was felt to be because schools were more demanding than the districts about the timely delivery of orders and correct titles and quantities, and the effort involved in selling school-by-school gave the more serious booksellers an upper hand in the market. Today decentralisation has been further elaborated to incorporate School Development Committees under the leadership of the school head but involving teachers' and parents' input on textbook-ordering decisions. The ministry, the schools and the commercial sector are all agreed that the effect has been exceptionally beneficial, particularly the element of sharing textbook problems with the parents. As a result of the erosion of the purchasing power of the per capita grant in recent years, parents are playing an increasing role in supplementary funding to the entire system. In 2003 a new phenomenon appeared in the urban centers: parents were given a list of books to purchase for their children, and also on the list was a request to purchase one library book as a donation to the school. The response caught publishers by surprise, and stocks of primary school textbooks ran out nationwide before they had reprinted for the 2003 seasonal textbook sales.

District-level, as opposed to school-level, procurement is frequently unavoidable where schools do not have bank accounts to pay suppliers, and the 'ordering authority' must, of necessity, be the district. In other cases, there is no supply network of booksellers in remote districts that could take on deliveries to scattered schools, and therefore the district again ends up as the ordering authority. But district-level procurement often has the same problems as those associated with central procurement, albeit on a smaller scale.

The bureaucratic processes involved in compiling accurate orders may be reduced if schools make their own lists against a budget ceiling, but those involved in consolidating these orders, dealing with suppliers, ordering, warehousing, and finding the means to deliver from a district to all the schools on time are practically very difficult. When Tanzania was beginning various pilot schemes in procurement via districts to schools in the 1990s (including textbooks, stationery, library books and other school requisites), the districts, despite their best efforts and often ingenious solutions, experienced huge problems in warehousing and effecting delivery to schools. In some cases it could take over six months for a consignment to be delivered from district to school. Almost identical problems have been witnessed in Zambia. In Zimbabwe, the district-level phase of decentralised procurement (1983–1989) functioned reasonably well, but was always problematic.

Choice of supplier

The second choice is about where to order and on what terms. The ideal position for a school would be to order from a local bookseller, which then in turn consolidates and orders from many publishers. This 'consolidation' role is an important service that frees a school from the administrative burden of having to place orders with a number of different publishers. The common theory is that, as soon as the market is decentralised, booksellers will follow. This is true in a general sense. The expansion of Zimbabwean booksellers into smaller towns was precisely a case of following the market because it became advantageous for them to be situated closer to the purchaser, a school or district. The expansion of Kenyan booksellers following the 1998 decentralisation of the selection of books to schools has closely mirrored this. The bookselling infrastructure in both Zimbabwe and Kenya has become possible because publishers agreed that they would not sell directly to the school consumer. The Tusome Vitabu project in Western Tanzania developed a similar role for booksellers in supplying schools in the project, and a surprising number of booksellers opened new branches in the remote province. The pilot decentralisation project in four districts of Uganda has shown a similar pattern.

As a consequence of state-monopoly approaches, African booksellers are concentrated in cities, where the market has been able to sustain their business, with or without a large textbook component. Where the decentralised system and market has taken root and matured, bookselling has decentralised, usually quite effectively. But where the system is new, where booksellers are fragile, and when schools or districts are ordering for the first time from untested local booksellers, problems occur. Abuses can become common in an environment where 'briefcase booksellers' are allowed into the system. Most countries have sought to solve this by creating a code of professional conduct for booksellers.

In some instances the district or school then reverts to ordering direct from the publishers, or from the established booksellers in a major city. Depending on distance, this can work adequately, but it defeats the major purpose of decentralisation – efficiency. There is hardly a situation in Africa where the major commercial publishers, even as a group, can deliver to all schools in all parts of the country. There must by definition be a process of consolidation and delivery mechanism between several supply points (publishers) and thousands of consumers (schools).

Publishers in some countries, working as a consortium, have attempted to establish distribution companies to address this. This was the case in Tanzania during the last PPP phase (1999), when publishers were faced with the mammoth undertaking of delivering to all 72 districts. It has proved to be an *ad hoc* solution that has not resulted in booksellers being established. It is also a solution that depends on single, large-scale (and therefore 'economic') deliveries, and in this sense was a return to centralised approaches. This has worked, with difficulty, up to the point where small supplementary orders are needed, or where the original consignment has a shortfall that needs to be rectified. It is too unwieldy for this purpose. Sometimes district-level intervention is a practical necessity to undertake tasks that should be taken up by local commercial booksellers – that is, consolidation and delivery to school. The problems involved earlier come into play where the district is not geared to this task.

Choice of product

The third element of choice concerns choosing between a number of different textbooks for each subject and grade, all of which conform to curricular requirements. The decision to construct a 'multiple textbook choice' system is a watershed decision in textbook provision. The thinking behind this has been widely debated by educationists.

The argument in favour of a single textbook per grade and subject is founded on the belief that textbooks of genuine quality will emerge if textbooks writers are commissioned by a team with experience and expertise, guided from within the educational system under the curriculum development department. Since all this takes place under the direct control of the Ministry of Education, the needs of the pupil, the system and the priorities of culture and social awareness can all be assured. It can be argued that this has indeed been the case in Mozambique, where the production and editorial quality of primary school textbooks have been uniformly impressive, particularly for the early grades.

However, multi-textbook systems are rapidly becoming the aim of African countries because it is now recognized that commercial publishers possess both the competence and social responsibility to assure these needs. Indeed, it is difficult to find examples where commercial publishers have not exceeded the quality parameters of state textbooks. The standard of books produced by Tanzania's so-called 'fledgling' commercial publishing sector exceeded previous efforts by the state. Both Zambia's and Uganda's commercial publishers have recorded similar quality successes.

Arguments supporting the use of different textbooks are that quality in educational delivery also requires a diversity of inputs, while still conforming to overall principles. Interestingly, school textbook-selection committees in Zimbabwe developed a practice of trying to ensure that the school has, in addition to one core textbook, a few copies of every other local textbook as a resource for the subject for both teachers and pupils. These extra copies often form the beginning of a small, useful classroom library.

No single textbook at any level contains every useful feature in the learning process; books become outdated, and in practice competition between textbooks creates conditions for innovation – a constant search for new and better methods. This is driven by the primary aim of every author and publisher – to secure a larger market share than their competitors. The more freely the market (in this sense meaning the 'book-user') is able to select, and the greater is the choice, the more effectively the quality will appreciate. This has certainly been a major factor in the high quality of Zimbabwean textbooks. It is not unusual for one publisher to launch a new or updated series of textbooks, to be followed within a few years by new or updated series from competitive publishers to regain market share they will have lost.

Multiple textbook use invariably requires some form of 'standards authority' to approve new textbooks, usually at the 'camera ready' stage of the manuscript. As far as the role of the state is concerned, book approval in effect replaces book creation. Textbook approvals are often, but not always, located within the curriculum department since that is where the responsibility for educational content lies. This is the method adopted in Zimbabwe and Zambia. In Tanzania and Uganda, however, it was decided to locate textbook approvals outside the curriculum authority, mainly because of perceived conflicts of interest, since the previous generation of textbooks were frequently authored by curriculum development staff.

Another form of 'public/private partnership' soon emerges. Authors commissioned by publishers find it necessary – in order to ensure that a textbook matches curricular requirements and does not omit essential pedagogical features – to work with both curriculum designers and teachers to produce better books. This has been the case in every situation where multiple textbook approval has been adopted.

All curricula contain both purpose and method, as well as content, in an overall strategy towards pupils' attainment of a prescribed level of ability and knowledge. While content may be relatively straightforward to define, purpose and method have many variables, many possible approaches which can improve 'quality in classroom use'. The interface between specialist author, curriculum developer and end-user (the teacher) in textbook design throws up new ideas and innovative methods.

Selection from multiple textbooks pre-supposes the decentralisation of procurement decisions. A single central consumer (the Ministry of Education) will inevitably select a single textbook per grade and subject –as with the tender model in Zambia. In Uganda, the middle road has been taken – a limit of three approved textbooks; but this came only after some determined lobbying by Ugandan publishers, since the Ministry had initially proposed a return to a single textbook per grade/subject. Generally, devolution of selection brings the decision to the point of the user (the school) or close to the point of the user (the district), and this brings many new factors into play.

Schools have different reasons why, in their own circumstances and responding to specific needs, they might select one book over another. Why should one textbook be better than another from a school's perspective? Past experience with a certain textbook might be a determining factor. The need for diversity, new inputs to the learning process might lead to a different conclusion. Price is a consideration. Production quality, which determines a book's life-span, is another factor. However, the primary reason will always be how helpful a textbook is to the teacher in delivering education, within defined financial limitations. Because of this, there is always scope for new products that offer more effective tools to the teacher and pupil.

This has exceptional significance to issues of quality of education, a prime objective in education ministries everywhere in Africa. The diversity and innovation of textbook products provided by the commercial sector in a multi-textbook system with school selection have far surpassed those of any equivalent state-monopoly publishing system. There are no exceptions to this in Africa.

The major concern of education ministries has been the perceived relatively higher cost of commercially produced textbooks in multi-textbook systems, especially when the commercial sector is responsible for delivery and therefore has to factor in the cost of delivery. It is frequently assumed that, in the commercial sector where a profit motive exists, the books must, by definition, be more 'expensive'. In this study, little evidence has been found to support this. No studies have been found that accurately analyse the comparative total costs of state publishing and distribution, tender (commonly with state distribution of some form) and multi-textbook decentralised and commercial distribution; there are many hidden costs and wastages with state and central tender systems, buried within ministries' administrative structures.

It is, however, not difficult to check the costing structures of publishers – which, by and large, are based on standard percentage costings for each component of the manufacturing and distribution process – and to establish control mechanisms to eliminate over-pricing. From the commercial perspective, competition is the most effective 'price control mechanism', though there are concerns that publishers might act as cartels to determine retail prices such that the benefits to the consumer of free-market competition are eroded. The spectre of poorly applied 'price controls', on the other hand, that set unrealistic price parameters for commercial publishers, would create another problem.

Intra-ministerial co-ordination

In a liberalised textbook-supply system, a number of separate departments are engaged with various aspects of textbook provision. The planning department may be collating figures on enrolments that are essential for correct budgeting. The curriculum department has a keen interest in the quality of textbooks being produced but is no longer directly involved in the writing and development of textbooks. Instead, the textbook approvals mechanism (whether inside or outside the curriculum department) will act on its behalf. The accounting section will be directly engaged in the disbursement of funds for decentralised procurement, and in the monitoring of these funds. In all this the ministry will find it necessary to streamline its own internal organisational capacity to deal with textbook issues that cut across many of its head office departments and filter down to provincial, district and even school or school-cluster levels. Ministries have found various ways to tackle this. The most common is to create a specialist textbook unit within the ministry to co-ordinate the decisions and activities of the state and the communications with the commercial sector. Alternatively, the office of the permanent secretary itself might perform this role, but the workload during the transition phase will be considerable, which means that additional staff will be needed.

In Zambia, the mechanism within the ministry to effect these changes has been a specialized textbook unit, the Educational Materials Unit, located in the curriculum authority, the CDC. Among its tasks are the administration of textbook approvals, receiving manuscripts, and organising the reading and recommendations that results in approval. Zambia's Educational Materials Technical Committee (EMTC) is an 'advisory' body that meets to discuss critical textbook issues and make recommendations, particularly on decentralisation of supply. It also oversees the work of the Educational Materials Unit, which is staffed by two people.

Box 13: Coordination in Ministry of Education

- Textbook Unit/Educational Materials Unit in CDC?
- Educational Materials Technical Committee?
- Office of Permanent Secretary?
- Book Management Unit in Planning Department?

In Tanzania, the organisation was considerably larger. The now defunct Book Management Unit (BMU) was staffed at its peak by eight people, had a vehicle and driver, a computer on every desk, a photocopier and a constant stream of technical consultants. It fell under the Planning Department, and had responsibility over all aspects of liberalisation in the Pilot Project for Publishing (PPP) programme. It advised the ministry, liaised between the ministry and the commercial sector, organised training programmes, and managed the bidding process that led to the first generation of new textbooks produced by commercial publishers. It also co-ordinated the phasing out of the old printing programme with the introduction of commercial titles.

The BMU was mirrored in the Ministry of Rural Administration and Local Government by the Education Co-ordination Unit (ECU). The ECU frequently undertook field visits to districts to monitor textbook supply, sometimes accompanied by BMU staff, and was responsible for the nationwide training programme for district education offices (as the new selection authority). The field monitoring work at ECU proved a key component of the liberalisation process, and, as is so often the case, localised supply problems in the districts presented a completely different picture from that seen by the head office of the ministry.

A comparable textbook unit in the Ugandan Ministry of Education, the Instructional Materials Unit (IMU), is the principal facilitator at ministry level between commercial publishers and booksellers and school and district selection systems. It manages the tenders awarded to publishers on the basis of selection at school level.

Single-textbook systems in all the countries had been under the control of the education ministry. If problems arose, remedial action could be taken internally: *ad hoc* or crisis decisions could avert catastrophe. With decentralisation, however, textbook provision was no longer under the ministry's direct control but was dependent on a system with many new players. For a ministry schooled in direct control, it was not quickly understood that the new system could not be administered in the same way.

Experience has shown that the new participants in a liberalised textbook system – chiefly commercial publishers and booksellers, as well as authorities in charge of the devolved purchasing (districts, schools, etc.) – are quite capable of carrying out their responsibilities, providing that the capacity exists and the foundation has been laid with systems of accountability. Setting up these new systems is the main challenge for the education ministries, and virtually every one is grappling with this task, though the tendency to control rather than to manage is still prevalent everywhere. The Ministry of Education is still seen to be, politically, the agency responsible for textbook provision, and if things go wrong it is the ministry itself that must be brought to account.

Forward planning and budgeting

A commercial textbook publishing system and a devolved purchasing system require considerable forward planning and budgeting. District and/or school purchasing authorities require textbook budgets, based on per capita calculations or special needs (for example, for supplementary books). Determining the funds available for textbook purchases and allocating the global budget to each purchasing authority (school or district) is an enormous and time-consuming undertaking, particularly in the first years when the tasks are new and the system is not mature. And after being budgeted, the funds themselves have to be disbursed.

As far as the publishers are concerned, books take years to commission, edit and publish, and signify a large investment. The decision on the actual print-run, especially the large print-runs needed for primary schools, is the most risky one that publishers can take, and requires accurate information about overall textbook budgets as well as a good picture of their own market share. Without advance information about what is likely to be allocated for textbook purchases, publishers cannot take these decisions. The longer the budgetary information is unavailable, the greater will be the delays in production decisions.

Box 14: Forward planning for devolved purchasing to schools

- Allocation of funds available for TB purchase to schools or districts.

- TB budgets in schools or districts (based on school enrolment or special needs).

- Publishing decisions on size of print run based on:
  - overall budget
  - own market share

- Importance of transparency of TB funds.

This brings into sharp focus another dimension of the public–private relationship – transparency regarding textbook funds. Questions and concerns over budgets are communicated constantly by the commercial publishers to the education ministry. Where booksellers are engaged in distribution, they are also keenly interested in what is to be spent on textbooks, but, unlike publishers, they do not have to invest large sums of money in printing costs so don't need the information as early as publishers do.

The system of per capita grant funding applied by Zimbabwe provides a good example. The grant used to be split into two tranches, 70 per cent being disbursed in the first term and the balance some months later, after publishers had supplied the initial stock to schools and had a clear idea of shortfalls or special needs. The actual amount of the grant has always been considered of vital strategic consequence because it serves as the basis for accurate re-prints of textbook stock. Booksellers and publishers literally counted the days until the grant came out, and then a flurry of sales activity began on the part of the booksellers, and publishers received stocks from printers and began processing orders.

Two tranches:
• 70% disbursed 1st term (*for initial despatch of books to schools*).
• 30% some months later (*to meet shortfall or special needs*).

This system does not remove the element of risk and competition in the publishing sector, but it does serve as a basis on which informed decisions can be made. More importantly, it propels both the producer and consumer towards an annual planning cycle that increases the efficiency of the entire book chain. The continuity inherent in the system laid the foundation for an efficient seasonal pattern of textbook production and supply in Zimbabwe. It allowed the consumers and distributors (schools, parents, booksellers) to assess new products, look at the impact of price increases, compare services of suppliers, and work out priorities and budgets. In Zimbabwe's recent hyperinflationary years, the buying power of the per capita grant has been severely eroded and is of less importance, but at its peak it was an important pivot on which the system hinged and the result was streamlining and efficiency.

In assessing future roles for the state in the growth of liberalisation, effective methods of state intervention in previous book provision should be borne in mind, especially where these concern public–private co-operation. In several instances, lack of commercial capacity propelled the state into publishing. The problems related to insufficient commercial capacity are still evident, even with its growth in an environment of liberalisation. This is particularly acute in the most risky areas of publishing, including local language and supplementary educational materials.

The ministry's role in quality management

The Ministry of Education is affected by liberalisation in various ways. It will have to adapt itself and make concessions, but it will also have to take on many new tasks. From a situation in which the ministry had total control of the content of education, it now faces the somewhat worrying fact that textbooks will be developed by commercial publishers. It is reassuring that the curriculum remains safely in its hands; the educational goals and general principles are firmly established by the government. But if liberalisation is to bring pedagogical benefits, the ministry will have to relax its control over content, to some extent. In a single-textbook system, the syllabus is often so detailed that it can be used for teaching if textbooks are not available. In a multi-textbook system, however, a detailed and prescriptive syllabus limits the scope for educational innovation and variety and hampers development.

Correspondence with the syllabus is one of the criteria for the approval of a textbook, and it is difficult to write an innovative and captivating book for, say, Grade 2 if it risks being rejected because it contains some 'Grade 3 words'. In a liberalised system the syllabus needs only to define 'the broad area that textbooks must cover in each subject and at each level' (Garzon, 1997). The rest can be left to the discretion of the writers.

The Ministry of Education can offer guidance to inexperienced publishers and writers to help them interpret the intentions of the curriculum. In Zimbabwe, the Curriculum Development Unit (CDU) has for many years offered pedagogical guidance, for a fee. As the CDU is also responsible for the approval of textbooks, using the services and following the advice offered means that there is very little risk that a book will be rejected. Although not a prerequisite for approval, the advisory service is used by many publishers.

It is in the interest of textbook writers to implement the aims and ideas of the curriculum developers and to follow the syllabus as much as possible. But if the writers are practising teachers they have practical (sometimes negative) experience of how curriculum-based material functions in class. This means that they can also help curriculum planners make the syllabus more 'realistic' and relevant to the classroom situation. With good working relations between publishers and curriculum developers, such issues can be discussed openly for the benefit of the entire education system.

Ministries of Education in Africa have in the past often introduced curriculum changes from one day to another, without prior warning; this would be disastrous in a country with liberalised textbook provision. Development of a textbook series takes several years to complete and is a large investment for the publisher. Books in stock will be worthless when a new curriculum is introduced, and unannounced curriculum changes might bankrupt publishers. This must be taken into account when curriculum changes are discussed. The content of education is important for the entire nation, not just for the education system, and curriculum revision is nowadays planned years in advance so that there is time for wide consultation to ensure that changes are supported by all interested parties – parents, teachers, teacher training colleges, universities, publishers, chambers of commerce, trade organisations, etc.

The approval of textbooks can be the responsibility of the curriculum department or of a separate approval committee, depending on local conditions. In Zimbabwe, the evaluation and approval of textbooks is just one of the duties of the CDU, but in Tanzania it is the task of a dedicated Education Materials Approval Committee, within the ministry. This solution was chosen because the Tanzania Institute of Education still receives royalty on many of the existing textbooks on the market and many curriculum developers have been engaged as freelance writers. It was decided that staff who had financial relations with publishers could not also be involved in approval of their books.

It is important also that the criteria for approval are made public so that publishers are familiar with them before they start developing books. Bernard Gatawa of the CDU in Zimbabwe stresses the need for objectivity in a handbook for textbook evaluators: 'Textbook evaluation is a national activity guided by clearly defined criteria. ... It is these criteria, and not the moods and whims of individual evaluators, which should direct the evaluation exercise. Among other things, textbook evaluation looks at syllabus coverage, language level, readability, ideological orientation, gender neutrality and cultural compatibility' (Gatawa, 1992). The book was published in 1992, but the text is still very valid. The entire process must be transparent, but as the rejection of a title may have serious financial implications for the publisher it is prudent not to disclose the identity of individual evaluators, thereby reducing the risk of 'unwarranted interference'. Publishers whose titles are not approved should be able to appeal against the decision if they wish.

The Ministry of Education should also introduce standard technical specifications to ensure that the quality of paper and binding will give textbooks an expected life of at least three years (the usual target). In practice, of course, the life of a textbook will also depend on how it is stored and how it is handled by the pupils. In Zambia, the Ministry of Education is therefore producing guidelines for schools on care and maintenance of textbooks.

Although publishers are responsible for marketing their own titles there is also a need for objective information to schools about available books and their prices. This could be the responsibility of the Ministry of Education, which could add such information to a list of approved titles, but a joint catalogue could also be published and distributed by the publishers' association.

The Ministry of Education must define how the selection and purchase of textbooks (at district or school level) should be organised. The ministry needs to distribute instructions on procedures and selection criteria and should also organise some form of training for those who will deal with the procurement issues. It is important that selection is not done by administrators alone but that the teachers who will use the books can also influence the choice. Here, transparency is again very important. In Zimbabwe, the book selection is done by a school committee on which the teachers are represented and on which the parent–teacher organisation can have an observer.

Experience shows that many teachers prefer not to use textbooks, thereby limiting the subject content of their teaching to old notes and ignoring new subject matter, new teaching methods and denying the pupils access to modern pedagogical illustrations. The ministry should therefore also see to it that training in the evaluation and selection of textbooks, and how to use textbooks in the classroom, is included in teacher training programmes.

Monitoring the use of textbooks in schools by inspectors or other officers of the Ministry of Education will show to what extent and how effectively they are used and whether the teachers are satisfied with their quality. Monitoring is also necessary to detect distribution problems, corruption or the misuse of textbook funds. Such problems must be corrected before they become a permanent part of the system. The ministry therefore needs to have, among its employees, technical staff with an understanding of commercial publishing and bookselling, who can monitor the system, advise the ministry on textbook issues, and prevent *ad hoc* decisions and interventions from distorting the market, which will make the system stable and the ministry less dependent on external consultants.

Box 16: Changing Roles in Zambia's Ministry of Education

As Zambia moves rapidly towards decentralised textbook procurement in 2004 and 2005, its Ministry of Education has had to undergo a major and quite complicated internal transition in relation to textbook provision.

Authorship and Textbook Approvals
In 1996 the staff of the Curriculum Development Unit (CDC) still authored most basic (ie primary) school textbooks, in a single-textbook system. Gradually, every title under the former state-monopoly system has been replaced by titles from the commercial publishers. By 1999-2000, the ministry had put in place a quality control 'textbook approvals' mechanism in CDC, under a new unit styled the 'Educational Materials Unit' (EMU). After early teething problems, especially delays and mistakes in producing lists of 'approved and recommended textbooks' and sending these to all educational institutions, the textbook approvals system has achieved notable efficiency. Today, every commercially produced textbook is evaluated by three independent evaluators, trained by the EMU in a number of workshops. An evaluation panel sits to review these, and makes a final decision on whether a textbook is approved, recommended, or rejected. The latest round of evaluations, for new curriculum grade one materials, in four subjects from about 8 publishers, was completed within a record two weeks. Approved and recommended booklists are up-to-date to June 2003, and this, plus an addendum covering approved textbooks up to June 2004, will shortly be sent to all schools and districts education boards. The EMU produces stringent quality controls for technical specifications of books to be produced, including format, paper, layout and cover board quality.

Planning and Finance
Up to 2002/2003 all textbooks in Zambian primary education were centrally procured from commercial publishers in a tender system. Planning hinged around known and perceived shortages from previous centralised procurement. There was little knowledge of the exact quantities of books reaching schools, since they would often be stuck at DEO level for many months, awaiting delivery to remote schools. Payment was effected through a tender system, to a single commercial publisher that had won a tender and delivered the books centrally in Lusaka.

As of 2004, the entire system is being decentralised. The Planning Directorate is concentrating on creating procurement and ordering systems with the 72 District Education Boards as the formal 'purchasing authority'. A new task concerns that of creating statistics to enable funds for textbooks to be disbursed to each district as a 'per capita grant', whereby each school has a ceiling against which it can order the books of its own choice, from a bookseller chosen by the school. The finance and accounts sections, meanwhile, are disbursing textbook budgets directly to districts and ensuring, together with the EMU, that these are correctly spent on textbooks, within strict guidelines. The current priority is that schools order new curriculum grade one materials. Next year, this will shift to new curriculum grade two and five materials.

While schools have a new task in selecting books in a multiple choice system, District Education Boards, have the task of monitoring and supervising school selection, and placing the order with the bookseller concerned. Since booksellers will deliver directly to schools, there will be a need to verify delivery and to ensure that the bookseller is paid. A major new task of the ministry as a whole, managed by the EMU, is ensuring that the payment system, covering disbursements from Accounts to District, payments from District to bookseller, and finally payments from bookseller to publisher, functions smoothly.

Central Procurement
Since centralised procurement is being phased out in 2004, the Ministry of Education Procurement and Supplies Unit (MEPSU) finds itself in a completely new role: that of registering booksellers as 'official suppliers to Ministry of Education'. There is a strict registration protocol to ensure that so-called 'briefcase booksellers' cannot enter the supply chain.

Textbook Management
Whereas previously the Ministry of Education had little to do with the publishers and booksellers associations in Zambia, except with the individual publishers that won central tenders, today the EMU holds regular meetings with both the Book Publishers' Association of Zambia (BPAZ) and the Booksellers Association of Zambia (BAZA). These meetings cover every aspect of the supply chain for textbooks, including ministry budgets and disbursements to districts, problems with shortage of booksellers in some districts, prices, publishers' production schedules, and textbook approvals. All this has to be coordinated and fine-tuned in such a way that commercial publishers are producing and marketing books according to an annual cycle of procurement being put in place. There are many problems and delays in this transition.

Similarly, the EMU finds itself engaged in constant internal ministry meetings to coordinate the work of Curriculum, School Inspection, Planning, Finance and Procurement (for registration of booksellers), in so far as textbooks is concerned. Sometimes these meetings bring all stakeholders in the process together to discuss principles.

The EMU also undertakes training of booksellers in the decentralised procurement system and training of district education officials in ordering and selection procedures. It produces several manuals and guidelines covering both the new system and care and maintenance of textbooks at school level. It produces strict guidelines to districts with information on what subject areas and grades particular textbook financial disbursements are intended to cover. This is because a curriculum reform is taking place and most existing textbooks are being phased out for a new curriculum. Eventually, such guidelines will be unnecessary, since each school will order 'top-up' quantities of any textbook they need, from their per capita grant.

Ministry of Education Skills
Through EMU, the ministry is, in effect, producing a group of textbook specialists, well versed in commercial publishing and bookselling, and able to play the coordination role between ministry and the private sector. The EMU also plays an essential management function ensuring that each department in the ministry plays its part in the overall process, communicating with districts and provincial education levels, keeping the top management of the ministry informed and solving problems as they arise. This has given rise to new working methods and systems. Communication and information flow throughout the system, to every district and throughout the ministry, and to all booksellers and publishers, has emerged as the single most important function of the EMU.

Relations with indigenous publishers, trade associations and NGOs

As has been discussed earlier, indigenous African publishers, independent of the state and commercially orientated, did not initially receive much support from education ministries or funding agencies. In most cases they were excluded from school textbook markets altogether, even while their multinational competitors derived considerable turnover and profit from the education market in Africa. Nevertheless, their inherent advantages in being able to respond in the most direct manner to local readership needs and interests, and in publishing an ever-growing pool of local authors, kept many indigenous publishers in business.

The cultural and social importance of this eventually attracted the interest of some funding and international partners, and the momentum towards an indigenous African publishing response to African book needs grew rapidly from the mid-1980s, culminating in the establishment in 1992 of the African Publishers Network (APNET). One of its first achievements was to give African publishing a unified voice.

There has been an extraordinary transformation of attitudes in the African education sector, both in education ministries and in funding agencies, since then. The predominant view in African education circles in the 1980s had been that local commercial publishers profiteered from the education of children, or were not competent to take on the weighty tasks of educational publishing, or both. This view was mirrored in the majority of textbook-funding programmes in the 1980s, which ignored any role for indigenous publishers. The multinational publishers, who had ceased operating in key African markets (such as Zambia, Ghana, Tanzania and Kenya) after state-monopoly textbook systems were enforced, were often exempted from this negative view – a reflection of their long-standing position of dominance in the African textbook market. By the late 1990s, however, the majority of education ministries in Africa, and all the major funders of African education, had, in principle, accepted the need for indigenous publishing to be a component of all textbook programmes.

Incorporating local publishers into textbook programmes and establishing a supportive environment for indigenous publishing are gradually becoming part of the policy considerations of education ministries, a new development in Africa. While it is appreciated that multinationals bring important technical and financial capacity to textbook provision, indigenous publishers have vital cultural, language and local-development strengths, and are invariably more responsive to national book needs, in the broad sense, than foreign companies.

There are difficulties, however, in those situations where state-monopoly educational publishing has weakened or eroded any role for indigenous publishers, and moves towards liberalisation have resulted in the return of multinational publishers through a process in which indigenous publishing remains marginalized. Liberalisation in Zambia did not result in the emergence of indigenous commercial publishing to any notable extent, and indigenous publishing remains on the periphery. A similar situation has prevailed in Uganda.

A different style of communication becomes necessary between the core decision-makers and sub-sectors in education, in publishing and in bookselling. In managing rather than implementing textbook provision, the ministry learns that communication is its most critical management task. The ministry cannot in practice communicate with the commercial sector on a company-by-company basis: not only do rivalries emerge between competing companies, but it is also very time-consuming. The increased information flow requires streamlining and it is at this stage that the functions of the publishers' and booksellers' associations become critical to the effectiveness of textbook provision.

In Zambia there was for many years a combined association of booksellers and publishers – the Booksellers and Publishers Association of Zambia (BPAZ). Booksellers and publishers had good reasons to co-operate in those days in order to defend the common interests of the commercial sector *vis-à-vis* the government's interests. But when the commercial system began to function, they each found that they also had specific interests to defend, and the two separated in November 2002. It was a natural and timely separation, with liberalisation of textbook publishing in place and decentralisation of procurement imminent.

Box 17: From mistrust to dialogue

In Zambia, Kenya, Tanzania and Uganda, there has been a history of mutual hostility and mistrust between the Ministry of Education and the trade associations. The ministry has complained that publishers and booksellers have allowed profit motivation to override educational and national interests. The trade associations, on the other hand, have pointed to unfair state-monopoly publishing and the government's disinterest in the development of the local book industry. It is a well-worn African story, repeated countless times in ministry corridors and boardrooms all over Africa. But the situation is changing rapidly. The Zambian Ministry of Education now actually provides an office within the CDC for the benefit of the publishers' and booksellers' associations, giving publishers constant access to curriculum developers. In Kenya, the development of the Primary Education Textbook Policy has been distinguished by a mood of conciliation and mutual interest between the ministry and the publishers' association. Ten years ago in Tanzania, workshops debating the 'future of textbook provision' were uncomfortable occasions, more than once resulting in a string of accusations and public vilification of ministry officials and private publishers. Since then, however, publishers have been constant visitors to the Book Management Unit, and it sometimes became difficult to distinguish between the publisher and the ministry official, since each understood the nature of the other's problems well.

There is considerable evidence that effective trade associations, and good communications between them and the ministry, facilitate important innovations in textbook provision. Moreover, aid interventions become more stable in a triangular relationship (ministry–funding agency–commercial sector) than in a simple horizontal one between funding agencies and the ministry. This is an important consideration because it helps achieve balance between the educational concerns of the ministry (i.e. good-quality textbooks reaching pupils' desks) and the commercial concerns of the private sector (the 'standards and conventions' that underpin the entire book chain).

Commercialisation of the textbook sector provides the education ministry with an enormous number of new resources to enable it to fulfil its mission in textbook provision. These resources include commercial publishers and booksellers, and a pool of independent authors, as well as the variety of print and production facilities that are brought into play. The driving force of the commercial system is competition, and commercial entities will always seek flexibility in production options in an effort to obtain competitive advantage. In addition, stronger commercial publishing tends to stimulate NGO activity in areas such as training, reading campaigns, book fairs, library development and alternative book-provision methods. The commercial book sector invariably finds ways to strengthen its industry in terms of broadening readership and developing both the market and the scope of products they produce. Since books represent a means of transmitting culture and information, the more publishers there are, the greater this capacity develops. The book sector is able to harness resources that are far greater than those within the control of the state, and can directly and indirectly benefit the quality of education by generally improving the supply of books to the population.

Inevitably, ministries of education are drawn into issues of strategic importance to the overall development of books and reading, since the link between education and books underpins all publishing activity in Africa. Ministry officials find themselves confronted with book-related issues beyond the basic provision of core textbooks. The development of libraries, the provision of supplementary books, and methods of stimulating bookselling activity at district level are typically among their areas of responsibility. There is pressure on the ministry to respond to changing priorities and to set objectives for the next or a future phase of book provision and development. Publishers and booksellers will respond to this by encouraging the creation of NGOs and strengthening their trade associations in order to develop capacity to deal with issues concerning long-term development. Hard-pressed education officials, often implementing reforms in the education sector, find it equally difficult to find the time and skills required to understand and respond to the needs of the book sector, and to provide the necessary leadership. Hence the development of book-related NGOs is a key element of public/private partnership in textbook provision and book development generally.

Conclusion

Throughout Africa, and in particular in the countries in this study with such widely diverse patterns of textbook supply, there is broad movement towards new forms of co-operation between ministries of education and commercial publishers and booksellers. In some cases, as in francophone Africa and Ethiopia and Mozambique, this has been a gradual process, especially where the state has no alternative but to continue centralised approaches while commercial capacity is being developed to replace it.

In East Africa, and especially Kenya, there has been a more rapid and definitive process of change precisely because of the greater commercial activity. Developments in this regard are not linear; everywhere, tensions, set-backs and contradictions arise in the growing public and private-sector linkages. Development 'blueprints' seldom conform neatly to the situation on the ground. On the contrary, evidence suggests that solutions to the many problems posed have to be found among the participants in the process themselves, even when mistakes occur. From the interviews conducted in the course of this study, interaction at all levels and forums between ministry officials and the commercial sector is growing, and differences in attitudes are narrowing, despite tensions arising in every stage of liberalisation.

Liberalisation does not mean that the Ministry of Education can relax and leave textbook issues to the commercial sector. It is still in charge of textbook quality, and decentralised procurement places new demands on financial planning and control. The ministry needs to find the ways and acquire the competence needed to fulfil its obligations in the new context. As with many other elements of changing roles in emerging commercial textbook systems, its responsibility becomes one of managing a process, in which many partners and interests are active, rather than implementing it.

Chapter 5

SOME AFRICAN CHALLENGES IN LIBERALISED SYSTEMS

A major finding of this study is that continuity of policy, with long-term stable planning and systems, is essential for liberalised textbook provision. As we have noted in the preceding chapters, liberalisation of textbook provision brings new commercial actors into the system as well as many more textbook choices in a multi-textbook approach. It requires new methods of management to achieve co-ordination among the Ministry of Education's stake-holders, both between the departments in the ministry's head office and from head office to districts and schools. Roles and responsibilities necessarily must be transformed. In effect, centralised 'internal' approaches are replaced by management of a complex public/private 'partnerships', that incorporate many diverse interests, and a new decision-making role for thousands of schools in dozens of districts. The dilemma of most countries is to establish continuity in a transitional period when systems are changing. In reality, this transitional process is accompanied by set-backs, conflicts of interest, policy reversals, *ad hoc* decision-making, and interventions and influences from funding partners and consultants. At the same time the transition opens new oppor-tunities.

This chapter explores some of these realities and the conflicts of interest involved, with examples of policy reversals and set-backs, and also some successes and resolutions, so that we may gain a deeper understanding of the practical challenges of establishing public/private partnerships with a multiplicity of interests involved.

Zambia's liberalisation: The realities

In 2004, Zambia is scheduled to decentralise the procurement of all its new Grade One textbooks. For the first time, publishers will be working in an environment where there are no central tenders and deliveries, but where the market itself will decide which textbooks to purchase. The challenges facing the Zambian publishing industry are fascinating, intricate and exasperating. They are, in many respects, typical of the range of issues facing publishers in Africa in the transition to a free market.

Having received the new curriculum and syllabuses, with a new range of subjects, publishers have been working flat out to commission authors and produce manuscripts to meet the deadline for the submission of their titles for inclusion in the approved textbook list to be sent to schools. Normally in commercial publishing, commissioning a new textbook (involving contracts, authorship, editing, illustration, design, marketing, etc.) would be viewed as a 12–18-month exercise. Zambian publishers are required to undertake this within about four months to ensure that textbooks reach users in time.

Major financial and investment considerations need to be taken into account before this exercise even starts. The deadlines are tight. Many of the authors will be found within the curriculum department that developed the new syllabuses and where textbook-writing skills were previously concentrated. At least in that respect there is some capacity, and publishers are determined to meet the deadline.

After the approval of their manuscripts as core textbooks, publishers will be faced with a series of critical decisions that will determine their viability. The first will relate to print-runs and pricing. Publishers will require data on the gross budget available for the purchase of textbooks in the new phase (essential to determine their print-runs), as well as on disbursements to schools and districts and on enrolment figures (to determine their marketing strategy). These figures are not yet available (at the time of writing, late 2003), and the publishers will depend on the ministry to obtain them in advance of production schedules. It should be remembered that neither the publishers nor the ministry have undertaken this task (i.e. decentralised textbook procurement) before. Then the publishers will have to decide on a print-run that takes into account their estimated market share, in competition with other publishers. How many publishers will compete is also not yet clear. The market share will further be determined by the retail price of the books, and for the first time publishers will be required to embed the costs of nationwide distribution and marketing into their retail price.

Inevitably, most of the printing will be done outside the country, since, for a variety of reasons, Zambian printing tends to be more expensive and of a poorer quality than imported printing. Printing could take place in South Africa, Mauritius, the Far East (e.g. Singapore) or Zimbabwe, and publishers will be evaluating their options. Customs duties and transport will have to be meticulously calculated, as will the lead-time for delivery in their negotiations with printers.

Simultaneously, the publishers will be engaged in marketing, working on promotional materials, and working out how to reach the 5,000 primary schools, or at least the 72 newly re-structured district education boards, with their message. This will probably require them to employ travelling sales representatives (and to provide them with transport), or agencies, or both. Remote and far-flung provinces will present acute problems and additional costs. Establishing trade relations, especially credit terms, with a host of new and mostly untried booksellers will be one of the biggest challenges. In many cases, booksellers will have been only recently established and will lack experience and skills. Supplying large numbers of books on credit to booksellers with no track record will be exceptionally risky, and yet the means must be found to deliver the books to schools, since this is the aim of the ministry.

All these decisions entail investment and risk, and the margin of error is high, given that there is no precedent on which to base many decisions. Zambian publishers have been used to a tender system in which the winner had exact numbers to work with – a definite quantity at a pre-determined price, with central delivery. The move into a new phase of decentralised procurement requires that all components of the book chain fall into place almost immediately – authorship, printing, costing and pricing, marketing, bookselling, delivery – and this will depend on ministry decisions and access to information about the textbook budgets. As in other countries undergoing similar transition, relations between the Ministry of Education and the commercial sector are not fully developed. Mutual trust, founded on continuity of policy and the integrity and capacity of both commercial and ministry stake-holders to achieve the goals of decentralised, fully liberalised procurement, has been slow to emerge. A major reason for this is that previous textbook procurement policies in Zambia have suffered from many different approaches and methods, *ad hoc* decisions and aid interventions, making the current transition more difficult.

Zambia's transition had begun in 1991 with a broad policy to liberalise textbook publishing and decentralise procurement. But by 1995 the CDC was still centrally engaged in textbook writing, and the state-owned ZEPH retained publication rights on a number of existing and new titles, and was still being funded through ZEMP. It took a further five years for CDC to withdraw from textbook preparation and concentrate its core activities on curriculum development and the approval of textbooks developed by commercial publishers.

It was unequivocally stated in 1996 that funds would be devolved to districts and schools and that publishers and booksellers would undertake commercial marketing and distribution. By 2003, this process was still at the planning stage, earmarked to begin in 2004 for Grade One textbooks only, as discussed above. Liberalisation has largely remained at the point of central tenders and centralised purchase of textbooks – to all intents and purposes a single-textbook system, since there can be only one winner in tender-based supply, despite there being multi-textbook approvals in place. Some twelve years into liberalisation policy (1991–2003) there is no direct role for Zambian booksellers.

To a large degree the delays in fully liberalising the system have been caused by the need to continue supplying schools while the new system was established, using existing (central tender) mechanisms. It has proved exceptionally difficult in Zambia to establish a parallel or dual system, where, for example, the central-tender-based supply continued to function at the same time as an open-market, competitive system of decentralised purchase has started to operate. The growth in Zambia's commercial capacity has suffered as a result.

In Zambia, over a ten-year period from the initial liberalisation announcement in 1991, and despite the clear-cut liberalisation policy statement of 1996, aid interventions and textbook-procurement exercises have included:

- World Bank ICB tenders with books provided by foreign multi-national publishers;
- funded state textbook authorship, publishing and distribution (ceased by 1999);
- local tenders for previously state-published textbooks to locally based commercial publishers;
- several methods of haulage tenders to deliver textbooks to districts and schools;
- funding agencies directly organising the writing and printing of some educational books;
- funding agencies resorting to Crown Agents method of supply (by-passing both the local tender arrangements and local publishers);
- pilot (district level) decentralisation of procurement in some provinces;
- central funding by the ministry to secondary schools for 'school requisites', including textbooks;
- *ad hoc* funding to other schools or districts at certain times by funding agencies.

In addition, there have been about a dozen or more small-scale textbook-provision initiatives through NGOs. In effect, textbook provision exhibits the features of a series of procurement exercises, not necessarily co-ordinated, to meet increasingly alarming textbook shortages.

It may seem that this presents a diverse textbook market with opportunities, and in many senses this is true, but the effect on the book chain has been singularly negative. This 'patchwork' of textbook-provision systems since liberalisation is applying different methods of production and supply that do not allow for continuity in the emergence of a book chain. The publishing of trade and supplementary educational books has been in decline, even compared to the 'heyday' of the state monopoly. Indigenous publishers have not emerged to compete at the same level as their foreign-owned counterparts. There are barely twenty retail bookshops offering a wide range of textbooks; some provinces have no bookshop at all. The same atmosphere of mistrust between the ministry and the commercial actors, and confusion over roles and responsibilities, that was so pervasive in Tanzania in 1991, is still evident. For all this, it must be accepted that liberalisation in Zambia has not been a failure, but it has suffered from such a myriad of procurement-centred approaches.

Tanzania

Tanzania has achieved an effective public/private partnership in textbook provision insofar as relations between commercial publishers and the Ministry of Education are concerned. Tanzania presents a fascinating inter-relationship between these two sets of interests, which, with liberalisation at its core, became gradually mutually dependent. Centralised state procurement and distribution continued while the Pilot Project for Publishing (PPP) concentrated on creating commercial capacity and putting into place a new system in which state-authored textbooks were to be tendered to commercial publishers.

At the start of the process, a deep mistrust existed between the education ministry and the commercial publishers who had been marginalized by the state textbook-publishing system. The ministry was under considerable pressure at the time because textbook–pupil ratios had fallen consistently in the 1980s, and the immediate priority was to expand centralised state provision to address this. Tanzania's commercial sector was, at that time, in no position to replace the centralised state system; no matter how dysfunctional it was, it still represented the only immediate solution to textbook shortages.

The response of the PPP, reflecting the concern of the ministry, was to incorporate with liberalisation the building of the capacity of local publishing in an effort to ensure that the new system could replace the state system without any break in supply. It was a long-term vision. Gradually, between 1993 and 1999, commercial publishers – and, in some cases, booksellers – went through training and pilot exercises, discussion workshops, field visits and the like. Even the tender system, in which the publishing of state textbooks was tendered in various PPP phases to commercial publishers, was designed as a training exercise as well as a formal tender. The Tanzania Children's Book Project (CBP) played a prominent role during this period in support for children's book publishing that kept quite a few publishers in business during the transition. There was a standing joke at the time that Tanzanian publishers, being among the most highly trained in Africa, might eventually be able publish some textbooks. An exaggeration, but one that reflected realities.

By its conclusion in 1999, such a degree of mutual dependence had developed between the Book Management Unit of the Ministry of Education and the commercial publishers that it was inconceivable that the ministry could undertake any policy reversal. The publishers, both as a result of extensive training and through their determination to succeed – where the state had failed – produced textbooks of higher quality and delivered them to districts with greater efficiency than the state had previously managed. The remnants of the state system fell away naturally and quickly. The ministry moved swiftly towards multiple textbook approvals and a textbook-approval mechanism. The transition from state monopoly to commercial textbook provision was complete, in so far as the publishing of textbooks was concerned.

With an eye to the future, Tanzanian publishers invested heavily in developing new series of textbooks. In hindsight, the key factor was the stability of policy and the longevity of the PPP (7–8 years), which allowed for a gradual changing of attitudes and the emergence of 'standards and conventions' in commercial indigenous publishing. In effect, the transition was marked by a sense of continuity, against a background of the gradual replacement of one system by another.

Kenya

In contrast, Kenya emerged with a functional local commercial textbook system in 1998 precisely because of the existence in that country of commercial capacity, energy and the tenacity of Kenyan publishers. However, a history of inconsistent government textbook policies, *ad hoc* decision-making, inappropriate funding interventions, and dominance by multinationals undermined the commercial publishing sector, and in particular the newer, weaker indigenous publishers.

About ninety publishers, mainly British (a number of which had locally incorporated), had a presence in Kenya in the 1970s. Between 1963 and 1977 about ten local publishers attempted to establish themselves. The East African Publishing House was formed in 1965, aiming to establish an outlet for the academic and creative writing output of the East African Cultural Trust members. As Henry Chakava notes, 'by 1977, Nairobi had become the enviable educational, cultural, and publishing center of East Africa' (Chakava, 1996).

The Kenya Institute of Education (KIE) developed syllabuses and course materials for the new curricula, and the Jomo Kenyatta Foundation was set up to publish primary school materials developed at KIE. At this stage, it was possible for commercial publishers to reach agreements to publish materials for and on behalf of these two institutions. The Kenya School Equipment Scheme (KSES), in collaboration with KIE, generated order lists which it distributed to schools. Schools selected the books they wanted and the KSES supplied. Mainstream publishing was left largely in the hands of commercial publishers, mostly local branches of multinationals.

From this promising base, a series of setbacks, policy reversals and aid interventions followed that proved ruinous to the expansion and development of indigenous publishing and undermined all commercial publishing in Kenya. In 1977, the East African Community collapsed and, with it, the regional market for Kenyan books. In the same year, the Ministry of Education attempted to award the annual tender for textbooks, in which the books of a number of different publishers featured, to one 'favoured' publisher. The Kenyan Publishers' Association disputed the arrangement and it was withdrawn the following year, but not without cost to the book industry. On the back of charges of corruption and other factors, KSES became moribund and was replaced by a system in which parents had to share the costs of textbook purchases. Gradually the government shed responsibility, eventually leaving most of the buying to parents, in a rapidly deteriorating economy.

In 1983 government abruptly changed the structure of education, rendering nearly all current textbooks irrelevant. In 1985, the ministry ended tenders for primary-level books to commercial publishers, who had experienced great difficulty in adjusting to the new education system, mandated KIE to write textbooks, and instituted state-monopoly textbook publishing in basic education through its parastatals. The explanation was that Kenya had obtained a loan from the World Bank and the government had decided to use some of these funds to revive the two state publishing firms and operate them commercially, although they were not set up for this purpose. After three years, the system was again changed, and books from commercial publishers could be recommended as supplementary materials.

All this created havoc in the Kenyan publishing industry. So it was that, by 1987, most indigenous local publishers were bankrupt. Multinationals, able to draw on greater resources and withstand the setbacks and policy reversals, fared better. Of interest is the response of the few surviving commercial publishers. David Muita explains: 'Many publishers were forced to ... close down altogether, a scenario created by the state monopoly. ... But not everyone could be pushed out of the business. Together with the 'never-say-die' attitude ... [o]ne way was to inject more professionalism ... with a view to having a superior product ... This was done admirably' (Muita, 1998). So much so, in fact, that schools and parents frequently 'invisibly' obtained the 'supplementary' titles of commercial publishers in preference to the drab, poorly written parastatal books. In this way Kenyan commercial primary school textbook publishing survived. This later proved the foundation for moves to develop a new textbook policy through the Kenya Publishers Association in the early 1990s, under its then chairman Gacheche Waruinge.

South Africa

The policy reversals and absence of long-term policy stability that have held back the progress of commercial publishing in Kenya are evident even in African countries where public/private partnership has been the bedrock of textbook provision. In South Africa, in 1997, it emerged that the senior provincial curriculum planners had far-reaching plans to reverse private-sector textbook publishing and implement a state textbook system (with parallels to Kenya's so-called 'textbook wars' in 1985) on the back of new of syllabuses, requiring a new generation of textbooks. At the time, the Department of Education put forward a rationale behind possible state publishing, which more or less reflected the thinking behind state publishing elsewhere in Africa. They claimed that commercial publishers could not meet the deadlines imposed by the urgency of developing materials for the new syllabus, and that a state model could be more efficient and more responsive in this respect. They saw a state publishing model as a means of empowering teachers, who would be drawn into the textbook-writing process. They felt that state publishing would be more cost-effective, and viewed commercial publishers as making excessive profits. They alluded to the perceived lack of commitment of publishers to ongoing democratic transformation in that country. In part, this may have reflected problems of inequity and the legacy of apartheid peculiar to South Africa, especially so in view of the high levels of foreign investment in the South African publishing industry.

The 120-member Publishers' Association of South Africa (PASA), representing the most sophisticated and lucrative publishing industry on the continent, embarked on a furious counter-campaign that was ultimately successful, and plans for state intervention in textbook publishing were shelved (McCallum, 1998). The uncertainties, however, combined with a massive fall in expenditure on textbooks surrounding the implementation of the new curriculum, played havoc with publishers' planning and textbook commissioning activities.

Interestingly, the flurry of discussions between PASA and education officials over the issue helped raise the profile of commercial publishing as a partner to the state in strategic matters concerning education and educational materials, and helped resolve some of the lingering mistrust. For example, PASA had to draw up a code of conduct to regulate the behaviour of its members and their relations with education department officials, essentially to counter (admittedly isolated) allegations of corruption over textbook orders. Even in a more advanced commercial book sector, the problems and arguments over state relations with the commercial sector are evident.

Zimbabwe

Public/private partnership had also characterized textbook provision in Zimbabwe, but a recent event here illustrates how aid inventions and aid dependency can divert even long-term stable policy. In June 2003, a tender appeared in Zimbabwean newspapers for a textbook 'project' amounting to Z$3.5 billion (about US$1.75 million at the time) that flouted basic tenets of the textbook-provision system. Textbooks were to be centrally pre-selected, rather than schools being allowed to select freely, the practice for fifteen years. This, the largest single textbook order since independence, has been approached as a 'procurement project', using a tender system that will undermine, and may prove ruinous to, the 'standards and conventions' that have under-pinned the highly successful book chain developed over two decades. The tender was advertised on a Saturday with a Wednesday deadline, giving applicants all of two working days to cost around 300,000 copies spread among 120 titles, preventing most booksellers from outside the capital from participating. When asked why this tender has proceeded in this manner, the decision-makers concerned said the major consideration was that the funds had to be disbursed during their current financial year, in line with the agreement and obligations to the funding agency concerned.

Guinea

An interesting parallel to the Zimbabwean example – in terms of the influence of aid invention, even with the best of intentions – can be found in Guinea. From 1989, Guinea's curriculum institute took over the development of primary school textbooks, previously imported from France, in co-operation with some local publishers. The price of the books was heavily subsidized. Local booksellers distributed them and parents made a contribution to the cost. Thus a system developed in the early 1990s where booksellers distributed school textbooks, as a result of which a network of book outlets (including small traders) started to develop rapidly in the country.

Because of extreme rural poverty, the Ministry abruptly changed its policy in 1996 and decided to make textbooks free of charge under the World Bank Education for All programme. Distribution was tendered out to haulage contractors and the booksellers became redundant. Under the centralised single-textbook system that has been in operation since 1996, textbooks for primary schools are not published by the Ministry of Education but are bought centrally through ICB, a system that makes it difficult for local publishers to win any orders. Moreover, the duties charged on inputs to the print industry (for example, 20%–22% on paper) and the foreign-currency constraints on importing paper make it virtually impossible for Guinean publishers to print their books locally, even if they were to win any orders.

In addition, USAID's NFQE/EDC project, which has developed and published primary supplementary readers and distributed one million copies annually for free, has by-passed booksellers. The results have been a major setback for the development of booksellers that showed early promise, and in the growth of indigenous publishing in that country.

Box 18: Liberalisation in Francophone countries	
Ministry of Education curriculum institute takes over preparation of all textbook manuscripts in a single title system, eg	
• Mauritius	1977
• Senegal	1987
• Guinea	1989
• Mali	1995

Francophone countries

Francophone countries have tended to view the liberalisation of state publishing through the lens of international competitive bidding, and such funding and tender arrangements have not been conducive to the special needs of the indigenous publishers and booksellers. However, in a promising trend, indigenous publishers have found scope to grow as a result of their relative strength *vis à vis* multinationals in the field of indigenous language publishing.

Senegal's curriculum institute took over development and writing of primary school textbooks from 1987, although books from 6th Grade are still imported from France. In 2002 a new curriculum was close to being finalized and the education ministry decided that private publishers would develop the local-language books, but this will be through an ICB process.

When Mali localised its textbook preparation in 1995, the Ministry of Education took over the development of manuscripts but the books were still edited and printed abroad. According to World Bank policy, ICB procedures had to be used for selecting publishers and printers, and small companies in Bamako could not compete.

These countries have, however, seen a more positive environment developing recently, particularly through the introduction of local languages as the medium of instruction in the early grades of primary school. In 2001, the education ministry in Mali decided to allow the four major local publishers to take over the copyright of existing ministry textbooks. Rights were transferred grade by grade or subject by subject in a phased process, and publishers are still revising and improving the books. This is the first time that local publishers in Mali have been engaged in textbook publishing. For any new manuscripts from the ministry, publishers must once again be selected through an ICB process. Malian publishers feel that, since the next generation of primary school books is to be published in national languages, this will give them a competitive edge over French and Canadian publishers.

Ethiopia

Local language, as the custodian of cultural and regional 'identity', has in many respects been the central focus of Ethiopia's textbook-provision policies since 1991. Unlike in the francophone countries mentioned above, this has not necessarily led to a growth and development of indigenous commercial publishing in Ethiopia. In many ways the reverse is true, and it presents an interesting contrast. After the change of government in Ethiopia in 1991 there were high expectations that the pervasive state monopoly in textbooks could be dismantled. In 1993 a 'stakeholders' conference adopted wide-ranging recommendations on the liberalisation of textbook provision. In 1998, a draft textbook-liberalisation policy was commissioned. The education ministry, prior to the outbreak of hostilities with Eritrea in 1998, was formulating ambitious plans to embrace commercial publishing and competition. By 2003, as far as basic education is concerned (with a handful of exceptions), these plans remained stalled in a single-title (per region) state publishing system. In secondary education, which uses the medium of English, publishing tenders for textbooks are regularly awarded to the commercial sector, and this has led to limited commercial growth. In the meantime, the ministry bemoans the lack of commercial capacity. Only one commercial publisher with the size and resources to undertake large-scale educational publishing has emerged, in 1997.

On the other hand, the education ministry has invested considerable energy in expanding its capacity to write and publish primary school textbooks in local languages, devolving much responsibility to regional (i.e. provincial) education bureaux. It could be argued that Ethiopia has simply adopted an alternative path to decentralisation – local-language devolution of responsibility to regional education offices, as opposed to decentralisation towards the commercial sector. Yet it is difficult to envisage how the commercial sector can grow without any direct role in primary school textbook publishing.

Ethiopia's Educational Materials Production and Distribution Agency (EMPDA) stood out from the many state models adopted in Africa as an effective state publishing, printing and distribution instrument. It contributed massively to the development of skills in book production and in its output of titles up to 1998, when the devolution of primary school textbook writing and publishing to regions was fully implemented; it is still the major educational printing agency. Ministry officials might argue, not without justification, that given the problems of rural poverty, the vast size of the country, past political instability, and the diversity of the language, a more cautious textbook liberalisation approach is called for.

It is an interesting scenario. The ministry remains convinced that devolution to the regions is the foundation for basic-education textbook development because of the language issue. Commercial publishing (as in most African countries) is concentrated in the capital city. Therefore, until commercial capacity is able to embrace textbook writing and publishing across eleven regions and in twenty languages, it is difficult to see a deepening of liberalisation outside the production of secondary school textbooks.

Mozambique

Like Ethiopia, Mozambique has a largely underdeveloped commercial book infrastructure, in part because of the government's strong early socialist commitment which was relatively successful in terms of textbook provision and appeared to present an effective state textbook model. In complete contrast to Ethiopia, however, Mozambique has embraced the liberalisation of its state textbook sector, with a drive towards privatisation and foreign investment. This appears to have undermined rather than increased local commercial capacity in textbook publishing and printing, and for the time being one might conclude that privatisation policy in textbooks has not been consistent with the need to create a strong, indigenous, commercial Mozambican book industry and print sector.

From a background of massive initial investments in state-monopoly textbook publishing and provision, with public ownership of major economic sectors, Mozambique looked towards liberalisation in 1998. The state printing company CEGRAF was sold to the private sector, which invested heavily in new equipment suitable for textbooks; there were several other printers with modern equipment in Maputo. However, the primary school textbook market was not open to local printers, as the Canadian International Development Agency (CIDA), which financed the printing of primary school textbooks, used only Canadian printers.

A new curriculum for primary schools was completed in 2001, and commercial publishers were invited to compete for contracts to develop the textbooks. According to the rules of the World Bank, the main funding agency, publishers were to be selected through international competitive bidding. The state-owned textbook publishing and distribution agency, Diname, was not allowed to participate. After two decades of investment and skills development in monopoly state publishing of textbooks through Editora Escolar – the main primary textbook publisher, itself owned by Diname – indigenous commercial publishing in Mozambique was still very weak. Three foreign companies (one British multinational, one Portuguese, and one Mozambican subsidiary of a Portuguese publisher) are set to develop and compete for the new generation of Mozambican primary textbooks under the liberalisation programme. As with most countries moving towards liberalisation through publishing tenders, a textbook-approval mechanism has been established. In the long term, book selection will take place at school level and, in the medium term, at provincial level. In the immediate future, however, for 2004 and 2005, books from the 'approved textbook list' will be centrally selected on a single title per grade/subject basis. By November 2002, publishers still did not know if they would be free to arrange printing for themselves or whether Canada would continue to be involved.

For many years Editora Escola, under Diname, has functioned both as a publisher and training institution for editors, designers, illustrators, photographers and printers. It was expected that, with liberalisation, these state assets could be revitalized and provide the lead in a new generation of Mozambican indigenous publishing, perhaps in joint ventures with foreign firms. Instead, as it currently stands, only foreign publishers are competing for the primary school textbook market in Mozambique. In the early 1980s all textbooks for Mozambique were printed in Maputo. Today they are printed in Canada.

Mauritius

In stark contrast, the printing sector in Mauritius presents perhaps the most compelling example in Africa of the effectiveness of public/private partnerships and long-term policy cohesion. In the area of printing Mauritius has made a singular impact in Africa. There are not less than 300 printers in Mauritius, some fifteen of which are engaged in print exports of textbooks, mainly to Africa. Government support for the printing sector is channelled through the Development Bank of Mauritius, which provides medium- to large-scale loans at lower interests rates for investment in print machinery and computer technology. The policy of the government is to encourage local printers to upgrade machinery and technology regularly to enable them to compete internationally as an offshore printing center. In addition, virtually all foreign trade delegations and export programmes feature printers, and the Mauritius Investment Development Programme provides further support. All this is supplemented by an excellent air-freight service from Mauritius, and a range of taxation, duty and investment regulations that strengthen local print manufacturing. There is a close co-operation at all levels between the government and the print sector that, taken alone in the area of printing, is without comparison or precedent in Africa as an example of public/private partnership. It is an incredible success story by any standard, so much so that a large number of textbooks published in Tanzania, Uganda, Kenya, Zambia and parts of West Africa are being printed in Mauritius.

In textbook provision however, Mauritius combines a mixture of state and commercial systems that appears to function and co-exist reasonably well for the needs of Mauritius. It follows a pattern more in keeping with trends in other francophone African countries, and quite unlike the print sector it retains a strong state focus.

The curriculum authority retains a monopoly over core-textbook provision at primary school level, writing and developing materials ready for printing, meeting costs of production, and providing books free of charge to all primary schools. The parastatal Editions de l'Océan Indien (EOI), established during a turbulent economic period in Mauritius (then dependent on imports from France and the UK), effectively localised textbook provision after 1977.

From 1977 to 1994, EOI (60% owned by the State Investment Corporation, and 40% owned by multinational publishers and printers) was in the privileged position of publishing virtually all textbooks at primary school level. This is changing. The actual printing of books, and publishing of extra copies for the open market, has since 1994 been put out to open tender. A private company has emerged and started developing textbooks to compete with EOI. At the same time the curriculum institute has developed its own 'publishing' capacity, essentially by-passing EOI and taking work directly to printers. At junior-secondary level a multi-textbook system operates, in which publishers develop textbooks. Selection is undertaken by schools from the approved-textbook list, and the state provides the books ordered free to schools.

Mauritius has at least sixty bookshops, fifteen of which are permanent and well-stocked, a fairly high number for a developing country with a population of just 1.2 million. A substantial number of higher-secondary and tertiary-level books are imported from both the UK and France, and, with a literacy rate of 80% in a booming economy, there is a fairly active reading public.

Uganda

This chapter concludes with an example from Uganda that shows the conflict of interests between purely pedagogical concerns and the perspective of industry, which sought policy continuity and an unfettered free market in order for the long-term investment in textbooks to be commercially productive.

In Uganda, where a multi-textbook system had been adopted in 1993/94, any textbook approved by the textbook-approval authority in the ministry could be ordered. On this basis, smaller (that is, mostly indigenous) Ugandan publishers successfully entered the textbook system with new products. In 1998/99 the Ministry upgraded the entry level for textbook tenders, a move that, however well intentioned, had the effect of limiting the role of indigenous publishers. In 2001, the policy of unlimited textbook approvals was reversed, and a maximum of three approved textbooks per subject/grade was imposed. There were sound pedagogical reasons for these decisions – to ensure quality and to prevent too many textbooks entering the market – but the absence of continuity in textbook provision systems has set back the development of local publishing. Publishers that had invested in new series of textbooks, had had these approved by the ministry (in terms of quality, curriculum requirements and price), and in some cases had them previously purchased, will not be able to sell them, except to parents, for three years – the life-span of this new decision.

These examples show some practical realities of textbook provision in Africa. They illustrate conflicts of interest, the effect of *ad hoc* interventions and lack of long-term policy cohesion, and in some cases the converse of this. They offer some lessons on the type of set-backs that occur even when public/private partnership is expanded and the textbook sector is liberalised. From the viewpoint of the authors of this book, they offer compelling reasons why long-term, national book policy remains such a major strategic priority for all those engaged in developing the African book sector.

Chapter 6

AN EXAMPLE OF LIBERALISATION: THE CASE OF TANZANIA

From Antagonism to Partnership

At the beginning of the 1990s, the effects of state intervention in the textbook sector had reduced the relations between Tanzania's publishers and the MOEC to an all-time low. The publishers were frustrated for many reasons. The government's monopoly system prevented them from publishing and marketing primary school textbooks and had forced the closure of most of the country's bookshops. A clause in the copyright law made it legal for a minister to override a publisher's copyright in the public interest.

Publishers were allowed to sell supplementary readers, but the books had to be printed before being submitted for approval. The evaluation process could take months and if the omnipotent commissioner didn't like the book for some reason the whole print-run would be worthless. On top of this, there were rumours that the Institute of Curriculum Development (ICD) intended to establish a big publishing house with World Bank financing. Ministry officials, for their part, seemed to look upon publishers as ignorant profiteers who should not be in the education sector. Rare encounters between the publishers' association and the Ministry were marked by antagonism and suspicion and usually ended in an outright quarrel.

The monopoly system did not function very well. Schools were frustrated with the low quality of the books and erratic distribution. Sida, the Swedish International Development Co-operation Agency, which supplied all the paper and other inputs for the printing and had invested heavily in Tanzanian education for over a decade, was dissatisfied with almost all the performance indicators. When, in 1991, the MOEC announced that it was going to open the school market to local commercial publishing, it did not come as a complete surprise. The publishers, however, did not believe it was a genuine conversion – and they were partly right: the ICD argued against liberalisation and also had many supporters within the Ministry. The Institute attempted to block the idea, but had to give in.

Implementation of the liberalisation policy started in 1993, under the Pilot Project for Publishing (PPP), financed by Sida. The goal was clear, but to estimate how long the transition would take was difficult. Textbook development is both time-consuming and costly, and Tanzania's publishers were inexperienced and poor. Relations between the public and private sectors were frosty and all those involved feared that this was going to be a long and difficult process; but Sida was determined to see the project through to the end.

The transition did take a long time, as expected, but apart from some initial problems it was remarkably free from friction. When the PPP came to an end in the year 2000, the essential components of the commercial system were in place, and mistrust and antagonism had been replaced by a spirit of co-operation and mutual respect. The PPP is an interesting example of the transition from a state-monopoly system to public/private partnership in the book sector, and it is for this reason that what happened in Tanzania forms a separate chapter in this study.

Many factors were important in order to achieve a positive result, but some have been identified as decisive.

Longevity and Consistency

There was a commitment from the funding agency to see the transition process through to the end, in spite of the knowledge that it would take at least five to seven years, perhaps longer. The consistent, guaranteed support of a single agency, plus consistent technical consultancy, served as a solid platform for the work. The Book Management Unit (BMU) of the MOEC was responsible for the management of the PPP. Its head was a very senior Ministry official, and this gave the BMU a high degree of independence from the start: its work was never disturbed by frequent changes in the political leadership of the Ministry. The BMU was also provided with the necessary technical assistance and material requirements to make it work.

Transparency and Confidence Building

Because of the tension between the public and the private sides from the start, two consulting firms were used during the first two years. One was based in the BMU and assisted the Ministry with the planning of the project and negotiations with publishers; the other assisted the private sector through seminars, on-the-job training and advisory services. This latter consultant also dedicated much time to the consolidation of the publishers' association and the booksellers' association and acted as the publishers' adviser in negotiations with the Ministry. The project had no previous experience from other countries to build on, which meant that procedures had to be worked out, discussed and revised throughout the project period, always involving close co-operation between the BMU, the publishers and the consultants. Sida's evaluators of the PPP described the approach as follows (Pehrsson and Grahm, 2004).

"PPP started ... with a goal hierarchy and indicators to control progress. As time went on, this project management method was toned down. Goals were redefined from phase to phase, dependent on what had been achieved and learnt so far. The project was coming closer to a process-oriented approach, similar to Open Project Management methodology. The evaluators understood that this dynamic project approach was very popular among all involved parties. The first reflection was that this would be because of the positive results. A deeper look into the project tells that this is not the only reason. The explanation is probably that a more open project management invites participants to influence the project, since it makes the 'top down' conception of the project disappear. The success is partly based on the fact that participation ensures real support to relevant persons to implement the project ideas."

Capacity Building

It was obvious that those who were going to develop teaching/learning materials – publishers, writers, editors, designers, illustrators and photographers – would need training in how to develop quality material. Publishers would also need to develop business and financial skills. But a market system delivers only what the market demands. The quality of the books would therefore also depend on the competence and integrity of those in the Ministry who would evaluate and approve them, and of those who would procure books at district level. Seminars and workshops in book evaluation were therefore organised both in the Ministry and in the districts. Representatives of the public sector also participated in many activities for the private sector in order to understand the conditions of commercial publishing. Both sides took part in study tours to Zimbabwe and Sweden, where they saw market systems functioning. Over the years, the staff of BMU acquired a broad understanding of all aspects of educational publishing and the market system, knowledge that was invaluable for the Ministry to manage the transition.

The Publishing Tradition

Tanzania already had a publishing tradition when the PPP started. Before the monopoly era, both the East African Language Bureau and subsidiaries of British publishing houses had published books in Tanzania. Oxford University Press was the only British company that still had an office in the country, but many Tanzanians who had experience of publishing in the early days of independence were eager to get back into business. Some had taken the opportunity, offered by CODE's Children's Book Project, to publish illustrated books for children, with sales of a small print-run guaranteed by the Project.

The Textbook Monopoly

A short background to Tanzania's monopoly system and a more detailed description of the Pilot Project for Publishing and the transition process follows. Two recent studies of the textbook situation in Tanzania show that, although Tanzania's publishing industry is thriving, there are many problems in the district-based procurement (Pehrsson and Grahm, 2003). We will also, briefly, look into these problems and the solutions proposed in the reports.

Box 19: Tanzania's experience of a monopoly system

- Books produced by Government institutions very expensive.

- Impossible to accurately estimate or control costs

- Decisions made by Curriculum officers with no technical production expertise or budget responsibility.

- Pupil/book ratio 1:3 (at best).

- A black market developed for stolen books.

- Insufficient time for editing.

- No trialling or monitoring of how books used.

- Books reprinted each year without revision or correction.

- Books distributed according to central plan (rather than according to need).

- Exclusion of local publishers from textbook market negative impact on other types of book publishing.

The birth of the monopoly

Tanzania's first President, 'Mwalimu' Julius Nyerere, gave high priority to education and was very successful in mobilizing his people. At independence in 1961, there were only 500,000 students in primary school, but four years later there were two million. The campaigns to eradicate illiteracy were also enormously successful; small indigenous publishers started to publish material for the literacy campaigns. Using Kiswahili in primary education and literacy courses gave Tanzania a great advantage in comparison with most other former colonies, which had to use a European language.

Financing the rapid expansion of the school system was a heavy burden for the new nation, however, and not least financing the textbooks, which were imported from British publishers or purchased from their local subsidiaries. Although the government bought very large numbers of copies, it failed to negotiate reasonable terms with the publishers, who offered Tanzania little more than normal bookseller discounts. In 1966, Tanzania Publishing House (TPH) was started as a joint venture between Tanzania's National Development Corporation and the British publisher, Macmillan Educational Publishers. The new company was given monopoly status as supplier of textbooks (on the proposal of the owner of the British company, the former British Prime Minister, Harold Macmillan).

In 1971, however, the MOEC accused Macmillan of overpricing the books published by TPH and began to reprint them without involving the publisher. The takeover was made possible by a provision in Tanzania's first copyright law. Macmillan pulled out and TPH became a parastatal company in the following year.

Tanzania's education system had become dependent on a single foreign publisher for educational materials and, in the political climate of the 1970s – nationalization was the logical solution. The MOEC would have total control of the content, and, if all the best pedagogical experts in the country contributed, the best possible books could be produced. The large print-runs in the single-textbook system would give low unit costs, and no commercial publisher would be able to profiteer from children's textbooks.

Tanzania had no difficulty in getting international support for the policy to dispense with publishers altogether. UNESCO and UNICEF financed a project for editing and printing manuscripts from the curriculum institute and assisted in the establishment of a book-production unit within the MOEC. They also donated printing machinery, and Sida agreed to supply paper and other inputs for production. The so-called 'confinement policy', in 1981, gave a parastatal company, Tanzania Elimu Supplies (TES), total monopoly over the distribution of textbooks for primary schools. This meant that Tanzania's bookshops lost their most profitable trade, and most of them closed down. For the commercial publishers this was yet another change for the worse.

The monopoly system

Responsibility for the provision of textbooks was shared by a large number of institutions. In the 1980s the system functioned in the following way:

- Manuscripts were written by the ICD, which had also, gradually, taken over the functions of a publisher – editing, page design and illustration – from TPH.
- Production – i.e. the ordering of typesetting and printing – was co-ordinated by the BMU.
- Books were printed by two parastatal printers under the Ministry of Industry and Trade.
- All inputs for the production – paper, cover board, stitching wire, glue and film – continued to be provided by Sida.
- The Education Co-ordination Unit (ECU) of the Ministry of Rural Administration and Local Government (MRALG) determined the print-runs needed, paid the printers, and was responsible for the transport of finished books from the MOEC's warehouse to the districts. (TES was now out of business.)
- District Education Officers handled the distribution of books to individual schools.

Disadvantages of the monopoly

1. Cost aspects

In Tanzania, as in many other countries with a monopoly system, the costs of textbook development, production and distribution were hidden in the general running costs of the government institutions and parastatal companies which shared these responsibilities. No realistic budget for the production of textbooks could be made, nor was it possible to calculate the real cost of a printed copy.

Decisions about the extent of a book, the number and type of illustrations, the use of colour, etc., were made by officers at the curriculum institute, who did not know the technical production process, were not aware of the cost implications of their decisions and, of course, had no budget responsibility. Without a budget for an individual title, no one strived for an economical layout. In 1993 the BMU was able to reduce the extent of certain old textbooks (and thereby the production cost) by 25 per cent simply by eliminating preliminary pages, blank pages, and lengthy prefaces of no interest to pupils.

The government could finance one copy per three students – at best. If at least some parents had been allowed to buy copies for their children, it would have been a good way of sharing costs, and would also have benefited pupils from poorer families through an improved overall book–pupil ratio. But textbooks were government property and, since they were not available through normal sales channels, a black market developed for stolen books.

The fragmentation of responsibilities within the monopoly system also made it difficult to control how inputs were used: in the 1980s, it was found that large quantities of donated paper had been misappropriated by the printers.

2. Pedagogical aspects

Monopoly textbooks were written – often in haste – in workshops involving curriculum developers and teachers. There was little time for editing, there were no classroom trials, and manuscripts from the ICD were automatically approved for use. The BMU simply co-ordinated the printing and had no responsibility for the content. There was no system for following up how books functioned in the classroom and what teachers thought of them. Books were reprinted, year after year, without revision – in some cases, still with errors and misprints after ten years. Ordinary teachers could not question the accuracy, selection or sequencing of subject matter in a book published by the Ministry. When generations of pupils get exactly the same presentation of school subjects, the damage done by uninspiring, unclear or even incorrect learning materials can be serious – especially if poorly trained teachers cannot provide supplementary information and if there are no reference books to consult.

3. Distribution

In the monopoly system, books were distributed according to centrally made distribution plans, not according to the needs of the individual schools. When distribution is not demand-driven, books also tend to be distributed when it suits the center, not when schools need them.

4. Effect of monopoly on the book sector as a whole

In most of Africa, the large primary school market is the only sector in which publishers and booksellers are able to make some profit. If they are excluded from this market, they will not be able to provide the trade books, reference books, fiction and children's books that every country also needs.

The New Textbook Policy

In December 1991, the MOEC issued a new Textbook Policy, which stated: 'The Policy aims at transforming the Textbook Production and Distribution to a completely commercialised system, whereby the entire book provision would be marshalled by publishers.' The monopoly on textbooks for primary schools was to be phased out and it was expected that competition between commercial publishers would result in improved pedagogical and technical quality, while at the same time keeping the cost of books down. The Textbook Policy was in line with the ongoing general liberalisation of trade in Tanzania and the region.

The implementation of the Policy would take place in two phases:

The *transition period*, during which the government would continue to be responsible for the development of manuscripts and textbook distribution, while publishers would be contracted to handle the publishing. The length of the transition period could not be defined at the outset, but would depend on the performance of the public and private sector in building the new system.

The *long-term goal*, when the commercial sector would 'assume the entire activities of production and distribution'. The government would then be responsible for curriculum development but would have no direct involvement in the production and distribution of textbooks but 'simply recommend suitable titles for use in schools'.

The long-term *production model* was to be as shown in Figure 1.

FIGURE 1: PRODUCTION MODEL

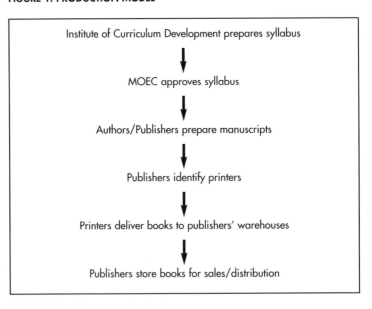

Regarding *book distribution*, the Textbook Policy foresaw a development in five stages, where each stage signified a reduction in the government's direct involvement in the process (see Figure 2).

FIGURE 2: BOOK DISTRIBUTION

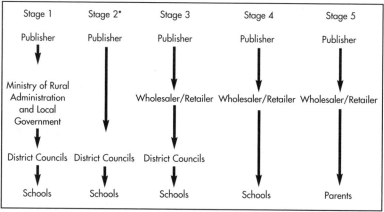

*This was the situation at the end of the PPP.

The goal was a multi-textbook system, i.e. with various titles on the market for each subject/grade. The responsibility for *selecting and purchasing* textbooks for primary education with government funding was to be devolved first to district and eventually to school level. Books would also be available on the open market so that parents could buy books, which, as suggested above, might improve the pupil–textbook ratio in the classroom and also benefit poorer pupils.

The Pilot Project for Publishing (PPP)

Sida had been the main funder of the textbook monopoly and it was natural for them also to fund the implementation of the new policy. The Pilot Project for Publishing began in 1993 in order to manage the transition. There was consensus between the Ministry and Sida that only local publishers would be invited to participate in the exercise. The Publishers' Association of Tanzania (PATA) had several members, but all were very small and would stand little chance of winning contracts in international competition.

The Project's goal regarding the distribution of textbooks was to be stage two, i.e. each of the (then) 113 District Councils would procure textbooks for its schools. The publishers would deliver the selected books to the District Councils, who would deliver them to the schools. It was considered premature to try to devolve selection and procurement to the 10,000 schools, although that remained the ultimate goal.

The Pilot Project for Publishing was designed

- *to guarantee an undisturbed supply of books to schools* during the transition from the centralised system to a market system by co-ordinating the introduction of commercial publishing with the phasing out of the government's printing programme. This was facilitated by making the Book Management Unit also responsible for the management of the PPP.

- *to continue centralised purchasing during a transition period*, which should be long enough to allow the commercial actors time to build a commercial distribution system capable of reaching districts, schools and parents.

- *to cover the basic needs for new textbook titles as quickly as possible.* The original plan, to contract publishers to take over, revise and improve existing titles, had to be abandoned. A radically revised curriculum was under way, where the number of school subjects would be reduced from thirteen to seven, and the existing titles would therefore soon be obsolete. A number of manuscripts had already been written to the new curriculum by the ICD, and others were under way. Publishing of these manuscripts would be the fastest way of covering all school subjects and grades with one new title.

- *to strengthen the local publishing industry's pedagogical and technical capacity* through technical assistance so that they would be able to meet the demand from the schools and future competition from abroad.

- *to compensate the local publishing industry's lack of working capital* by contracting them to deliver the entire first print-run of each title (in most cases, over 200,000 copies for a pupil's book) in bulk to the central warehouse of the Ministry and be paid for these books on delivery.

Technical assistance

The consultants had no resident representative in the country working with the PPP. The head of the BMU was the project manager, assisted by the consultants on a needs basis, especially in the planning phase, in the bid evaluation and in the capacity-building activities.

The bidding procedure

The selection of publishers for the manuscripts from the ICD was done through local competitive bidding. Interested publishers first had to go through a pre-qualification process to ensure that only serious companies were participating. Qualified publishers were invited to collect manuscripts and develop a proposal for each title.

The proposals consisted of:

- A *technical bid*, which included a thorough review of the manuscript, specifying strong and weak points, and defining what alterations would be made to improve it; sample pages demonstrating typography, layout principles and type of illustrations; a dummy, showing format, extent, quality of paper, board and binding; a production plan, showing the number of additional copies to be printed for the general market; and a marketing plan for these copies.

- A *financial bid*, with prices of the copies to be delivered in bulk to the central warehouse, and of the copies to be sold to the general public through bookshops.

Technical evaluation

Bids were graded on the basis of quality criteria. Merit points were awarded for the quality of the content (which in this case referred to the quality of the publisher's pedagogical evaluation of the manuscript and proposed alterations), legibility, design, illustrations (of the sample pages), marketing strategy, and the technical quality (paper and binding of submitted dummies). Bids with a quality rating above a certain minimum level passed to the next phase.

The technical evaluation was done as group work, with the entire staff of the BMU and the consultants present; representatives of other departments of the Ministry often took part as observers. The organisation of the work in this way contributed to objectivity and transparency, and was also an important training event for all present, as all possible aspects of textbook quality came up for discussion. A large number of bids were submitted, and each of the four batches (see below) took at least seven full days to evaluate.

Financial evaluation

The financial bids were opened in the presence of the Ministry Tender Board and participating publishers. The lowest bid was not necessarily taken if a bid with a considerably higher quality rating was within 10 per cent of the lowest bid.

Tendering of the titles

The tendering of contracts for publishing took place in four batches:

- In 1993 (PPP1), manuscripts of eleven titles, written by staff at the Institute of Curriculum Development, were tendered for publishing. A total of 782,000 copies were purchased by the Project. The publishers were obliged, by contract, also to produce copies for the general market and to make these available to parents through bookshops.

- In 1995 (PPP2), a second batch of manuscripts, containing 10 titles, was tendered, and 960,000 copies were purchased by the Project.

  In 1997 (PPP3), the third batch of manuscripts, containing 28 titles, was tendered, and 3,192,000 copies were purchased by the Project.

- All copies purchased by the Project under PPP1–PPP3 were delivered to the central warehouse of the Ministry and the publishers were paid on delivery. The Education Co-ordination Unit then distributed the books to the 113 districts, exactly as under the previous centralised production system.

- In 1999 (PPP4), the final batch of 30 titles was tendered for publishing. These were the last textbook manuscripts to be written by the ICD, which had now changed its name to the Tanzania Institute of Education (TIE). A total of 3,420,000 copies were purchased by the Project, but this time the publishers were also required to take responsibility for the distribution of the books, and they were paid only after completed delivery. Most publishers opted to use the services of independent distribution companies and the distribution functioned reasonably well.

- The completion of the fourth batch in 1999 meant that a total of 79 new titles, covering all the primary school subjects and grades, had been published and distributed under PPP.

The transition to market system completed

When the PPP ended in December 2000, the centralised system had been wound up and the essential components of the new system were in place: Tanzania Institute of Education had stopped writing textbooks and was concentrating on its key functions: curriculum development, research and in-service teacher training. The best curriculum developers were still writing textbooks, but as individuals; and, like all other authors, they were receiving royalties. Writers were also recruited among teachers and teacher trainers. Two new structures had been introduced by the PPP to handle important tasks: the Education Materials Approval Committee and the Textbook Selection Committee.

Textbook approval

In some countries in Africa, such as Zimbabwe, the curriculum institute is responsible for the approval system. This was not possible in Tanzania, as the ICD was the copyright-holder of all

PPP textbooks and several members of its staff were busy writing alternative titles. A new body, the Education Materials Approval Committee (EMAC), was therefore established as a sub-section of the Department of Policy and Planning in the MOEC for the approval of textbooks. The new system had the capacity to handle a large number of applications and great pains had been taken to make it objective and transparent: clear criteria for approval had been published, and each new title was evaluated by three independent reviewers whose identities were not revealed to the publisher. There was a fixed timetable for the evaluation process, and publishers would have the right to appeal against negative decisions. By the end of the year 2000, a total of 129 alternative textbook titles had been submitted to the BMU, which now functioned as the secretariat of EMAC, and 53 of these had been approved, most of them after the publishers had made changes requested by EMAC. The districts and schools were now free to buy and use alternatives to the PPP titles – as long as they had EMAC's approval stamp on the copyright page.

Textbook selection and procurement

When the PPP ended, the responsibility for selection and procurement rested with the District Councils. The District Education Officer (DEO) would be the manager of the process, but his or her function was purely administrative. The selection was to be done by a Textbook Selection Committee, the majority of whose members would be teachers from different parts of the district. The Committee was designed on the pattern of the well-functioning Textbook Purchasing Committees in Zimbabwe's schools, on which parents were also represented. Apart from the obvious pedagogical reasons for engaging teachers in selection, this was also seen as a way to create transparency in the procurement process and reduce the risk of 'unwarranted interference'. All DEOs had taken part in seminars on the functioning of the new procurement system, as had the District Education Directors and District Logistics Officers.

Training activities

Throughout the PPP, local publishers and their staff participated in training courses given by expatriate specialists in areas such as page design/desktop publishing, illustration techniques, copyright, marketing, and how to organise the book development process. The most appreciated type of training was the hands-on assistance provided by specialists to editors, illustrators and designers during the development of a new title.

None of the PPP textbooks had photographic illustrations. Publishers did not know any photographers, and the photographers had never realised that educational publishing could be a market; neither was aware that a photographer could be entitled to a fee for the publishing of a photograph. A joint course for editors, designers and photographers was therefore arranged, covering issues such as copyright, remuneration principles, technical and pedagogical demands on illustrations, and the organisation of picture libraries.

Training activities were also arranged for booksellers, and joint workshops for publishers and booksellers were held where they could discuss issues of common interest and learn how the textbook market functions in other countries. Representatives of MOEC, MRALG, PATA and the Booksellers' Association of Tanzania (BATA) travelled together to Zimbabwe and Sweden to study market systems in operation.

Seminars were held for teachers who wanted to work as book evaluators for EMAC. During the last two years of the PPP, the training activities were extended to the country's District Councils, in order to prepare local education staff, as mentioned above, for the new responsibilities of managing the systems for the selection and purchase of textbooks in a commercial multi-textbook system. Seminars were carried out in 'clusters' all over the country and reached all officers concerned in the 113 districts. Similar activities were also carried out at regional level.

Research studies

The PPP commissioned studies in areas of direct interest both to public and private partners: The study 'Textbook Usability in Tanzanian Basic Education' was undertaken by researchers from the Morogoro Teachers' College and two researchers from Stockholm Institute of Education. The team made more than 180 classroom observations and interviewed teachers and pupils to find out how they related to the new books and to what extent the books were accessible and easy to use. A study of the economics of bookselling and a study on gender issues were also carried out (Minzi and Saiwaadand; Mbilinyi and B. Omari).

The funding agencies

As mentioned earlier, Sida financed the monopoly system, and the PPP also started as a Sida project. In 1998 three 'new' funding agencies expressed interest in contributing to the financing of textbooks published under the Project. This new phase would signify a dramatic increase in the budget for books, but as the agencies had different demands on payment procedures, reporting, etc., it was a year before the agreements could be signed. During this period, the local project management was almost entirely occupied by discussions with the agencies: procurement decisions had to wait until it was clear when funds would be available, and in the meantime no book could be printed. Finally, in October 1999, the PPP was formally succeeded by the Interim Textbook Programme, financed by Sida, the Netherlands (DGIS), the European Union and the British Department for International Development (DfID). The delay in project activities, however, led to the extension of the Technical Assistance contract for the PPP, first to 30 June 2000, then to 31 December 2000. In 2001 the Primary Education Development Plan (PEDP) started. Its sector-wide approach replaced practically all previous bilateral and multi-lateral project support.

How the plans worked

Who could participate?

Participation was limited to 'local commercial' publishers, but the term was given a generous interpretation and no publisher in Tanzania was excluded. Thus, Tanzania Publishing House was accepted as 'commercial', although it was a parastatal (under the Ministry of Industry and Trade), and the Tanzanian subsidiary of Oxford University Press (OUP) was accepted as 'local' (after some debate). The only publisher in the country with a foreign owner, OUP had been in Tanzania long before independence, its staff was Tanzanian, and it had been the publisher of President Nyerere's works. TPH did not manage to get any PPP orders, but OUP won some PPP titles: its high-quality bids were due to technical assistance from its sister company in Kenya. A couple of the other local publishers also had former links with British publishers. The following publishers are currently active in educational publishing: Macmillan Aidan, Mture, E and D, Ben and Co., OUP, Educational Books Publishers, Tanzania Publishing House, and Readit.

Slow start

Textbook reform did not have the full support of some institutions within the monopoly system, and the development of the PPP was slow at the beginning owing to a reluctance by the decision-makers to give the go-ahead for various stages of the project plan. One of the most crucial issues was the monopoly status of the Institute of Curriculum Development with regard to textbook development. It was eventually agreed that the Institute, then called the Tanzania Institute of Education, should withdraw from the development of manuscripts, and as a result the publishers were free to take the long-expected step towards publisher-initiated titles. Some curriculum developers soon became engaged by the publishers as freelance writers.

Financing of the production

The publishers' lack of working capital was seen as a serious problem at the Project's planning stage. The editorial process was no major problem, but the print-runs would be very large – over 200,000 copies for a pupil's book – and the printers demanded 50 per cent payment up front: printers in Tanzania were also under-financed and needed the advance money to be able to buy paper. The publishers could not borrow money from banks – they had no collateral, and interest rates were around 30 per cent. But the publishers' money problem was solved when the MOEC guaranteed payment on delivery, in bulk, of the entire first print-run to the Ministry's warehouse. With the contract in hand, the publishers contacted printers abroad – in Kenya, South Africa, Mauritius and India. The foreign printers accepted the contract as collateral, and some even offered the publishers up to 90 days' credit.

For the system to function, it was absolutely essential that the publishers could pay the printers' invoices promptly. This they could do only if the MOEC met its obligations immediately. Experience had shown that disbursements made in the normal way through the Treasury did not meet this requirement; the PPP was therefore allowed to use dedicated project accounts.

The long validity period required for the publishers' bids caused some problems. First it made it difficult for publishers to get firm estimates from printers. Substantial fluctuations in the international market prices of paper led to the re-negotiation of prices of the PPP1 titles: all prices were adjusted upwards by a standard percentage. In the last year of the PPP, drastic changes in the rate of exchange between the Tanzania shilling and US dollar led to demands for compensation from the PPP4 publishers.

The PPP books were printed abroad for several reasons. The large parastatal printers, Printpak and NPC, which had produced the books for the monopoly system, were out of operation. It was impossible for Tanzania's commercial printers to compete with the generous credit terms offered by printers abroad, and an additional problem for them was that Tanzania's paper mill in Mufindi had stopped producing suitable paper, which meant that they would have to import paper. In Tanzania there is 10 per cent import duty on printing paper, and paper represents 65%–70% of the total production cost for large-volume products like textbooks; the publishers could import finished (printed) books without duty.

A total of eleven local publishers had managed to win orders from the PPP. Without exception the publishers managed to deliver the very large print-runs ordered. Considerable improvement took place over the project period, both regarding delivery and quality. The large print-runs of the PPP titles, which for some time enjoyed a monopoly position in their respective subjects/grades, signified a substantial boost to the financial position of their publishers.

The publishers tendered for and won PPP orders for individual titles, not for entire series. The fact that a series of books in a certain subject came to be divided between two publishers was initially seen as a problem. It turned out to be favourable for the development of parallel titles, however, as publishers who had part of a series immediately started developing their own titles to 'fill the gaps'. In some subjects, two complete series soon emerged, each one characterized by its own graphic design and style of illustrations.

Competition is now gradually reducing the annual sales of the PPP titles, but their publishers have re-invested the profits in the development of new textbook titles. They have also invested in new staff, in better office equipment, and in the publishing of readers, novels and trade books.

Decentralised procurement

Textbook procurement by districts was finally introduced in the last phase of the PPP. The process, which was managed by the ECU and the BMU, turned out to be more complicated and time-consuming than expected. Both the government's procurement regulations and the new funding agencies prescribed local competitive bidding – a method that is not very suitable for buying books. Buying textbooks was also a new experience for the districts, and some DEOs had difficulty in calculating textbook needs and costs. The central authorities found it difficult to relinquish responsibility, and prescribed that the District Councils send all documents such as tender invitations, draft contracts, etc., to the ECU for approval before invitations could be advertised or orders sent to suppliers. The first full-scale test of decentralised procurement was therefore a time-consuming learning process for all involved.

Bookselling

When the Pilot Project for Publishing ended, booksellers had not been engaged in sales to schools and bookselling had therefore not developed to the same extent as publishing. This can be seen as a failure of the PPP, as the increased availability of books on the market is one of the desired effects of book-sector liberalisation. However, there were only between 10 and 20 small booksellers in the country when the Project started, and it was not possible to entrust the nationwide distribution of the PPP books to these: they were too few and too weak for this.

Booksellers have complained that they did not receive as much support as publishers. They have, however, benefited from the PPP in various ways. From its beginning, publishers were obliged to make copies of the book available through booksellers. As the government could finance only one copy per three students, primary school pupils and their parents represented a large market also for bookselling. (A book–pupil ratio of 1:3 continued to be government policy after the end of the PPP.) When the Project started, most booksellers had very little contact with publishers and there was a lot of confusion regarding sales conditions and discounts. The PPP therefore organised workshops where booksellers received basic training and where they could meet publishers and discuss issues of common interest.

In a market system, sales channels will develop if and when they are needed. Publishers could handle distribution themselves during the PPP, but they have realised that it is not rational for them to continue marketing and delivering their books to 113 districts. When 11,000 primary schools start purchasing books, they must buy them from booksellers. With the further development of the textbook market, the bookseller will be indispensable as a link between the publisher and the district/schools.

Positive side effects of liberalisation

The content of education is no longer simply a matter for the curriculum developers within the walls of the Institute; it is discussed at many levels of, and even outside, the education system. Writers, publishers, editors, EMAC reviewers, DEOs and teachers selecting books will discuss the content of textbooks and the curriculum. In Tanzania, the syllabuses have traditionally been very detailed, as a teacher should be able to teach using the syllabus if textbooks were not available, as so often happened. A detailed and prescriptive syllabus is not an ideal basis for a multi-textbook system, however, as it gives very little scope for creativity and the development of alternative methods. The new actors involved, and the new openness, are likely to influence curriculum development in the future and may help revitalize education in Tanzania.

Teachers can discuss the qualities and shortcomings of textbooks more freely than before, because books are published by commercial companies and not by their employer. The education system in Tanzania is hierarchic and seldom attaches great importance to the opinions of teachers. But teachers should be involved in the selection of books, and publishers should welcome feedback from teachers, as this will help them to improve their products.

Post script

Experience has shown that transition to an open-market, commercial system from a state-monopoly background introduces many new challenges, and setbacks also occur. Nowhere is this a straightforward, mechanical process. The transition is not an event, but a process, and in Tanzania developing a procurement mechanism to replace central state deliveries of textbooks has met with many (expected) problems. In common with much of Africa, the Tanzanian example shows that it is in establishing decentralised distribution and procurement systems that complex problems often arise. It was assumed that once the commercial system was set up it would be, by definition, self-regulating.

To some degree this has been true, since the commercial textbook-publishing and -approvals system has functioned well. But the need for co-ordination and management of the entire system by MOEC, essentially requiring innovative problem-solving, did not end automatically once commercialisation had started. The dismantling of the Book Management Unit after the PPP, both as a management and co-ordination center and as a repository of accumulated book knowledge for the Ministry, was therefore perhaps premature.

The following is an attempt to summarize how the textbook provision system in Tanzania is functioning a few years after the PPP ended. It is based on a country visit and on two recent consulting studies (Pehrsson and Grahm, 2004; Smart, 2003).

The publishing industry

The consultants' reports confirm that the positive development of the publishing sector during the PPP has continued:

'There is no doubt that Tanzanian textbooks have improved from the start of the PPP and onwards. This stands out as very clear in all interviews with DEOs and teachers, and the children who are lucky enough to use the books in schools are equally happy with them.' (Pehrsson and Grahm). 'Many local publishers have clearly benefited greatly and now operate from well-appointed premises with professional skills and resources. The publishing industry is in good shape and well able to respond to educational publishing opportunities (Smart).

Distribution

There is a variety of books on the market today but, unfortunately, there do not seem to be more books in schools than before the liberalisation. The target of PEDP is a book–pupil ratio of 1:1, and, although the current funding is not quite sufficient for this, a ratio of 1:2 in the schools could be expected. However, data collected by a PEDP review found that it varied between 1:4 and 1:7, and consultants found ratios of 1:20 or worse in some rural schools.

According to the consultants, one contributing factor may be that irregular and piecemeal disbursement of funds makes it impossible for Districts to purchase books in bulk at low prices. The schools need to have textbooks delivered once a year, but funds are disbursed four times a year, which means that districts cannot supply schools at the beginning of the school year. Funds come from different sources:

- Basket funding from donors channeled to the MOEC
- World Bank credito to the President's Office – Regional Administration and Local Government (PO-RALG)
- The Treasury, which makes quarterly transfers through PO-RALG

Another reason may be that the Book Selection Committees, which were introduced by the PPP in order to increase transparency in the procurement process and involve teachers in the selection of books, have not been institutionalized. In nearly all Districts it is the DEO, who negotiates with publishers and orders educational materials on behalf of the schools. There seems to be little dialogue between DEOs and the head teachers, which means that teachers cannot influence the choice of books and that feedback from the teachers does not reach the publishers. In the few cases where a Book Selection Committee has been formally established, no teachers are members.

At present, booksellers are not involved in the sale of educational materials to state schools, but they should use the new opportunity to sell textbooks to parents. Unfortunately, the publishers seem reluctant to print more copies than the exact quantity ordered by the education system. It is obviously more attractive to deliver books in bulk and be paid promptly than to sell on credit to booksellers and have to wait for payment; but the publishers should realise that it is in their own interests to pave the way for booksellers. Nevertheless, the Booksellers Association of Tanzania (BSAT) has approximately seventy members today, which is a considerable increase from 1993, when there were twenty. BSAT has drafted a Code of Practice, which it is intended will be binding on all members.

Management and supervision

The authority for delivering primary education in the field now rests with MRALG's successor PO-RALG. It is responsible for disbursing funds to the districts, and for supervision and auditing of the use of them, including funds for procurement of textbooks. But access to quality textbooks is one of the key components of education, and the overall responsibility for the system therefore rests with the MOEC. Before the PEDP started, the BMU was the natural focal point for all textbook-related activities, but today most of the staff have been dispersed, and the Ministry does not make use of their special competence and knowledge about the new system. The BMU still exists, but only in a very reduced role as the secretariat of the EMAC.

Since the BMU's leading role fell away, there seems to have been an unfortunate lack of clarity regarding the responsibility for textbook issues, both within the MOEC and between the MOEC and PO-RALG. The Quality Improvement Technical Working Group within PEDP and the external consultants seem unanimous that there is a need for a separate unit, located in the MOEC, with responsibility for managing all aspects of provision of educational materials. That unit would need to have an understanding of the teaching and learning process as well as an understanding of the book industry (publishers and booksellers) and would also provide the 'institutional memory' for all issues related to educational materials. The requirement for stricter production specifications for textbooks is only one example of the issues that such a unit would handle. It is therefore probable that the BMU will soon be resurrected in its former capacity but as a permanent sub-section within the Policy and Planning Directorate of the MOEC.

Considering the large amounts of money spent on textbooks, EMAC, with its key position in the system, ought to have no problems financing its important work. Nevertheless, EMAC's capacity has been affected by lack of funds to the extent that it is no longer able to arrange evaluation exercises, or to train evaluators. Publishers in general are positive to the EMAC process, but some complain about the length of time currently taken by EMAC to evaluate submissions and that it lacks vision regarding the development of methodology. The latter complaint is probably due to the fact that EMAC's freedom of action is restricted by the detailed syllabuses.

School-based selection and procurement

From the start, the goal of textbook reform has been to give schools full responsibility for selection and procurement. District-based procurement was introduced as an intermediate stage, to enable publishers and booksellers to gain experience and skills in educational publishing and marketing, something that was not possible under the monopoly system. District-based procurement has not functioned as planned, however, and, rather than trying to set things right in the current system, the MOEC seems determined to go ahead in implementing school-based selection and procurement (stage four in the 1991 Textbook Policy). The Ministry has opened bank accounts for the 12,700 schools and wants to hand over responsibility to them as soon as possible. According to the consultants, the MOEC had planned to introduce the new system already in 2003, but this was found not to be feasible.

Box 20: Essential factors in school-based selection

- Existence of bookshops

- Access to samples of all textbooks.

- Teachers trained to select books effectively.

- Head teachers trained in procurement.

- An effective system of follow-up and audit of accounts.

- Training of District Education Officers (or Inspectors) in checking accounts.

- Piloting in a number of districts.

There are many advantages in allowing schools to select and procure their own educational materials and choose their own supplier. Experience in many other African countries has shown that procurement by schools is more efficient and more cost-effective than centralised procurement. Procurement by the end-user (the school) is also more transparent and less vulnerable to 'interference' than centralised procurement, especially if it is done by a school selection committee rather than by the head teacher alone. By empowering the teachers, this system of school-based selection may also give teachers increased self-assurance and renewed pride in their profession.

The weak bookseller infrastructure in Tanzania is a restraining factor. There is no doubt that the prospect of marketing such a large volume of books will attract both booksellers and other entrepreneurs, but the fact that textbooks are distributed only once a year means that it is unlikely that many permanent bookshops will be established simply to service schools. Established booksellers can use travelling representatives to cover large areas, however, and distributors of other types of products, with wide distribution networks, might take on textbook marketing as an extra seasonal activity.

Chapter 7

NATIONAL BOOK POLICY IN AFRICA

In the preceding chapters there have been numerous references to book-policy issues, the problems related to *ad hoc* decision-making and textbook policy creation. While a number of countries have articulated a 'textbook policy', either within one policy statement or comprising a *de facto* policy made up from many separate decisions and documents, none has an all-embracing 'national book policy'. Moreover, virtually every issue in this study concerns policy (or its absence) in some form. In this chapter, with an eye to the future, we look at the major debates and issues surrounding book policies and their creation in Africa.

Why is a national book policy necessary?

The purpose of a national book policy is to enable the co-ordination of the myriad regulations and other factors that affect each component of the book chain so as to stimulate the local book industry and encourage increased access to books. The components of the book chain include: authorship and book creation; printing and production; publishing and publishing services such as editing, design and illustration; bookselling and distribution; readership; library services; book statistics; and issues relating to literacy, language, copyright, imports, etc., as well as state policies regulating the flow of information to the public.

In all African countries book industries are relatively small industries, in comparison with other manufacturing sectors, and are usually 'located', from an industry and commerce policy perspective, within the 'printing' sector. Although ministries of information and culture tend to create policies inculcating social and national awareness, it is the policies of the education ministries that dominate the environment in which a book industry operates, because textbooks are such a significant proportion of book consumption. Two aspects of education ministry policy control textbooks: the curriculum policies that regulate content, and the book-provision policies that determine what books reach schools, how, and in what quantities.

All countries have policies affecting book provision in some form – laws, regulations, and economic and social controls – but they are often of a scattered and patchwork character and sometimes contradictory.

Defining national book policy

A national book policy may range from a statement of broad objectives through to meticulous legal instruments that establish the legal framework for the rights and obligations of parties in the provision of books. A 'book' policy is distinct from a 'textbook' policy in that it is an all-embracing framework for the production, distribution and readership for all types books. It considers the book as a manufactured product, as a product that is commercially traded, and as a product with intangible 'cultural and spiritual' qualities.

Box 21: A Comprehensive Book Policy

• Encourages literacy creation.

• Provides a legal framework for protecting authors' rights.

• Provides fiscal, credit and administrative incentives for the publishing industry.

• Facilitates nationwide distribution.

• Removes taxes from books.

• Establishes nationwide library networks.

• Introduces new methods for teaching reading.

• Promotes human resource development in the different skills in the book sector

---

(adapted from Garzon, A. 1997).

Álvaro Garzon, in his wonderfully succinct manual *National Book Policy: A Guide for Users in the Field* (1997), describes a national book policy as follows:

'The main objective ... is to ensure that access to books is made easier for all. To achieve this it must reckon with the complex chain of cultural, industrial and commercial relationships that links the author to the reader.

'... when formulating policies to develop books and reading one must identify and regulate a series of partial objectives specific to each of the protagonists in the book chain, taking into account the situation in the country ... and the delicate equilibrium between educational and cultural policies of the state and the industrial development of the publishing sector.

'Setting in motion a national book policy entails bringing together all of these elements, and seeing to it that they develop harmoniously, in line with ... established objectives.'

Meaningful national book policy is a practical matter and can be interpreted as the appropriate means for mobilizing and co-ordinating the book sector (state, commercial and NGO interests) towards a defined set of results, which, in Garzon's view, is simply easier access to books for all. However, of the thirteen countries in this study, none has formulated and adopted a national book policy that meets Garzon's definition. According to the available documentation there is no such precedent as yet in any African country, although several have national book policy drafts or reviews in various forms.

Among these, the Zambia Draft National Book Policy (1998) is the most far-reaching, and is clearly the product of considerable thought. While it does not respond to some immediate practical concerns, and may be criticized as being distant from realities, it is nevertheless a finely articulated vision of long-term objectives. The approach taken by book professionals in Zambia was to develop this in such a way that it could be debated in Parliament with the ultimate aim of being adopted as a Statutory Instrument. It was felt that this was the best means of ensuring that the govern-ment of the day, and its staff, was legally bound to its application. In itself this aptly sums up the scepticism that if it were simply endorsed in a government policy statement this would be insuffi-cient to ensure that it would be implemented.

At the other end of the scale, the 1991 one-page Tanzania Textbook Policy statement, which has been broadly implemented, defines the textbook liberalisation policy and makes no attempt to determine or develop any sort of national book policy.

Countries undergoing textbook liberalisation in this study virtu-ally all have some form of 'textbook-provision policy statement that defines the way in which the provision of textbooks would be transferred from a state monopoly to a partnership with the commercial sector. African textbook policies, their formulation and processes have been discussed in preceding chapters.

The process of policy formulation

For the purpose of a discussion on 'national book policy', we may first note that it is possible that the process that has resulted in African textbook policies may provide the basis for a compre-hensive national book policy in some countries. In particular,

Ghana and Kenya appear to have established an extensive dialogue between commercial stakeholders, such as trade associations, and the government. This dialogue is an important foundation in the process of developing a national book policy, distinguished from those examples where a policy is merely a statement of government without any participatory process. Examples of this include the draft textbook policies of Zimbabwe, Ethiopia and Mozambique, essentially established unilaterally by government, with the help of technical consultants.

The process of policy formulation begins with setting objectives and the submission of these broadly political objectives to the scrutiny of the practitioners who advise on the technical aspects of their implementation. This is no easy task. The sheer number of practitioners and concerned parties, who have diverse interests in the outcome, and the absence of established trade organisations require delicate balancing of interests and tremendous investment in time.

There must be capacity to drive this process, and such capacity is rare in all African countries. In other parts of the world, this is undertaken within the education ministry, which usually also handles cultural issues, or a by specialist institution, such as a book development council, which may be given authority to undertake the task. Whatever system is adopted, this policy process can be led only by technically proficient people.

Participatory approaches

On the one hand the education ministry is the *de facto* lead government agency in book policy because its textbook procurement decisions alone define the nature of the entire book industry. And yet it is rare, if not impossible, to find technical proficiency covering the entirety of the book industry within the education ministry alone.

National book policy is a long-term vision in which textbooks cannot be separated from books in general, since the book sector is one indivisible industry. Education-centred policy concerns have propelled the idea of an insular 'textbook policy', in which 'education' and not 'the book' is at the core of goals and results. This is not objective reality. Printers do not exist to print merely educational books. Authors write all kinds of books. Publishers do not produce books only for schools. Booksellers do not sell only educational books. All these sub-sectors of the book industry interact with a diverse range of other industrial, commercial and other actors over issues including training, paper, print inputs, writing skills, book imports and exports, and readership.

From the perspective of an all-encompassing national book policy, it is the book as a manufactured and cultural product that is at the core. The textbook policy that sees the pupil (or consumer) at the center of the process is a distortion. On the other hand, those bodies with the professional expertise in a wide range of book issues – for example, publishers' and booksellers' associations or book development councils – do not often have the political or executive authority to lead a policy process that is national.

Without a participatory process, a book policy invariably becomes a document that nobody refers to because it has no practical use. Ownership by all the sub-sectors – literally all the stakeholders, which will use and benefit from the policy – is the key to a workable book policy. The government arm with the biggest stake in books, i.e. the education ministry, must set in motion the mechanics of creating a policy, but the creation of a realistic policy requires the active participation of book professionals and commercial stakeholders.

In most African countries, however, the Ministry of Education is generally unwilling or unable to delegate this authority, even though it does not have the internal capacity and technical proficiency to lead a book policy process. Nigeria provides a good example of this. With its well-established commercial publishing foundation and highly skilled resource base, Nigeria is in an ideal position to establish a national book policy. A number of high-level conferences in the 1990s attempted to do just this. Yet the dialogue established between government and the private sector has never been enough to sustain the degree of trust that would automatically lead to a national book policy that is led by the technical proficiency of industry but under the authority of senior federal education officials and political interests. Nigeria produced a document entitled 'Final Draft of the National Book Policy' in 1992; however, the Federal Government has yet to give it formal approval thirteen years later.

Core policy targets

To begin the process of creating a national book policy, it is necessary to define core policy targets (literally the 'purpose' and 'desired results' of the policy), which might initially be drafted by the education ministry but would eventually be accepted by all stakeholders through a process of consultation. In Africa, although there is a huge diversity of opinion, there is consensus over priorities among the commercial actors and the NGO sector.

This was evident at the Zimbabwe International Book Fair Indaba on National Book Policies for Africa in July 1996, the most wide-ranging and representative discussion on national book policy to have taken place in Africa to date (McCartney, 1996). We have drawn extensively from the proceedings of that conference, from interviews with book professionals met in this study and from various other sources for the following discussion of national book policy objectives in Africa. This is not intended to be exhaustive, but to give the most common perceptions about book policy needs and priorities in Africa.

Publishing output

Africa currently contributes only about one per cent of world book output. Some ninety per cent of the titles published are educational, and of those the majority are textbooks, as opposed to supplementary and reference educational books. There is consensus in that Africa must increase its proportion of world publishing output over the next twenty years by developing those areas in which most countries show a high degree of dependence on imports: fiction, children's literature, technical books, professional and vocational books, and scholarly publishing generally. This could be expressed as a need for greater diversity in publishing output and for a concentration of policy measures to achieve this.

Structure and ownership of publishing

It is generally accepted that publishing is a commercial and therefore private-sector activity. The role of the state should simply be to provide curriculum content, guidelines and quality controls for textbook publishing and procurement.

Within African publishing circles there is a strong opinion that, in ten to twenty years time, publishing in Africa should have developed a 'national character', expressed in terms of its ownership and market share. It is widely believed that this should be achieved without restricting foreign investment in the book sector, but that African publishing must itself raise its profile. It is felt that this can be accomplished if governments accept that publishing is a strategic industry and that securing its national character is important to national development.

Taxes and the affordability of books

Poverty is seen as the main factor undermining the growth of the book industry and weakening bookselling. The problem is typically expressed in terms of 'affordability', or the price of books in relation to average (formal-sector) incomes. While there are diverse ideas about methods of confronting the problem, most are concentrated around three areas:

- the removal of all taxes and import duties on finished books;
- the removal of all taxes and import duties on paper and other print inputs;
- the introduction of methods of low-cost book production and incentives to reduce book prices – for example, through subsidized editions, and book clubs, by stimulating increased print volumes and reducing profit margins for certain books.

Although most countries have already removed taxes on finished books, many still have high import duties on printing paper. As a result, many publishers in Africa are forced to have their books printed abroad, sometimes as far away as Singapore, instead of creating business for their own printing industry.

Cultural relevance, language and authorship

The direct relationship between higher retention and learning skills in early schooling and the use of books in the mother tongue is widely accepted. There is also a commonly held view that cultural relevance in books leads both to higher quality in educational attainment and to the development of readership. Therefore, a growing emphasis is placed on local authorship of all types of books, and more specifically local-language writing and the development of authorship. There are major problems to be tackled at a national level in terms of policy, including development of orthography, support for local-language writing, and innovative ways of publishing for small or minority language groups.

In more general terms, the development of writers' associations, the provision of training to authors, and public recognition accorded to authors (for example, through book prizes) are consistent themes.

Copyright and photocopying

Copyright infringement is a huge problem in parts of West Africa and it is worsening elsewhere in Africa. Publishers are concerned that governments should show far greater urgency and commitment to the protection of intellectual copyright. At the same time there is a need to nurture reproductive rights agreements (RROs) between publishers and consumers to allow the legal use of photocopying of educational materials at a small charge.

Bookselling

The major theme in bookselling development, endorsed by APNET and PABA in their 2001 accord, (African Publishing Review, 2000) is that booksellers become fully integrated into all educational book supply; and that the costs of distribution are accepted by consumers, including, importantly, the Ministry of Education and schools.

Another main theme is the adoption of policies that will encourage the establishment of retail bookshop services outside the capitals and major cities. To a large extent this is incumbent on the Ministry of Education to develop decentralised textbook-procurement policies that favour booksellers close to the users of book in schools.

It is generally acknowledged that there is need to support and protect professional and ethical bookselling practices, through means such as a strictly enforced 'code of conduct' for booksellers.

Readership, book awareness and the role of NGOs

There is, in general, an emphatic belief that readership development and book awareness is the foundation of book industry growth, and that this should be the main thrust of book NGOs. More problematic is the problem of transforming 'book awareness' into a book-buying culture. The number and range of activities of NGOs supporting readership and book awareness needs to grow, and this growth must be recognized and supported through national policies. Activities such as national and local book fairs, public readings, book reviews in the media, author promotions and children's reading need to be massively promoted at state level.

Library development

A priority must be to work towards the financing and functioning of a basic, school library in every primary and secondary school, and to facilitate the necessary library management skills throughout the educational system to this end. In addition, the co-ordination activities of a 'school library service' will be necessary.

Furthermore, the development of public library services, to both urban and rural communities, needs serious attention, in many cases now in the form of the rehabilitation of those services that, throughout Africa, have declined in recent years.

Parental and community responsibilities

In most African countries, book-industry professionals hold the view that the culture of 'free textbooks' and, more generally, 'book dependency' is inimical to broader book development aims. On the other hand, many education professionals are concerned with the equity in education that is achieved through 'free textbooks'. It would seem, however, that there is consensus that parents and communities should be encouraged and empowered to assume greater financial responsibility for the provision of textbooks, and in particular to take responsibility for the improvement of school libraries and the availability of supplementary reading.

Co-ordination of the book sector

Most book practitioners are concerned about the poor communication and relations between the book industry and Ministry of Education, leading to misgivings and mistrust. Many feel that only by creating systematic contact through regular, focused meetings can this be addressed. Secondly, it is widely held that only through the institutional development of trade and professional associations (publishing, bookselling, authors, libraries, special interest groups, etc.) can co-ordination be improved.

Information flow

Information is viewed as the most critical and sensitive element in relations between the private sector and government. It is felt by the book industry that information about textbook procurement and financing should be publicly available in order to develop a spirit of partnership and transparency.

Data collection

The majority of African countries have very poor book data. Stakeholders in the book sector concur that it is vital to create the capacity for the collection of essential data, on an annual basis, of key indicators in the book sector, such as annual title output, number and type of publishers, number and type of booksellers, number and type of libraries, book–pupil ratios, relative cost of books, and similar data.

Incentives for growth

Book professionals are unanimous that governments should, by recognizing the book sector as strategic to long-term national development, adopt financial incentives that encourage growth in the book sector and that have little impact on state budgets.

Policy creation

While the above 'core targets' represent some themes and ideas currently uppermost in African book circles, they are necessarily incomplete because no single source can accurately portray the entire range of needs and perceptions in the book sector. It is through consultation that policy becomes comprehensive, and ownership becomes complete.

On the other hand, such core targets cannot be so diverse and representative of every shade of opinion that they are impossible to implement. An important principle in establishing book policy is that of 'trade-offs' – necessary compromises to maintain balance and stay within agreed overall priorities.

Garzon and other exponents of national book policies (such as Askerud) agree that it is vital to write up an 'inventory' and 'systems audit' of the existing systems by which the book sector functions, and those that regulate textbook procurement (Garzon, 1997; Pernille Askerud, 1996). In addition, a book-sector survey is required, to gather all basic relevant data. When the 'purpose' of policy has been ascertained (by setting core targets) and existing systems are defined (by a systems audit and book-sector survey), the basis for drafting a genuinely representative, and therefore workable, national textbook policy exists. Typically, such a policy would be structured to comprise a sub-policy for each component of the book chain – authorship, publishing, printing and production, bookselling and distribution, library services, readership, the NGO sector, and textbook financing and procurement.

The articulation of policy requires technical experts with extensive experience of working in the book sector. For obvious reasons, it also needs an investment in time, report writing and circulation, meetings and a co-ordinating function. It is advisable that this capacity is planned from the beginning, as an exercise in capacity building.

It is worth quoting the Indian scholar, Arvind Kumar, a frequent visitor to Africa in years past, who offered an Indian perspective to the *Indaba* on national book policy at the ZIBF 1996 (Arvind Kumar in McCartney, 1996). It is a useful reference in this context: the example of another developing country to Africa, a continent that still lagging behind in book output and readership.

'Books can play an important in not only promoting the country's scientific, technological and economic development, but also forging a sense of common purpose and identity among the people. Nehru [India's first Prime Minister] initiated a nation-wide movement to promote books and the habit of reading by establishing national institutions such as Sahitya Akademi (the academy of letters) in 1954 and the National Book Trust, India in 1957. ...

'What cannot be questioned ... is the national commitment to the promotion of books. Since independence in 1947, state and central governments have budgeted funds for the purchase of books by educational institutions and libraries, and this more than anything has sustained the Indian publishing industry.

'The industry has also enjoyed special benefits such as postal and railway concessions, income tax relief and exemption from import duty and sales tax.

'The national commitment was further reiterated through the following clauses in the 1986 National Policy on Education:

The availability of books at low prices is indispensable for people's education. Efforts will be made to ensure easy accessibility to books for all segments of the population. Measures will be taken to improve the quality of books, promote the reading habit and encourage creative writing. Authors' interests will be protected. ...

Together with the development of books, a nation-wide movement for the improvement of existing libraries and establishment of new ones will be taken up. Provision will be made in all educational institutions for library facilities ...

The Indian experience has proved that it is not sufficient simply to set up a National Book Development Council and adopt a National Book Policy. Despite the importance of these activities, not much can be achieved unless there are strong and responsible national institutions, voluntary and non-government agencies, and a private book industry, to take advantage of the positive environment created.'

The book chain

To facilitate the understanding of the relationship between the various components involved in book provision, the concept of a 'book chain' has entered into international book development debates over the last twenty years. Its main purpose has been to illustrate how and why these components are interlinked, and therefore why and how policies applied in one aspect of book provision necessarily affect the whole. We have therefore developed two charts that attempt to apply this in an African setting.

FIGURE 3: MAIN LINKS IN BOOK CHAIN SYSTEM

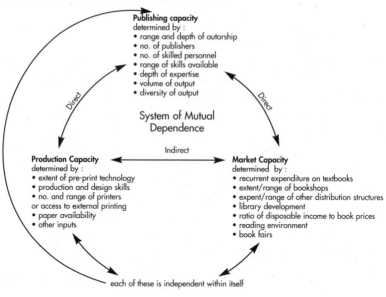

Publishing capacity
determined by :
• range and depth of autorship
• no. of publishers
• no. of skilled personnel
• range of skills available
• depth of expertise
• volume of output
• diversity of output

System of Mutual Dependence

Direct

Indirect

Production Capacity
determined by :
• extent of pre-print technology
• production and design skills
• no. and range of printers or access to external printing
• paper availability
• other inputs

Market Capacity
determined by :
• recurrent expenditure on textbooks
• extent/range of bookshops
• expent/range of other distribution structures
• library development
• ratio of disposable income to book prices
• reading environment
• book fairs

each of these is independent within itself

FIGURE 4: FACTORS DETERMINING DEVELOPMENT OF LINKS IN BOOK CHAIN

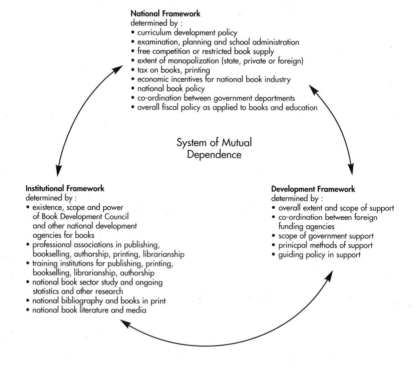

National Framework
determined by :
• curriculum development policy
• examination, planning and school administration
• free competition or restricted book supply
• extent of monopolization (state, private or foreign)
• tax on books, printing
• economic incentives for national book industry
• national book policy
• co-ordination between government departments
• overall fiscal policy as applied to books and education

System of Mutual Dependence

Institutional Framework
determined by :
• existence, scope and power of Book Development Council and other national development agencies for books
• professional associations in publishing, bookselling, authorship, printing, librarianship
• training institutions for publishing, printing, bookselling, librarianship, authorship
• national book sector study and ongoing statistics and other research
• national bibliography and books in print
• national book literature and media

Development Framework
determined by :
• overall extent and scope of support
• co-ordination between foreign funding agencies
• scope of government support
• prinicpal methods of support
• guiding policy in support

Book NGOs

The few African book NGOs in existence, such as book development councils, are playing a critical role as partners to both the state and the private sector. In most cases, book NGOs have arisen as a direct corollary to the emergence of the commercial sector, often established by professionals such as writers and publishers. The effectiveness of these NGOs arises from their flexibility. Book NGOs, typically small, local and specialist, have shown ability to adapt project activities to changing needs, without the constraints imposed by large bureaucratic structures. Their impact can far exceed the immediate aims of their project. At their most effective NGOs are neutral in their relations between the state and the private sector, providing resources, facilitating dialogue and book awareness, and playing a supportive role in the process of developing a national book industry.

Aid-dependency is, however, an acute problem in the NGO sector. NGOs do not have adequate sources of income outside grant funding. Indigenous publishing is not yet in a position to provide corporate sponsorship, and multinational publishing has, on the whole, shown little interest. Where the state is not able to provide support, NGOs look to funding partners for institutional and project support. Nowhere in Africa, except in a limited way in South Africa, is the state in a position to fund the activity of book NGOs. African book NGOs are dependent on international funding agencies, and their fortunes rise and fall with the commitment of international funders.

In recent years debates have raged around the issue of 'institutional' versus 'project' support. NGOs argue that project outcomes are a result of institutional support; the two cannot be arbitrarily separated. Without offices, wages, transport and communications long-term project work is undermined. In turn, funding agencies have been hesitantand expressed the view that institutional support without tangible outcomes specified in contractually binding time-lines leads to a 'top-heavy' institution that is not 'result-driven', but motivated by job benefits. As a result, NGOs with a track record have benefited from greater institutional support over longer periods, whereas new NGOs have struggled to win the confidence of funding agencies. Overall, very few African book NGO initiatives have successfully managed a transition from 'limited-term project' to 'permanent institution', mainly as a result of constraints of financial dependency.

Subsidies towards books and readership are a pattern in book-related NGOs globally; they are not in any sense an African phenomenon. A cursory investigation of book-development initiatives throughout Europe (numbering thousands of organisations, projects and institutions) reveals massive, diverse methods of support provided through or by the state, or by state-sponsored institutions, by funding agencies, or in partnership with corporate funding, all in the 'national interest'.

In the case of research-based support, such is this level and range of support to authorship and sometimes directly to publishing that even within African studies, the output of published books in the West by far exceeds that of Africa itself. In a more general sense, one finds innovation and diversity in the support that underpins publishing industries of developed countries: book-marketing promotion, export promotion, subsidies to 'cultural/educational' products, to research, to language development, libraries, book technology, and all manner of book and authorship sponsorship. Corporate funding in profitable publishing countries typically extends to areas where the publishing industry derives direct benefit, such as training, book fairs and book prizes.

The significance of this support to publishing as a strategic national industry and its applicability to Africa is not one of scale but of principle. P. G. Altbach and D. Teferra in their introductory chapter to *Publishing and Development: A Book of Readings* state that 'publishing remains central to educational systems, to the creation and distribution of knowledge, and to the nurturing of an independent intellectual culture. Without books, a civil society cannot exist, educational systems suffer and knowledge cannot be communicated (Altbach and Teferra, 1998).' Such thinking underlies the conventional perception, almost universally held in the West, guiding policies in books as a strategic national industry.

Elieshi Lema locates these issues within the African context: 'In order to link the role of publishing to its strategic nature, there are critical issues that will need to be addressed. These are: the colonial framework in which are education systems function, that makes formal education only marginally linked to social reality ... and the development of which is donor driven; the ... trend of consuming knowledge and culture created by others; as a result ... an intellectual culture more aligned to the West than to our own societies (Lema, 2002)'

She continues: 'How does the publishing industry, involving all actors and stake-holders, take the lead in ensuring that publishing becomes an effective channel of personal and social development, so that organic literature reflective of people's educational, cultural, social and economic aspirations is produced? When answers to questions such as: who is writing? for whom? for which purpose? are clear, we shall no longer be ... guessing at the book market ... books will have found its place in the priority list of life's necessities. This definition of strategic industry reminds us that to sell books and realise returns and a bit of profit will not make us a strategic industry.' Lema argues that African publishers are, in reality, so busily engaged in basic economic survival that the broader concerns of the relationship of a book industry to social and political realities are neglected. It is a very common perspective of African book professionals.

Lema reminds us that no East African country has put in place a national book policy that addresses books as a strategic national industry. Indeed no African country in this study has done so, and we are not aware of any other African country that has adopted a comprehensive national book policy, as distinct from a textbook policy. In this context the work of African NGOs and trade associations is crucially concerned with its capacity to mediate between stakeholders, to motivate national debate and book-awareness, and, more in keeping with project outcomes, to facilitate the myriad linkages required in a book chain, and strengthen its components, from authorship to readership promotion.

The Tanzania Children's Book Project

The Tanzania Children's Book Project (CBP) played an immensely important role in setting professional standards in Tanzanian publishing in the lean years of the 1990s, and in mobilizing all aspects of the development of commercial publishing. Many Tanzanian publishers recognize that their survival was, at some stage, dependent on CBP support, and virtually all have benefited from training and subsidies. Support to publishers was not restricted to the subsidy of children's book publishing through the buy-back system. It has included training in every facet of children's book publishing, standards control, advice, support to the trade associations and setting up dialogue among commercial and book-development interests. Faced with a dearth of illustrating and writing skills for children's books, CBP trained illustrators and writers, many of whom today are producing textbooks. At the same time, CBP has adapted to changing needs, starting a school readership programme, working with teachers on reading skills, and establishing libraries, while continuing to train and support writers, illustrators and publishers. Over ten years (1991–2000), 151 titles from over 40 publishers were subsidized through the buy-back method, in which nearly one million books were produced and 547,000 copies were purchased and distributed to school libraries, making Tanzania an exemplary children's book producer in Africa. Overall, CBP's efforts have helped to facilitate the emergence of new NGOs by promoting dialogue amongst commercial publishers, booksellers, writers and the Ministry of Education at certain times. There are two important new NGOs – the Tanzanian

Book Development Council (BAMVITA) and the Writers Association (UWAVITA). BAMVITA has a mandate to provide input to book-policy formulation; UWAVITA has a strong training profile to develop writing. There is significant new NGO activity, inspired by CBP, in the Tusome Vitabu Project, which is structured so as to put funds into the market (for school libraries) and support procurement through booksellers. The pilot phase of this project was an unprecedented development in that schools ordered books directly from booksellers, and booksellers consolidated all orders to publishers.

A study on the activities of CBP and constraints written in 2001 states (Brickhill, 2001):

'The most intractable problem in the book sector is that the distribution capacity has not developed in tandem with publishing. There has been some growth in bookselling in Dar es Salaam and major centers. But on the whole bookselling remains weak. Book buying and readership, for self-enrichment and leisure, is under-developed throughout Tanzania. The book market is weak.

'Only a tiny proportion of parents understand the value of reading in children's education. The legacy of dependency on the state for free provision of books undermines initiatives aimed at community and parental responsibility. Very few libraries exist at primary level to support readership, and the capacity of the state... is limited.

'One commentator said that CBP should take a "holistic" view of children's literature, looking at every aspect of quality and promotion of reading, and adopt a role equivalent to a permanent Children's Literature Institute, as opposed to the project approach. Most commentators agreed that the buy-back subsidy system had worked so well that it would be a pity if CBP abandoned this. However, all agreed that the "dependency syndrome" was inappropriate and that "the focus is now on creating a market". Every interviewee without exception noted that "the market" was THE problem, and that all efforts in book development were being thwarted by inadequacies in the commercial distribution.'

CBP aptly illustrates the core issues confronted by African book NGOs working in the realities of the African book environment, simultaneously balancing institution-building and capacity to respond to broad structural development challenges with short-term project activities. Notably CBP's impact has not been restricted to projects but has been extended to a facilitating role and many innovative initiatives far beyond its remit.

The Zimbabwe International Book Fair

An NGO of a completely different nature, but comparable to CBP in the sense of the multi-faceted effects emanating from one core NGO activity, is the Zimbabwe International Book Fair

(ZIBF), which developed over the same period, 1991–2000. Quite apart from the expected results in terms of contacts, trade promotion and dialogue among African publishers, ZIBF has spawned an incalculable number of projects and book development initiatives. ZIBF was the initial springboard for the early development of both APNET and PABA. At least fifty networks and collaborative initiatives can be traced to meetings initially held under the auspices of ZIBF according to the first Executive Director, Trish Mbanga when interviewed for this study. These have ranged from research and academic publishing through to library networking, trade promotion, and many different kinds of writers' and publishers' initiatives. Within the ZIBF programme the annual *Indaba* (conference) has itself garnered a reputation as a forum for debate and exchange of information on book issues throughout Africa. All this has come from an NGO whose sole core activity is, in reality, a commercial trade fair, facilitating trade and contact in the African book industry.

Other African book development bodies

There are book NGOs throughout Africa, similarly able to outline diverse outcomes significantly beyond their core project mandate. While focusing on specific projects, many are, in effect, engaged in creating the capacity and environment for overall book development, involving all stakeholders in the book chain. To some degree all are engaged in stimulating debate around national book-policy issues and books as a strategic industry. It is difficult to estimate their number; few if any studies have focused on the particular role and effect of NGOs. The ADEA *Compendium of Successful Reading Projects* (ADEA, 2003) lists twenty-five such NGOs from fifteen countries in the area of reading promotion. One may surmise that there around 100 active book-development NGOs in sub-Saharan Africa, excluding professional and trade associations (of writers, publishers, bookseller and libraries), that are also engaged in NGO-type activities, especially training.

Noticeably countries with more developed commercial structures have a greater range of NGO activity, including professional associations. Thus Kenya, Zimbabwe, Nigeria, South Africa, and, to a lesser extent, Tanzania, Uganda and Ghana, have several specialist book NGOs, focusing, for example, on children's books, reading, libraries, general book promotion and training. These countries all have some form of book trade and promotion fair at regional, national or international level.

To cite a typical example, Zimbabwe has a Book Development Council (ZBDC), a prominent rural library project (Rural Library Resources and Development Programme, RLRDP), and international book fair, and a host of professional associations, particularly of writers. There are also a number of *ad hoc* and informal initiatives. The range of NGO activities in Zimbabwe, as in Kenya and Nigeria, includes training and workshops, book awareness, reading campaigns, library development, language development, trade promotion, relations with education ministries, and representation of members (as with trade associations).

The Nigerian Book Foundation (NBF), established in 1991, is held in esteem by many Nigerian book professionals and is one of the most prominent 'umbrella' NGOs in Africa, attempting to act as an intermediary between all stakeholders, including the state. The NBF is 'an umbrella organisation bringing together the key participants in book development, to ensure that all components of the book chain function maximally and that the state provides a conducive environment for the book industry to flourish. Its mission is to develop a vibrant book industry in Nigeria' (Ike, 1998).

The East African Book Development Council (EABDC), established in recent years, has had a major impact in stimulating debate around national book policy and in promoting trade and contacts, including several training initiatives, in East Africa. This is one of the most exciting regional NGO ventures in Africa, especially since East Africans had a *de facto* single book market until 1977.

In contrast, Ethiopia and Mozambique have very few such NGOs and associations. In Mozambique there is a state-run National Institute for Books and Records (INLD), similar to a book development council, but, as in Ethiopia, very little NGO activity because of its small commercial book sector.

The francophone countries also have less in the way of book NGO activity, although important initiatives have been established. Guinea has pioneered a 'network of book professionals' (REPROLIG); Senegal has an important NGO initiative in development of national language (Associates in Research and Education for Development, ARED); and both Mali and Senegal have notable library development NGOs.

It is not our intention to present any representative survey of NGO activities in the countries within this study, but simply to draw attention to the crucial role played by NGOs in the creation of a book chain and a supportive book environment. NGOs are a key link in the formation of public/private partnerships, facilitating dialogue, offering the state and commercial sector skills, vision and policy input, motivating debate on book policy and carrying out project activities.

Copyright and piracy

Copyright protects the intellectual property rights of an author in the literary or artistic work that he or she has created. It is governed and regulated by national laws, normally involving the accession to one of two international copyright conventions – the Berne Copyright Union founded in 1886 and the Universal Copyright Convention adopted in 1952.

Copyright protection entitles the author or creator to benefit from income arising from the commercial use or reproduction of his or her work by others. This income is normally earned through the payment of a royalty on each copy of the work that is sold and/or as a percentage of any subsidiary rights sold. The author is also entitled to claim the moral right of authorship, enabling him or her to object to anything that might be prejudicial to the author's honour or reputation.

There are, however, general provisions in copyright laws that allow 'fair use' of parts of a copyright work. Fair use includes the copying of extracts for the purpose of private study or research, criticism or review, and for judicial or educational purposes.

All authors are vulnerable to the infringement of their copyright as a result of piracy. Copyright infringement emerged in the study as a major issue, particularly in populous countries such as Nigeria and Ghana. In Nigeria photocopying played a significant part in copyright infringement, particularly when one takes into account that by 1993 there were 173 photocopy centers in just seven of Nigeria's thirty-six universities (and there are more than twice that number of polytechnics and colleges of education).If one were to extrapolate the frequency of photocopy centers it is likely that Nigeria's universities may host nearly 1,000 of them. The potential for significant illegal photocopying of educational and research material is easy to see.

The reasons (or excuses) given for copyright infringement through piracy in this study involve a number of factors. These include the inability of publishers and booksellers to supply sufficient copies of a title to meet high demand; the difficulty in distributing a popular title to far-flung corners of a country; retail book prices that are expensive relative to local people's income; unscrupulous agents and printers who exploit any shortage in the supply of books by illegally reproducing cheaper editions for sale; and long drawn-out processes involved in copyright litigation that encourage rather than deter piracy.

Every author and publisher invests heavily both aesthetically and financially in originating, developing and publishing a book. It is this investment that requires protection. Whenever a book is pirated both the author and publisher are deprived of revenue from legitimate sales of the original book. The genuine copy and the pirated book compete for sales, and invariably the pirated copy will sell in greater numbers as it is more cheaply priced despite its inferior quality.

The extent of the loss of revenue through piracy is more vivid in a situation where a pirated title is an approved textbook and millions of copies are required for use by educational institutions. The greater the number of publishing companies suffering huge losses, the more likely it will be that the nation's economy will be equally adversely affected.

In his book, *Book Publishing in Nigeria*, Okwilagwe states that during the period 1985–88 virtually all Nigerian publishers fell victim to piracy (Okwilagwe, 2001). More than fifteen publishing companies had one or more of their titles pirated, while about twenty per cent of their annual turnover was lost to pirates. In 2002, the Nigerian Publishers Association claimed that 30%–40% of the textbook market was lost to piracy. Some of the best-selling titles were being sent to far eastern countries where identical copies were cheaply but attractively reproduced and sent back to Nigeria for sale at very low prices. The net effect of such piracy was an estimated loss of US$200 million a year by the book industry in Nigeria.

On account of the devastating effect that copyright infringement has inflicted on its book industry, Nigeria has for many years waged a war against pirates. The Nigerian Copyright Commission has a mandate to monitor any copyright infringements, redress incidents of piracy and enforce the copyright law to the letter. The Nigerian Publishers Association works very closely with the police, immigration, and customs departments to eliminate all incidences of copyright infringement.

Combined raids by publishers and law-enforcement agencies are made at premises suspected to warehouse pirated materials. As a preventive measure, the Nigerian Publishers Association and the law-enforcement agencies have mounted public awareness campaigns through seminars, workshops, articles in the media and meetings of interest groups to alert the public to the dangers of piracy.

It was evident from the study that the incidence of piracy in Nigeria was higher than in most African countries. Copyright infringement in Ghana appeared to be a spill-over from Nigeria. It was acknowledged, however, that the paucity of copies or the unavailability of titles needed in far-flung parts of Ghana did give birth to piracy, albeit on a small scale. In this regard printers were also identified as unwittingly contributing to piracy by reprinting titles, for want of money, without establishing who was the original owner of the publication. Efforts have recently been made to re-examine the Ghanaian copyright laws in order to seal any loopholes and improve enforcement.

Conclusion

The African publishing community, particularly APNET, has increased efforts to engage both governments and funding agencies in developing book policies. This has arisen because *ad hoc* textbook-provision decisions – taken against a background of the transition to textbook liberalisation and frequently influenced and altered by new funding arrangements – have not yet led to stable, sustained and 'holistic' book development.

There have been opportunities for growth in commercial textbook publishing, but the very nature of the transition has led to anomalies and imbalances in the book chain. Some countries that invested heavily in print capacity over the last two decades are importing printing. Duties on finished book imports have been relaxed in many countries in recent years, while inputs to local book manufacture are being taxed. The role of booksellers in the textbook supply chain remains, in most countries, limited and uncertain, and, because of that, access to books (outside city centers) and the development of general readership is undermined. Trade relations between publishers and booksellers, and the 'standards and conventions' unpinning book industries, are under-developed. The tender models adopted in liberalisation have, in most cases, not matched the expectations of enhanced diversity in book output that authors and publishers in particular would wish to see. Problems related to access to books (through libraries, for example), readership and language development (as a corollary to stimulating readership) are largely unresolved.

This somewhat negative outlook is itself an indication of the higher expectations of African book professionals – and, ironically, a result of more positive and hopeful circumstances. Having turned away in varying degrees from state monopolies and offered the commercial sector scope for participation, virtually all African countries have witnessed renewed energy and enthusiasm among commercial actors.

The goal of a national book policy during the transition, for both the commercial sector and the Ministry of Education, would be a degree of rationalization that results in sustained textbook provision, as compared to the somewhat erratic performance that has often accompanied early phases of liberalisation. For individual commercial enterprises, this might be defined as a steady expansion in their market, planned production and commercial activity based on certainties of their role in the system, and budgetary provision for textbooks, broadly resulting in reduced risk that will encourage greater and long-term investment.

Over the years, many book professionals have alluded to a 'lack of political will' on the part of governments to foster their own national book industries. While this can be traced to the era of state monopolies and consequent tension between state and private interests, it also arises from uneven competition between multinationals and nascent African book industries. In its efforts to create an empowering environment, indigenous publishing has placed a lot of emphasis on national book policy. This is based largely on a perception that books form a 'strategic national industry', thus reinforcing the link between cultural nation-building, indigenous authorship and indigenous, autonomous publishing. In the same way, booksellers, previously excluded from textbook supply, see in national book policy the possibility of a rational outcome that recognizes their role and importance.

Whether the hopes that publishers and booksellers have placed in national book policies – as enabling instruments for their growth and development – will be realised remains to be seen. Certainly, an announcement by the first state in Africa to formulate and implement a unified national book policy would be an event of massive significance to the entire African book world.

Chapter 8

CONCLUSION

Woven within all textbook systems has been a thread affecting every policy decision – that of the resources and finance necessary for governments to provide textbooks. It is necessary to consider some aspects of funding partnership and the broad sweep of its background, from which perspective we may identify further factors at work in the confluence and divergence of public and private interests in textbook provision in Africa.

Monopolist state intervention in the book sector in the early decades of African independence was not as irrational as it may appear today with well over a thousand indigenous commercial publishers in sub-Saharan Africa. Not only was it a widely appealing concept in African nationalist political circles, it had the overt support of the World Bank, many bilateral funding agencies and sometimes multinational publishers, where they became the *de facto* supplier of textbooks under 'state' textbook provision.

Dependent on overseas examination systems, on imported materials and foreign authors, most newly independent African countries had virtually no indigenous publishing capacity except a few religious concerns. The longer-term perception of a commercial book sector, autonomous from both the state and multinationals, to sustain textbook provision was not then apparent. In African publishing and writing circles, such as they existed, debates centred around cultural emancipation and Africanist approaches to creative and scholarly literature, yet hunger for education was overwhelming in the new African states. Expectations were fiercely high that education would deliver a new generation from poverty. How was the textbook provision mechanism to function under the weight of such expectations?

The initial goal in textbook provision was to provide sufficient mass volumes of cheap, appropriate textbooks for school expansion alongside new African-centred curricula, as these were developed. Therefore, local subsidiaries of foreign publishers (where they existed in the early years of independence) played a dominant role in textbook provision, founded largely on importing books from their parent company and adapting and re-printing them locally as necessitated by curriculum development requirements.

Issues related to 'indigenous capacity' in textbook provision, mirrored in other segments of book publishing, became focused around authorship. The logical policy decision, so frequently reached, was that the curriculum authority would be empowered to pioneer and write new generations of textbooks, and a state distribution network would deliver these directly to schools, or districts or both. The 'publishing' function was reduced to 'production', since many editorial and specification decisions (paper, cover, design, format, colour, etc.) were effected within the curriculum authority, or in a quasi-publishing department attached to it, sometimes with the assistance of technical consultants.

Against this background, the question arose as to how to manage mass-volume book production. In some cases joint enterprises or co-edition arrangements were established with multinational publishers that could provide capacity and technical input to meet the volumes required; in other instances, multinationals largely supplied the materials required.

Approaches began to address the capacity issues to cope with school expansion, and development partners provided capital investment in the form of loans and grants for the establishment of state paper and printing capacity, textbook publishing and distribution companies throughout the 1970s and 1980s. At that time, large economy-of-scale textbook production capacity, under state control, was seen as a critical component of long-term textbook provision. Thus in Mozambique, Ethiopia, Zambia, Tanzania, Ghana, Uganda and francophone countries, various forms of state textbook writing, publishing, production and distribution took root, and took the form of monopolies. Nigeria and Kenya retained private textbook provision, in which multinationals had a dominant market share, alongside centralised procurement. Much later Kenya, in 1985, reversed its state/commercial partnership in basic-textbook provision and adopted the state monopoly textbook model on the back of World Bank funding.

The list of prominent state, parastatal and state-affiliated companies and government departments inside the ministries of education and local government across Africa engaged in large-scale printing, publishing and distributing of textbooks was formidable, as can be seen from the country reports in this study. It comprised state printing works, paper manufacturers, publishing enterprises, curriculum departments, textbook wings within curriculum departments, distribution and haulage companies (often with a network of warehouses), booksellers and educational material suppliers, and ministry of local government units engaged in textbook distribution through district councils.

As state textbook-provision systems and capacity developed in the 1970s and 1980s, supported extensively by funding partners, a 'state-provider' mentality became pervasive and the possibility of changing course grew more distant. The number of education ministry employees deriving their livelihood from state textbook systems grew, a bureaucracy of state textbook provision grew, adherents grew, and funding grew. The system justified itself. The budgets, unconstrained by profit-and-loss considerations, rationalized by the growing shortage of textbooks, grew accordingly.

The state-provider mentality, founded on monopoly and so difficult to dislodge in later years, became entrenched in the textbook-provision system. Arguments were constructed in the 1980s and 1990s, in different settings, to underpin the continuation of the state's monopoly over textbook provision, even as it entered crisis. The view that business interests were 'profiteering from the education of children' was the major one in the era of state monopoly. Where the local commercial publishing industry was weak, 'reversing dependence on foreign books and authors' was used as an argument in support of state publishing. Hence insufficient commercial capacity – an outcome of state monopoly itself – justified continued state monopoly. In Tanzania, Mozambique, Ethiopia, Guinea Bissau, Angola and Zambia (among others), the argument took a socialist ideological slant, focusing on the benefits of 'social ownership' over textbook provision, with central planning and state control over textbook content. By the 1980s, virtually all state textbook monopolies had become dependent on foreign aid. It is not difficult to appreciate that, in such circumstances, funding partners had considerable influence over African textbook provision policy.

The World Bank

From the 1970s and throughout the 1980s, the World Bank and major bilateral agencies worked on policy matters with ministries of education over textbook provision. While there was some contact between these agencies and private publishers and local NGOs –for instance, by Scandinavian bilateral government development agencies – typically these were confined to the 'cultural desk' or the resident in-country mission. From the 1990s the Bellagio Publishing Network provided a forum for such contacts.

The World Bank had minimal contact with African publishers when education projects were designed in the 1970s and 1980s, and, on the whole, input from independent African publishing professionals was absent from textbook provision project design until the mid- to late 1990s. This left education planners to work out the mechanics of textbook-provision systems, with consultants used extensively to provide technical input.

In November 1993, APNET dispatched a delegation to Washington to introduce indigenous African publishing to World Bank officials and find out about World Bank thinking. It became clear from this mission and subsequent contact that most World Bank officials, with one or two exceptions, were unaware of the extent of the activities of the indigenous commercial sector in African publishing; moreover, it was apparent that a certain amount of input or lobbying in key matters to do with African book provision was being provided, directly and indirectly, by British and French multinational publishers.

Initially, the growth and development of indigenous publishing hardly featured in the thinking behind the 'privatisation' of African textbook provision. By and large, in the liberalisation of African state publishing, there was little or no concept of a 'triangular' relationship – comprising the Ministry of Education, funding agencies and African publishing professionals – to replace the traditional vertical relationship between funding agencies and governments. Yet leading African publishers by the 1990s already had a strategic vision of how commercial African textbook provision might function.

The move to break up state monopolies and liberalise textbook provision came in the first instance from funding agencies, in which the World Bank played a decisive part. Elsewhere studies have traced the specific factors that stimulated the new thinking towards aid in Africa that emerged in the late 1980s. The decisions applied by the major agencies to African book provision were mirrored in most other sectors, reflecting a new wave of economic liberalism and greater accountability.

A key moment was reached by the time of the 1991 Manchester conference on African textbook provision, at which only two African publishers were represented (The British Council, 1992). After a decade of steadily increasing aid inflows to African education, donors reached a broad consensus that, in the long term, state monopoly textbook provision was futile: it had failed. The African education ministers and officials present were left with few illusions that change was imminent and necessary; differences seemed to arise mainly over the method of effecting the transition and whether a fast-track approach was preferable to gradual change.

The World Bank, a key player behind the Manchester conference, had been involved in textbook-provision schemes in Africa since 1963. By the mid-1980s the World Bank was deeply involved in project design and financing textbook development, production and distribution throughout Africa. By 1993, 70% of the bank's education projects had a textbook component. In that year the bank's budget for financing textbook provision worldwide was in excess of US$380 million (Chakava, 1994).

By virtue of its size and the extent of its operations, the Bank has had a profound influence on textbook-provision systems in Africa, chiefly because it was perceived as the de facto lead agency in textbook procurement in Africa. Where the Bank directly financed textbook provision outside state provision mechanisms, it adhered to its internal rules based on international competitive bidding procedures. Overall, the Bank's textbook-provision policies were guided solely by the need to provide sufficient appropriate textbooks to meet curriculum requirements. In addition, it commissioned a number of useful book-sector studies in the late 1980s and early 1990s (nine in Africa) as a means of determining the needs of recipient countries and to advise its education project designers.

Throughout the 1990s, in virtually all cases, tenders for textbooks to be supplied to African countries, financed by the World Bank, were won by publishers outside Africa. The Bank's core policy in procurement was to achieve the best value for money within given technical parameters, whether the books were obtained locally or internationally.

A critical issue in Word Bank lending is that, in principle, it lends only to governments and for specific projects. Governments, as the borrowers, have the right, within the broad lending frame-work, to amend regulations relating to procurement. With regard to textbook provision, it is therefore incumbent on a government, working with local publishers, to adopt borrowing strategies that incorporate building the local book industry. The World Bank has been amenable to more favourable lending conditions in other industries, but there is little evidence that any African government has lobbied on behalf of its national book industry in this way.

The most controversial aspect of World Bank policies in textbook provision has been the requirement that orders above a certain value must be procured through international competitive bidding. Critics complain that ICB favours foreign publishers, since emergent local publishers rarely can compete effectively for large textbook contracts against the expertise, track record and capital of multinational publishers. The late Chairman of the African Publishers Network, Victor Nwankwo, reflecting the views of African publishers, estimated in 1999 that for every book purchased from local publishers under World Bank lending, 50 books were bought from foreign-based publishers (World Bank, 2002). The World Bank system of procurement, mainly through ICB, provided more than 350 million copies of books in sub-Saharan Africa between 1985 and 2000.

The Bank's current procurement guidelines allow a margin of preference towards local supply in the evaluation of bids under ICB. This preference is, however, limited to the value of duties and other import charges that a local manufacturer has to pay to produce books, in comparison with foreign producers,[5] but it applies only when a supplier can show that 30 per cent or more of the bid price has been applied to local inputs (labour and raw materials). A complication is that in many African countries the printing components are imported and frequently represent more than 80 per cent of cost inputs.

Clearly, the mandate of the Bank did not extend to developing or even necessarily embracing the development of African book industries. Their job was perceived as 'putting books on pupil's desks' on a project-by-project basis by the fastest and cheapest route possible, and through ICB procedures where non-state supply was necessary. Local publishing was therefore on the periphery of the Bank's thinking, much less a factor in its procurement policies.

By 1997, perceptions at the Bank had started to change. At a conference attended by World Bank officers and task managers, publishers and government officials and other funding agencies in September 1997, it became clear that the Bank was ready to adopt new policies that would pave the way towards strengthening the role of local publishers (Chakava, 1997; Tumusiime, 1997). Participants accepted that state publishing monopolies were inefficient, bureaucratic and did little to develop the book chain. The conference explored ways in which local publishers could be incorporated into World Bank textbook projects. Participants recommended that all countries should formulate book policies, with clear guidelines and structures to support the local book industry. The need for information to flow freely between funding agencies – including the Bank, governments and commercial publishers – was emphasized. Bank officials revealed that procurement procedures relating to textbooks were to be re-written to give more focus to locally available and culturally appropriate books. The idea of selection by schools from multiple titles was widely discussed.

In March 1999, the World Bank presented its new draft policy on textbook provision to a gathering in Washington (African Publishing Review, 1999). In the Bank's proposals, for the first time, was a clear policy commitment to longer-term financing of book development and provision. Among the policy proposals was an acknowledgement that sustainability in book provision will be achieved only if there is a viable local publishing industry. It further recognized that a winner-take-all tender system was unlikely, in the long term, to provide maximum benefits to local publishing and the consumers because it fails to create conditions for a diversity of products and consumer choice.

In March 2001, the Bank adopted a revised Operational Policy on Textbooks and Reading Materials, with the following principles:

- Protection of copyright
- Articulation of agreed roles of the public and private sectors in the development, production and distribution of textbooks (hence an open acknowledgement that the role of the private sector must be recognized)
- Competitive processes in the selection and purchase of books (or printing services)
- Commitment to long-term financing of book development and provision
- Assurance that cost will not be an obstacle for poor students' access to books

The Bank has recently released its first review of support for textbook provision in Africa since 1985. The review covers 89 World Bank-financed education projects with a textbook component in 40 countries in Africa between 1985 and 2000. It is worth noting some of the major findings.

In terms of policy shifts during the period, the review confirmed that, while centralised state-dominated textbook provision was considered the most desirable mode of textbook provision in 1985, by 2000, private-sector initiatives and competition were 'indispensable to textbook provision'. Appreciation grew for the role of local private publishing industries in textbook provision. A new operational policy recognized the value of local production and acquisition, providing that the higher costs entailed were justified by clear educational benefits.

A clear trend emerged during this period towards providing 'free textbooks' as a matter of policy. This was based on experiences of various cost-recovery methods that had limited success, mainly because of widespread problems of poverty.

The review confirmed that few African countries still depend entirely on state resources to produce textbooks, and the confirmed the widespread growth in the procurement of publishing services using tender systems. It acknowledged that the move from state to private-sector textbook provision increased the perceived cost of textbooks. Commercial publishers have to recover all costs (production, distribution, cost of financing, overheads, etc.) from their sales, whereas governments typically budget in textbook provision only for the direct manufacturing costs. In the latter, the overhead and other indirect costs related to state textbook provision are buried in various 'non-textbook' budgetary allocations, and are not reflected in financial reports on textbook costs.

The review confirmed that the choice and use of multiple textbooks has been implemented in various African countries. It points out that this has had the effect of fragmenting the market to some degree and reducing economies of scale. The review also confirms some of the major findings of this study: that policies of decentralisation, multiple textbook choice, mother-tongue instruction, and support for reading programmes are having a positive and profound effect in creating opportunities for indigenous publishing.

The World Bank's findings on government capacity proved telling. In several projects, the Ministry of Education 'proved incapable of fulfilling all the demands placed on it by an over-ambitious design. The problem was particularly acute in small countries with a small corps of over-committed civil servants.' Project implementation has also suffered from frequent changes in government and project staff.

Among the recommendations in the report are several designed to further the development of the local publishing sector, including:

- Using African expertise and African examples
- Encouraging access to capital for African publishers
- Ensuring that textbook tender bidding documents are simple and inexpensive
- Supporting training.

Thus, there has been a clear movement in the Bank's thinking, policies and procedures towards acceptance of indigenous African publishing and printing as a serious component of long-term textbook provision in Africa. On the other hand, given previous inequalities, multinationals retain the major proportion (estimated at not less than 85 per cent) of tender-supply on all current Bank-supported textbook projects in Africa.

By late February 2004, the Bank had scheduled, in Uganda, the second in a series of regional gatherings in Africa around textbook policy. Whilst we can make no comment on the outcome, as this study was completed beforehand, we note three interesting features of the Uganda meeting. Firstly, the research groundwork required from participating countries (to be produced by ministries of education) resembles a partial book sector survey, and is a thorough examination instrument of the entirety of textbook provision. Seldom have African ministries of education themselves been requested to compile such extensive data on publishing, bookselling and textbook provision; the more usual method in previous years would have been to sub-contract a consultant to produce a book sector survey. In itself, this is a significant approach with positive signs. Secondly, the country teams invited to the Uganda meeting all comprise high-level Ministry of Education and commercial publishing participants. APNET is also represented. Therefore, the 'triangular' relationship referred to earlier in this chapter, between governments, funding partners and commercial actors, is being implemented, at least, in such discussion forums.

The third interesting feature is the regional focus, whereby experiences in one country are being transmitted to other countries in the region. In this context we note that the experiences of textbook liberalisation in Kenya and Uganda have strong focus on the agenda. These and other signals of policy changes at the World Bank reflect the positive new approach towards textbook liberalisation and multi-textbook systems, and growing recognition of commercial African indigenous publishing.

Aid Interventions and Other Funding Agencies

It has been outside the mandate of this study to investigate the effect of funding agencies on public/private partnership. Mostly this is because such an evaluation requires access to financial and project records of funding agencies and internal evaluations and reports by project consultants, and these are not generally available.

Whilst the World Bank has undertaken a wide-ranging internal study of its textbook provision funding policies in Africa from 1985-2000 and made this public; it is difficult to obtain parallel information from bilateral agencies operating throughout Africa.

There are of course numerous project reports and studies from all African countries, but little or nothing that draws broad conclusions from a neutral research perspective in the same way that the World Bank 1985-2000 study has done. It is unknown, in general, even whether this has been done internally by various bilateral funding agencies: *viz* an overall assessment of the effectiveness and results of textbook funding activities and policies over a substantive period, and in different countries. In the case of Tanzania, even the 7-year Pilot Project for Publishing funded by SIDA has not as yet been systematically assessed, although plans are underway to commission a study into its results.

The absence of such research is a drawback to the various textbook studies in Africa, including this one. A huge volume of information and experience about project design, textbook provision concepts and the financial policies pursued by funding agencies is not available. One cannot easily trace the changes in perspective that have taken place, for example since the mid-1980s, in the period when funding agencies were overwhelmingly responsible for financing state-monopoly textbook systems. Or for that matter the period from approximately the early to mid-1990s when funding agencies were encouraging the dismantling of state-monopoly textbook publishing bureaucracies, to be replaced largely by tender-based supply. This would seem to indicate a general weakness in cumulative retention of knowledge of textbook projects within funding agencies.

In the course of this study, interviews and meetings with both commercial publishers and Ministry of Education officials have revealed their perspective of the policies and activities of funding agencies. Due to the lack of verifiable data, the comments below are necessarily general, but we are satisfied they are sufficiently accurate to be included in a broad analytical discourse of this nature.

The major theme has been the past lack of co-ordination over aims and methods between agencies. Funding agencies have acted in unilateral direct agreement with governments in textbook support programmes over the past decade. The issue of co-ordination has come about because of the multiplicity of bilateral and multilateral support arrangements to education sectors, each with separate contract, frequently with a 'project' focus and moreover in which textbooks comprise one of many education-support components.

The growing practice of sector-wide methods of financing (sector funding for education within government plans and budgets, as opposed to project-based funding) appears to have introduced positive changes in this respect within the past 3-4 years. This has helped to centralise aid around overall ministry objectives. Never-the-less, even where sector funding is fairly advanced, significant volumes of aid for textbooks are designated to particular projects, reflecting the focus, policies and procurement regulations of the agency concerned. For textbook planners, the more the sources of such designated funds, each with a separate focus and quite often a separate procurement method, the more the complications arise in devising a singular and cohesive textbook strategy. It is not unusual to find in every African country moving towards decentralised procurement in a multi-textbook system, examples of designated textbook funding requiring direct procurement, tender procurement and even single-textbook approaches, attached to special areas of poverty and inequity, or a particular textbook shortage.

Thus the biggest challenge has been in situations where textbook provision systems have been in an unsettled transition from state-monopoly to commercial systems, and the government itself has been hesitant and unsure of exactly how to pursue commercial textbook strategies. Educational perspectives (getting textbooks to pupils by the fastest, cheapest means possible, to avert a serious textbook shortage) have often conflicted with book industry capacity concerns, as discussed at some length in chapter one. Whilst in general the advice to governments has been to develop a long-term cohesive textbook strategy, combining public/private partnership, in reality a number of the projects supported by funding agencies have been in conflict with this by supporting short-term, crisis and necessarily *ad hoc* responses to textbook shortages.

In most African countries, funding agencies providing long-term support to the education sector have responded to the need for inter-agency co-ordination by creating a forum for sharing of information. However, these seldom concern themselves with textbook issues in detail. The textbook component is seen as one amongst many components in overall education support programmes.

There is little information in African book development literature on the effect of project consultants in textbook development and the African publishing industry generally.

A large number of studies in textbook and general book provision exist, authored by consultants, in the offices of aid agencies. These are not for the public domain. Typically these have been commissioned to design or evaluate projects funded by aid agencies. The nature of such projects is diverse, both in scale and objectives: there is hardly any aspect of book development in Africa untouched by foreign financial aid. Project consultants, providing the interface between African governments and funding agencies have profoundly influenced how aid resources have been allocated.

Over many years Ministries of Education in Africa have been dependent on the technical expertise of externally based textbook project consultants. The preponderance of non-African consultants has been discussed throughout the 1990s and has been mentioned (by funding agencies) as a potential source of friction and a broadly negative component of aid-activity. APNET has attempted to redress the situation by publishing a portfolio of African book consultants. It is impossible to assess how widely this has been used.

However, in recent years there has been an increase in the involvement of African book professionals from the commercial sector in discussing textbook projects, as a direct corollary to growth in private/public partnership in the textbook sector. There is open willingness by some funding agencies and international consulting firms to contract African professionals in research and some aspects of textbook project design. This represents the beginnings of a watershed in appreciating the need for a dedicated core of African book consultants, based within Africa.

With the sheer number of funding agencies active in African education and the frequency with which consultants come and go, we must acknowledge the risk, at least, of differing signals, advice, nuance and emphasis. Very few consultants have been engaged in a particular country or project for periods exceeding two years. And yet, time frames in textbook development and long term book policy are closer to five to ten years in terms of objectives and results. Therefore, complications arise from a multiplicity of funding agency approaches, advocating different priorities, subsidising and stressing part but not all of a cohesive textbook system.

The Breakdown in Control in State Textbook Systems

Throughout the 1980s and into the 1990s, in state monopoly textbook systems, excessive but unavoidable state dependence on funding agency support produced debilitating effects on textbook provision. Wastage and inefficiency became evident throughout state systems. A stifling bureaucracy seeking to maintain monopoly over publishing and distribution of textbooks on the basis of donor support had simply strained all the linkages in the book chain to breaking point.

Governments embarking on the transition to commercial textbook provision have done so because funding agency supported state mechanisms failed to ensure adequate and sustained supply of textbooks to schools. This is well documented. A host of local factors have come into play in each country, but breakdown in control is a common theme. Productivity, defined loosely as books reaching pupils desks against total resources applied into state monopoly systems, was declining steadily as economic conditions deteriorated in the 1980s.

To compound matters, inefficient state monopolies placed enormous burdens on dwindling resources that could not be replaced without further external funding support. The critical weakness in state systems was that decisions, performance and results did not directly affect the large number of people engaged in textbook production and supply. Accountability in this situation was difficult to enforce.

This lack of control or accountability in state systems is well illustrated by the absence of reliable figures, and sometimes even estimates, of basic book data – for example, average pupil: book ratios, figures for which varied wildly depending on the source.

To give one fairly typical example: figures released in Tanzania in 1994 suggested that over the previous 5 years, 94% of 17,4 million textbooks printed were delivered to district offices, but that the delivery from district storeroom to schools was 'uncertain'. From statistics of books produced and sent to district level, book: pupil ratios appeared in the region of 1:3 or 1:4. A trial survey in 1995 on classroom usage of books in Tanzania concluded that book: pupil ratios were somewhat closer to 1:9 and there were extreme variations between schools and districts (Hedkvist, 1996). A considerable volume of books did not reach pupils. They either did not reach the school at all or were being held in school storerooms due to uncertainty over future supply. Similar results have emerged from various studies in all state-monopoly systems in the 1990s, including Ghana, Ethiopia, Zambia, Mozambique and most Francophone countries.

Less well documented is the extent of dependence reached. In the event of withdrawal of funding agencies, state systems in most instances would collapse. They were not sustainable without support, nor viable. This triggered serious questioning of long term textbook supply. Typically, the decision to embrace commercialisation has been a drawn out process, finally embarked on when government was made to appreciate the extent of crisis, acutely reflected in falling educational quality, and unavailability of textbooks.

Despite deficiencies, and the reason we refer to it in this context, previous state systems had a singular advantage. They were based on long-term stable policy, backed up by long-term capital investment. At the height of state-monopoly single-textbook systems there was policy-level unanimity about how textbooks were intended to be authored, manufactured, costed, paid for and distributed, and no question about selection and procurement method. There was little hesitancy in how funding partners might best apply aid resources within an overall strategic framework, given the state infra-structure already developed to provide textbooks. The major priority, apart from funding *per se*, was towards key inputs into the strategic resources required by the state system: such as paper, print machinery, technical training (such as in textbook authorship, or design), haulage and warehousing. Conceptually, there was a policy framework within which areas of acute shortage or state inadequacy might be addressed, namely tender-based supply, since it was one and the same state system which was designed to either produce the books or purchase them, centrally.

The current paucity of book policy

In contrast and as may be expected in any such transformation, whilst the transition to private sector involvement in textbook provision is in motion throughout Africa, it is characterized by widespread lack of certainty, and sometimes clarity, about specific public/private roles, time-frames and operational details of future phases. Few African countries have yet produced anything approaching a definitive 5-10 year plan (such as existed in state systems), addressing the strategic resources required of the new commercial systems. Understandably so, since the commercial system in itself is so frequently underdeveloped, lacks capacity and capital, and needs time to create a framework of book industry 'standards and conventions' referred to earlier chapters.

Never-the-less, the lack of a broad national book policy framework, within which commercial actors, independent professionals, supportive institutions and funding agencies, each in their own context, may apply technical and financial resources is acutely felt. Investment in commercial publishing, in bookshops, in institution-building and trade systems requires, in the same measure as state systems, a stable and specific policy framework within which long-term planning takes place.

There are major technical problems in developing new commercial systems in a situation where the flow of books must continue, and the establishment of commercial system can take a number of years to achieve. Ministries of Education, concerned that an over-abrupt transition will seriously disrupt textbook provision, are understandably cautious in delegating decisions and roles to an emergent, often 'untried' commercial sector to achieve required results. But the transition to commercial market-based textbook provision requires that decisions have to be increasingly decentralised to the commercial sector, within given parameters. Whichever way one approaches this transition, one is confronted with the capacity, resources, skills, investment and level of development of the commercial sector.

As understood by book professionals, a national book policy is a mechanism to create a supportive, co-ordinated trade and investment environment for a local, indigenous, commercial book industry to mature, in order to provide books for national development. We would add, in this context, to effectively partner the state in the provision of school textbooks for education development. African governments have, to this day, consistently failed to pay serious attention to the chorus of independent professionals arguing that a commercial book industry is a strategic national resource. As such it should be secured by a sound conceptual framework, comprising long-term development objectives and the means to implement these; in short a 'national book policy'.

Countless national and international fora have developed proposals along these lines. This study cannot trace an instance where an African government has established a national forum of stake-holders which has led to the adoption and implementation of a national book policy, based on consensus of stakeholders. This form of public/private partnership has not, as yet, developed. A number of textbook provision policies have been formulated with input from the commercial sector, around the issues of privatisation, liberalisation and decentralisation – by definition involving participation by the private sector. But this has yet to lead towards the creation of holistic national book policy, much must therefore be seen a further strategic goal, and one we would assume is within reach.

Any cursory examination of Europe's book industries, especially in smaller countries in Europe, reveals an array of direct and indirect support to the national publishing industry and profound respect accorded to national book culture. The methods are innovative, diverse and often sophisticated, from buy-back systems, research and institutional support for writers and publishers, to strengthening national language and incentives to export, or otherwise tax breaks and incentives allowing the growth of local book printing industry.

In Africa, there are equivalent and striking examples that have worked equally well. These have provided a specific foundation, to give a few instances, for Mauritian print exports, Zimbabwean bookselling and publishing of secondary textbooks, Tanzanian children's book output in the 1990s and its literacy achievements in the 1970s, Nigerian textbook authorship, local Ghanaian publishing through tax-free paper imports.

However, there are many cases of disincentives to national book industry development, such as those of consumer taxes on books largely purchased by parents or using public funds, or allowing imports of finished books duty-free (encouraging book imports), but taxing raw material and machinery inputs to the local print industry.

For African bookselling, disincentive to growth lies in its restriction from the educational supply chain. For indigenous African private sector publishing the over-riding constraint is lack of capital, particularly to invest in new titles, but also to provide a working capital base for entering the market. In an accelerated liberalisation, where emerging local publishers face financing problems and shortcomings in technical expertise, foreign publishers stand to capture a considerable market share. Ultimately, it is a matter of who is able to develop, publish and place appropriate quality textbooks in the market, or in the tender process. In most of Africa, it is unlikely that sufficient financial resources exist in the emerging local private sector to bear the risks of unrestricted competition with multinationals, many of whom have localised operations in the new environment of liberalisation.

African examples show that practical incentives and supportive measures really work as a catalyst to book industry activity, while the converse is equally true – disincentives stunt and distort growth and investment. Following this perspective, the purpose of national book policy might be construed as co-ordinating all of the components of a national book industry in both the public and private spheres around overall national strategic goals, such that an environment conducive to growth and investment is constantly reinforced.

Many African book professionals today argue that, in terms of policy, textbooks are artificially separated from the bigger goal of establishing the 'book chain' and that liberalisation of textbook provision is, in a broader context, one of a series of measures required to create a functioning, sustainable book chain. The book chain concept assumes a 'book market', in the sense of consumer and book-buying culture, encompassing textbooks. In this line of thinking, it follows that national book policy priority is to establish a functional book chain and that textbook provision is not sustainable in the absence of an indigenous 'book chain' that perpetuates its existence and finances its own growth.

Balancing interests

The findings of this study have shown that imbalance between commercial book industry (supply) interests and Ministry of Education (as a consumer) interests creates distortions. Narrow commercial interest at the expense of the educational consumer is reflected in manipulation of the market, over-pricing and dominance by commercial cartels. Policy decisions that ignore the development needs of a commercial book industry, often for reasons of short-term expediency, erode private sector enterprise and stable conditions necessary for investment. In Africa, book provision systems have suffered the effect of both types of imbalance, caused directly by monopoly-approaches to textbook provision. Both have the effect of undermining diversity of supply and choice for the consumer.

But the question of balancing interests is much broader than this. It equally concerns the necessary balance within the commercial sector between publishing and bookselling, and therefore the development of a commercial distribution infra-structure parallel to a commercial publishing. The interests of indigenous and multinational publishing, sometimes converging as commercial enterprises, sometimes in conflict as competitors for markets, must similarly be considered. In this study, no African publisher has recommended the restriction of multinational involvement in African textbook supply. On the other hand, policy measures that create conditions for equal competition, for opportunity and incentive for growth for indigenous publishing, given past inequity, is overwhelmingly seen as necessary. If genuine competition is not achieved, African publishers maintain, the commercial system will suffer many of the shortcomings of state monopoly. Such competition is only plausible when some emerging indigenous commercial publishers significantly reduce the gap, financially and technically, with vastly bigger multinational competitors.

We have referred in this conclusion to the potential of a triangular relationship, taking in government, funding agency and private sector, around which public/private partnership for textbook provision is gradually being centred. The different experiences of Kenya, Zimbabwe, Uganda and Ghana in this respect should provide ample evidence of how effective such triangular relationship can be, if it is brought into play.

Ultimately, all these activities and policy-approaches must be considered against one performance indicator - the quality, volume and scope of learning materials in the classroom, leading directly to improved education levels and to equity.

A Tanzanian education official argued that in the distant future, it is not curriculum experts who should be arbiter of what textbooks can be used in schools (as under textbook approvals systems), but schools and teachers directly, in a fully open market, from the supplier of their choice. Only then, he maintained, would the needs of the pupil be addressed, since the school consumer would decide directly their product and supplier of choice and be accountable for that decision in the classroom.

Yet, this is not such a distant future as we might assume. The phenomena of independent schools and colleges and private education is expanding exponentially everywhere in Africa. A growing segment of secondary and private school procurement, where parents provide financing for textbooks, is unregulated and fully liberalised. It is also the situation in vocational and technical training, where the private sector is heavily engaged.

In the context of emergence of commercial sector, it is this segment of the market that has kept booksellers from oblivion in many African countries. Booksellers are placing many titles on the market, both local and imported and in the latter case, increasingly from 'non-traditional' supplies (such as India, South Africa and Canada). These titles are competing in a free market environment, where market forces are determining choice by price and quality. From an educational standpoint, there are disadvantages in this highly liberalised procurement environment. Quality is difficult to monitor. However our interest in this is that checks and balances are being provided by the market itself – the fee-paying public. It is advisable to closely consider the performance of this 'free market' since it provides a working model, in Africa, of fully liberalised textbook provision.

At the other end of the pendulum lies the 'single or limited textbook per grade/subject' system, where textbooks are procured centrally, are 'theoretically' cheaper per unit, or at least 'price-controlled' and in which the ministry ensures pedagogical quality and content.

Central tenders for textbooks are often thought to be the best method of transition from state monopoly to gradual inclusion of commercial actors. But there are many cases in Africa where tender regulations have dictated terms of supply over and above the concerns of the either consumers or the book industry, since tender procedures create a 'winner-takes-all' scenario that undermines both diversity and consumer choice.

By way of a broad conclusion, it is the major finding of this study that multiple textbook systems, founded on a Ministry of Education textbook approval mechanism, are pivot in balance of interests in textbook provision at this time. Such systems encompass consumer choice over products and prices. The relationship between consumer and product is direct, and this empowers the consumer – the school. Competition between different titles leads to innovation, quality improvement and conditions for emergence of new publishers with new products. Multiple textbook systems lead naturally to decentralised selection, and this provides a basis to begin engagement of booksellers in the supply chain, providing the 'consolidation' interface between many consumers and many different products from many sources (publishers).

A multiple textbook system encourages diversity of output in the book industry and this is, without question, a positive development path on which to strengthen bookselling, publishing, readership and access to books generally. In the broadest dimension, the entirety of education needs from grade one to university, comprising all types of core, supplementary and reference textbook choices comprises many thousands of titles. Matching these products to the market, consumers and every kind of education institution throughout the country, is where the expertise of commercial sector lies. In its scale and diversity, it is a task that cannot be conceived, let alone undertaken or managed by one entity. It is for this reason that this study, from a policy standpoint, advocates diversity, as opposed to monopoly approaches, as the cornerstone of national and textbook policy.

The question of 'public/private partnerships' in textbooks may also be posed thus: how to increase the capacity, resources and diversity of the private sector in such a way that educational consumers – schools - are the direct and long term beneficiary. It is the correct balancing of these interests that is basis for effective public/private partnership.

COUNTRY STUDIES

Ethiopia

Ethiopia has centuries' old experience of writing and literature, with one of the world's oldest scripts (*Gee'z*) in use since the fourth century. Writing, illustrating, copying and binding of books has an almost equally long history.

Ethiopia combines a number of challenging features that are worth pointing out as a background to the textbook development strategies employed. About 65 million people live in Ethiopia, making it one of the most populous in Africa. They are among the poorest in the world, with a large proportion living on less than US$1 per day. Some 85% of the people depend on agriculture for a living. Rural Ethiopia is exceptionally poor. Food insecurity is a massive dilemma, exacerbated recently by catastrophic drought. In May 1998 hostilities commenced between the Ethiopian and Eritrean governments over a border dispute. The war was ruinous in terms of lives and cost. It ended in December 2000. In some instances, development efforts were temporarily halted during the war. On the other hand, in economic development terms Ethiopia has made good progress. GDP growth has averaged 5% between 1995 and 2000, increasing to around 7% in 2002. However, these improvements can be viewed against the considerable challenges facing the country, ranked at number 171 out 174 countries in the 2000 Human Development Index. About 30% of the population are estimated to be literate.

Since the 1974 socialist-orientated revolution, Ethiopia exercised state control over textbook publishing and production, and established several state enterprises to accomplish this.

The first independent, commercial publisher in Ethiopia came into existence as late as 1975. After political change in 1991, and a new era of political stability and peace, there have been moves to open up the economy to foreign capital, decentralise power, and create a new federal system of governance. In 1993 a conference took place on the liberalisation of the book trade, involving writers, publishers, editors, printers and others. The conference called for the strengthening of the private sector by allowing it to participate in textbook publishing. One of the important accomplishments of the new government has been to introduce press freedom and abolish most forms of censorship, an achievement that Ethiopia is justifiably proud of today. More than 600 private newspapers and periodicals came into existence in the aftermath of the new press laws.

Since the 1994 education policy under a new administration, there has been some limited movement towards a liberalised textbook-publishing system, but under the close control of the Ministry of Education. While writing and pre-production design of a few primary textbooks have been put out to tender, all textbooks at primary school level – that is, Grades 1–8 – have effectively continued to be produced by the Ministry in a single-textbook system.

Uniquely under the federal system, however, writing and production has been devolved to provincial level (referred to as the 'regional' level in Ethiopia), comprising eleven regions and twenty different languages. 'Regionalism' and mother-tongue instruction is the major principle in primary school textbook development under the policies pursued from the 1990s.

Although it is planned for the future, there is as yet no multiple-textbook system, and there is therefore one textbook per grade and subject per region. The concept behind this is that English is a foreign language and Amharic a second language for most people. In Grades 1 and 2 pupils learn their local language and are introduced to English. In Grade 3 they begin Amharic.

A 'standard syllabus' is produced at federal level by the Institute of Curriculum Development and Research (ICDR) for the entire country. This can be interpreted to some degree locally by each region. Each region has an education bureau with a curriculum department, monitored or governed by the ICDR.

While regional education bureaux of the Ministry have the authority to produce textbooks (using a form of local tender), the federal Ministry of Education (through the ICDR) has considerable influence over the form and content of regionally produced textbooks. The regional education bureau undertakes all aspects of writing and publishing primary textbooks by putting out tenders to authors and/or publishers to develop and design books up to camera-ready copy – all in the local language.

The books may be printed at the EMPDA state printers (see below), or printing may be put out to local tender. In practice, most books are printed at EMPDA in Addis Ababa. EMPDA is dependent on paper provided through funding agencies. All paper is imported

It has a chain of 36 bookshops; there are a total of 58 established bookshops in Ethiopia and an estimated 110 informal or small book outlets. A large of quantity of books are imported from India (which is the main external supplier),and is foreign is currency available for book imports. Importing books is not a problem but an import licence is needed and there is a 10% import duty on books.

There has been a massive increase in private schools and colleges, and this keeps the booksellers and the few commercial publishers in business. At tertiary level, institutions have autonomy and most books are imported.

The Ministry of Education retains copyright on all the textbooks it owns, so they cannot be reprinted for the general market without the permission of the Ministry. However, publishers that win tenders for writing and developing secondary school textbooks may reprint these and sell them on the open market with the permission of the Ministry, paying the Ministry a royalty as copyright holder. The open market comprises private schools, community schools and night schools, as well as parents and the general public reached through the bookshop network.

Ethiopia exhibits characteristics of the 'free textbook syndrome', where educational consumers are unwilling to buy books because they have historically been provided free by the state.

Commercialisation of publishing under the present system is slow and competition is weak. Publishers feel that the single-textbook tender system has undermined competition and diversity. Although there is, in effect, a positive trend towards 'indigenous production' of textbooks and multinational publishers have not been encouraged, international competitive bidding conditions (in library supply) have favoured foreign companies.

The Ministry of Education is keen to transform its system into liberalised market-based textbook provision, incorporating a multiple-textbook system, but, in common with other countries in a similar position, there are difficulties in beginning the transformation. Commercial Ethiopian publishers need assistance and working capital to grow, as well as training in all aspects of the publishing business. While government policy stipulates the liberalisation of textbook provision, Ministry officials bemoan the lack of commercial capacity in publishing to drive this policy forward.

Ethiopia has an inspiring legacy of scholarship and intellectual capacity, but this has not translated into a vibrant and diversified book industry. Independent commercial entities complain of too much control from the ICDR over authorship and also that the tender approach has stifled initiative. There are few book trade meetings to discuss the way forward, and few initiatives of an NGO nature, and therefore very little in the way of support mechanisms for the emerging book sector.

Ghana

Brief Background of Country Publishing

In character with British-colonized African countries, mission-aries from England established the first schools, and later intro-duced religious and primary school textbooks.

The emergence of political freedom, coupled with a desire for educational, intellectual, cultural and economic sovereignty, gave rise to the Accelerated Development Plan for Education in 1961.

This sought to localise the content of all textbooks and, to some extent, general books to suit the Ghanaian environment. At that time textbooks were developed and printed overseas and imported. A number of foreign publishing companies, such as University of London Press, Macmillan, Evans Brothers, Longman, Cambridge University Press and Oxford University Press, marketed books in Ghana through local agents. The launch of the Accelerated Development Plan for Education prompted publishers to commis-sion Ghanaian authors to write textbooks and general books in response to new syllabus developed by the Ministry of Education.

The arrangement under the Accelerated Development Plan worked and the first generation of Ghanaian-authored books were successfully published for use in the school system.

Six years after independence, the government in 1963 intro-duced the Free Textbooks Scheme for Basic Education. In the same year, Ghana Book Supplies (GBS) was incorporated to take charge of importing and distributing textbooks to schools on behalf of the government. In 1965 the Ghanaian Government established the Ghana Publishing Corporation (GPC) 'to print, publish, distribute and market books and other educational materials for schools, higher educational institutions and public.' Where local authors were not available, GPC was mandated to license foreign titles.

To a large extent, GPC was similar to the Kenneth Kaunda Foundation in Zambia (later re-named Zambia Educational Publishing House), the now defunct Milton Obote Foundation of Uganda, the General Egyptian Book Organisation, and the Jomo Kenyatta Foundation of Kenya.

The setting up of the state monopoly over textbook provision through GBS and GPC resulted in drastically reduced business for emergent Ghanaian commercial booksellers and publishers. Between 1963 and 1974, many textbooks were written by Ghanaians and published by British publishers. In effect, a large number of locally written materials were published by British multinationals on commission, or in collaboration with the Ministry of Education.

After 1974, the Ministry decided to publish its own materials exclusively. All books were authored by the Curriculum Research and Development Division (CRDD), which was formally responsible for 'developing, producing and supplying textbooks to government basic and secondary schools' alongside the GBS and GPC parastatal companies.

In 1976 the Ghana Investment Policy Decree restricted the business of publishing to Ghanaian companies. The Decree effectively forced foreign publishing companies to withdraw from Ghana and continue their business through local representatives.

Before the Decree, Afram Publications (Ghana) had been established in 1973 to publish textbooks for primary and secondary schools, teacher training colleges and technical institutes. The company was a joint private and public venture, with shareholding by Ghana State Insurance Corporation. Two years later, in 1975, Sedco Publishing was formed to publish textbooks at similar levels as well as general books. The three publishing houses, along with Adwinsa Publications and Edupress collaborated for sometime with the Ministry of Education to co-publish basic textbooks. Only the government, through GPC, published the mandatory core books and distributed them free to elementary schools, while Ghanaian publishers made their business by publishing supplementary textbooks for important examinations as well as for higher-level classes, where the market was still open, if not catered for by imported textbooks.

In 1980 a single textbook per grade/subject was adopted, completing the process of state monopoly textbook provision. The declining national economy, reduced funding support, and the overburdened GPC (by this time facing severe operational problems) adversely affected textbook output. GPC had been on a divestiture plan since 1985 and had not published any notable new books for some time.

In 1984, the government entered into an agreement with five local publishers to co-publish textbooks for primary schools. The Co-publishing Project, as it was called, was intended to combine state, parastatal and private publishing resources to publish core materials for formal education. It also permitted private partner-publishers to re-print extra copies for the open market. Implementation began in 1990.

By the early 1990s new private investors, prominent among whom was EPP Book Services, took advantage of the failing government system in the provision of textbooks and embarked on resuscitating the book industry. EPP Book Services, started in 1992, publishes mainly educational books, in addition to importing and distributing through its outlets in various parts of Ghana.

In 1996, the Ghana Book Publishers Association (GBPA) won approval for Ghanaian publishers to reprint required textbooks up to secondary school level. In the same year, government waived the 15% tax on inputs for books published by GBPA members only.

In 1996/7 twelve members of the GBPA were afforded the opportunity to participate in a Non-Formal Education Division programme (funded by World Bank) to publish post-literacy materials in fifteen Ghanaian languages. In 1998, the Ministry of Education announced an invitation for publishers to submit titles as supplementary readers for selection and purchase for primary schools; 60% of the books bought were from British publishers and 40% from Ghanaian publishers.

The language factor

Ghana has a long history, going back to the beginning of the nineteenth century, of writing in indigenous languages such as Twi, Fante/Akan, Ewe and Ga following the advent of missionaries. Teacher training colleges and elementary schools popularized the teaching of Ghanaian languages before 1950. Currently, the Ministry of Education has followed a deliberate policy to improve the use of Ghanaian languages in schools through the production of books in Akuapen Twi-Akan, Asante Twi-Akan, Fante Twi-Akan, Dagaare, Dagbani, Dangme, Ewe, Ga, Gonja, Kasem and Nzema. Ghana, however, has many other languages or dialects. The benefit of using mother-tongue languages for comprehension, effective communication and educational purposes has been well researched. The early use of indigenous Ghanaian languages enabled the Bureau of Ghana Languages to publish books and other literature in local languages.

The introduction of the Accelerated Development Programme for Education in 1961, brought about rapid school enrolments and less attention being given to Ghanaian languages, such that the young generation opted for the English language. This consequently affected the level of writing proficiency in both English and Ghanaian languages.

The quality of the country's writing and general book publishing is demonstrated at international level by the fact that Ghanaian book publishers have won two Noma Awards for African Publishing in 1982 and 1983. The Ghanaian Association of Writers, the Authorship Development Fund, the Valco Literary Award and the Ghana Book Development Council, which also established the Children's Literature Foundation in 1978, have greatly contributed to the development of local authors in various genres of books; a number of popular children's books and novels have been published and are successfully exported.

Liberalisation: The Genesis of Public/Private Partnership

In February 2002, the Ministry of Education approved a Textbook Development and Distribution Policy for Basic Education. In this context, basic education embraces Primary Class 1 to Primary Class 6, and Junior Secondary School Class 1 to Class 3. The Policy does not cover the senior secondary school sector or even technical and vocational institutes, but there is talk of drawing up a separate policy for this category. To operationalize the Policy, the Ministry also produced detailed Operational Annexes to the Policy.

Formulation of the Policy began in 1998 and the first draft was published in October 1999. A review and revision of the draft was done in 2000 that was subjected to further debate and amendment during detailed consultations in April 2001. A wide cross-section of 128 stakeholders that included individuals, trade associations of publishers, booksellers, printers, authors, illustrators, designers, librarians and development partners were involved at the initial and final stages of the Policy's formulation.

Policy heralded a major change towards liberalisation in the development of textbooks, teachers' guides, workbooks and supplementary reading materials, their publication, and the decentralisation of selection and procurement of textbooks at basic level. In a nutshell, the Policy aims, *inter alia*, at the decentralisation of decision-making on the selection of five textbooks per subject to enable teachers, parents and pupils to contribute fully, alongside other educational agencies, to the process of choice; active private-sector involvement in the implementation of a sustainable book development, production and distribution system; upgrading of local capacity in book development, publishing, distribution and printing and in the book industry in general; competitive textbooks from which schools may choose the titles that they prefer and which best suit their needs; and efficient and timely distribution of books to schools and pupils.

Bookselling and Distribution

The role of booksellers in the new Policy, however, has been limited to a pilot project in a district, while that of publishers is to distribute to the level of each district depot. The district depots will serve as the central collection points. It is from here that the Ministry of Education, through the District Directors of Education, will be responsible for the subsequent distribution of books to various schools within the districts. The general explanation given for this is that Ghanaian booksellers have no capacity to warehouse and distribute bulk quantities of books.

The association of booksellers, the Ghana Booksellers Association (GBSA), which was established in 1956 with membership drawn from booksellers including three university bookshops. Having been marginalized as a result of the introduction of Free Textbooks Scheme for Basic Education in 1963, the GBSA was somewhat disorganised and had effectively lost its voice until May 2002. The current active membership of GBSA is less than twenty (low compared to the GBPA's approximately 60 institutional and 20 individual members), but efforts are in place to mobilize the members and reorganise the Association.

Because of its marginalization, bookselling is perceived as diminishing in Ghana, thus affecting employment opportunities. Furthermore, booksellers had limited professional training, resulting in lack of recognition being accorded to them as professionals like their counterparts in publishing and printing. There is hope for the resuscitation of standard book-trade practices that will take into account their various functions as wholesalers or operators of retail bookshops, and cause them to abide by a code of conduct and obtain appropriate publishers' discounts. Other book outlets, such as kiosks and wayside or street vendors, may not require similar discounts because their operations are different and do not incur comparatively high overhead expenses, nor are their operations guided by a professional code of ethics.

Effects of Policy

Recognition of Roles

Incorporated in the Textbook Development and Distribution Policy is a detailed code of conduct to guide publishers and booksellers or their representatives when they visit schools or conduct promotional workshops.

Until the Policy was approved, the Ministry of Education, through the CRDD, was responsible for developing, producing and supplying textbooks to government basic and secondary schools in the country under the provisions of Free Textbook Scheme that had been in place since 1963.

With the Policy in place, the CRDD will be responsible for developing the curricula and syllabuses and thereafter ensure the quality control of all textbooks, teachers' guide, workbooks and supplementary reading materials through systematic evaluation based on detailed criteria. All textbooks submitted for evaluation will be in complete series ('lots') rather than as single textbooks. This arrangement is intended to ensure the continuity of textbooks from one Grade level to another.

According to the proposed publisher's contract pro-forma of the Policy, syllabuses will be reviewed and updated every five years.

Similarly, textbooks will be retained as approved textbooks for a minimum period of five years. To this end, the Ministry of Education would undertake to guarantee maintaining the approved titles on the Official Textbook List and Order Form for the five-year period. The Ministry would ensure that it maintained regular and close contact with respective publishers and the GBPA to provide early warning of any impending changes in the curriculum policy and syllabus. Publishers, in reciprocity, would undertake to make available for the duration of the contract sufficient quantities of the titles approved and included in the Official Textbook List.

Publishers, on the other hand, will identify qualified authors or writing panels to develop manuscripts that meet the requirements of the curricula and syllabuses and finance the entire production of the textbooks.

Furthermore, selection of textbooks will be made by individual schools. Each school will establish a Textbook Selection Committee to undertake the important work of selecting one of the five competing textbooks approved by the Ministry of Education. The quantities of books and number of titles will be determined by the annual school budget, based on the annual per capita allocation for that school.

Reference Point for Dialogue and Investment

Publishers in Ghana, while bemoaning the adverse effects of the Free Textbook Scheme on the publishing and bookselling industry, see the new Policy as a positive development that can resuscitate bookshops and enhance the private/public partnerships in the book industry. The publishers are of the view that the official Policy provides both a reference point and framework within which collaboration between the government and the private sector would function. They attributed most of the various existing limiting factors, including low investment in the book industry, to the absence of a policy. The Ministry of Education would henceforth have to agree with the GBPA on a price-inflation factor, and involve both the GBPA and GBSA in determining the criteria for selecting official district-level textbook suppliers.

The Policy should thus facilitate formalized dialogue between the parties concerned to address any issues that either had hitherto hampered national book development or would expedite the process. This is evidenced even at this stage by the government's offer to the GBPA to provide some tax or Customs duty relief on imports of paper intended for textbook production.

It is also envisaged that when the new Policy is implemented more publishing and printing companies will be listed on the stock exchange; Sam Woode Limited, a private publishing company, has been able to raise its capital through its listing on the stock exchange. With the Policy implemented, other publishing and printing companies may follow this route for raising additional capital to meet the new demanding challenges of massive book production.

While hope lies in the new Policy to address issues of limiting factors formally, it is speculated that the pre-financing of textbooks at development stage prior to selection may pose a problem. There are a number of costs to be borne by publishers that would have a bearing on the price of textbooks. Such costs include: purchase of submission procedures and syllabuses per specified lot at US$25; submission of proposal per subject and per package at US$100; fee for each textbook lot for which approved status has been awarded at US$500; and fee for claim against evaluation results per lot at US$200. In addition, publishers will be expected to fund post-evaluation trial testing by the CRDD. The testing will require submission of copies of each of five topics from each selected textbook and payment of a testing fee of between US$300 and US$500 per selected textbook.

Although the foregoing costs may appear to be manageable for multinational publishers, nearly 98% of the publishers registered with GBPA are in fact indigenous Ghanaians following the Ghana Investment Policy Decree of 1976. Multinational publishers such as Heinemann, Oxford University Press, Evans and Longman operate under agreements with local publishers. Macmillan, on the other hand, is represented by Unimax Macmillan Publishers.

More important is the fact that the Policy should go a long way towards creating transparency and accountability when it comes to implementing external funding for textbook provision by the World Bank or other co-operating partner, as ground rules and parameters would have been standardized. The Policy may also influence change in the way donor-driven programmes are governed by moderating certain restrictive conditions.

Despite the approval of the Policy in February 2002, implementation had stalled by the end of the year because the requisite funds were yet to be sourced. Essentially, implementation requires massive funding which the Ghanaian government cannot provide alone and for which it would seek funding from development partners.

Libraries

Sixty-four public libraries under the aegis of the Ghana Library Board have largely depended on donations of books from Book Aid International, as it has not been possible to purchase new books because of insufficient allocation of funds from the national budget over the years.

Copyright

Although the incidence of infringement of the Copyright Law is reported to be a spill-over from Nigeria, book professionals in Ghana acknowledge that piracy is gradually becoming a major problem. It is reported that the current law in terms of enforcement and penalty is ineffective or weak and amendments are in progress. Booksellers admit that pirated books are being sold cheaply, thereby affecting revenue from anticipated sales of original books. Photocopying of tertiary-level textbooks means that booksellers' capital expended on these titles is tied up in unsold copies. As a way forward a code of ethics among GBSA members may help curb piracy. Printers feel that professionalism may have been compromised when printing jobs are presented with ready cash for payment, as no effort is made to verify the ownership of copyright. There may therefore be need for appropriate inclusion of clauses in the printing code of ethics and for printers and publishers to specifically address this problem.

One explanation for piracy is that publishers are unable to supply sufficient books in remote parts of the country and this scarcity gives rise to unscrupulous booksellers who pirate titles.

Tax Waiver as Government Support to Industry

Taxes have remained a limiting factor in the development of the book sector in a number of ways. Printers, publishers and booksellers in Ghana are variously affected. There is a view that there is a need to revisit the effects on the local book industry – positive and negative – of the provisions of the Florence Agreement and the Nairobi Protocol to the Agreement. To enable the industry to develop there may be a need for some 'tax holiday' for a short fixed period. The current offer by government to waive duty on paper and ink with the firm proviso that publishers give foolproof guarantees against its abuse was greatly applauded. It was noted that that taxes affect the cost of imported production materials on locally printed books while imported books were duty-free. Booksellers bemoaned 20% duty, 15% tax and 12% VAT levied on catalogues and price lists that are currently not classified as printed matter. Whereas publishers experienced no major problems in accessing foreign currency, booksellers expressed concern over the delayed release of foreign currency, coupled with bureaucratic Customs clearance procedures that impact on delivery times and the cost of imported books. In addition, booksellers felt that violent exchange-rate fluctuations and the lack of ready foreign currency when it was needed adversely affected the value of booksellers' credit terms with overseas suppliers.

Printing

Ghana has a large number of printers that are able to meet the local demand for printing work, although some printers do need to upgrade their presses. The new Policy appears to offer prospects for further investment either by securing bank loans, using guaranteed massive textbook printing jobs from local publishers and government, or by offering existing plant and machinery as collateral. A printers' association that was dormant for some time has been reactivated.

On the other hand, because of competitive prices some publishers opt to have their books printed outside Ghana, using printers in Dubai, Mauritius and South Africa, for example.

Partnership Booster

Book promotion at all levels in Ghana has been the responsibility of the Ghana Book Development Council (GBDC), established in August 1975 under the Ministry of Education. The Council's membership is composed mainly of government ministries and institutions, while the private sector of the book industry is represented by major book-related professional associations.

There is general agreement that the new Policy provides a good starting point for the changing public/private partnerships in the book sector in Ghana. The Policy should be able to strengthen the contribution of various professional bodies and associations in the country.

In addition to the new Policy, stakeholders saw the need for a desk or focal person at the Ministry of Education to deal specifically with book professionals such as publishers, booksellers and printers. At present such an office does not exist, resulting in matters affecting the book being relegated to the GBDC, which is not well funded nor structurally empowered. To enable various book bodies to operate effectively there was a need for some internal reorganisation in respect of retraining, equipment and proper financing. Specifically, collaboration among stakeholders in the book sector in Ghana could be enhanced through a fully supported Ghana Book Development Council. Stakeholders have identified the need for technical capacity building to make the Council effective in its work. This view is further strengthened by the recommendation in the Policy that the GBDC will be expected to undertake an annual survey of local textbook printing and binding capacity, quality and reliability, as well as pricing, as a basis for the establishment of realistic annual textbook production targets. The annual survey would serve as a clear indication of progress towards local production targets.

Currently, the GBPA plays an effective role in cementing collaboration between the public and private sectors through liaison with government on book-policy issues, co-operating with development agencies and government, and being called upon to provide input into any book-related project. GBPA also supports the Department of Book Industry at Kwame Nkrumah University of Science and Technology in Kumasi by making publisher-members available to students for industrial attachment opportunities.

Other views expressed suggested setting up an apex forum on the lines of a Ghana Book League that would replace the current steering committees that deal with specific aspects of the book sector and make representations to government. The suggested apex forum would be broad-based, cut across some interest or pressure groups, and would effectively bring together the public and private sectors without being specialist in any segment of the booksector.

Of special note is the Ghana Association of Writers that is active and has benefited greatly from an Authorship Development Fund set up in October 1973 by the government. The fund was initially intended to help the Curriculum Research and Development Division of the Ghana Education Service to organise workshops for the writing of basic textbooks as a way of implementing the new structure and content of education in Ghana beginning in 1975.

Statistics

Book professionals generally acknowledged that accurate statistics on school enrolment are available, and that the Ministry of Education's inspectorate regularly updates, through questionnaires and visits, statistics on what books are available and what books are needed. However, the country needs to initiate data gathering in the book industry. Such data would help to establish the output of books every year, and the industry's contribution to Gross Domestic Product. Such information would enable the sector be identified as an industry. The situation in Ghana, as in many other African countries, is that the book industry is normally treated as a cultural or service activity and rarely attracts attention during national strategic or economic planning.

Non-Governmental Organisations

There are fewer NGOs in West Africa than in Eastern Africa that participate in book provision. In Ghana, NGOs ask for books from publishers to donate to a worthy cause rather than provide support to the book industry. Star for Hope International is one NGO that prepares, produces and distributes books free to pre-schools. Rotary

Clubs also donate some books. One local NGO of note is the Ghana Book Trust, established in 1990, whose objectives include supporting the promotion of indigenous publishing for primary-level education and adult literacy programmes, rural library development, donating and distributing books in support of adult literacy and post-literacy programmes, and co-operating with other bodies engaged in the book industry and library development in Ghana.

Training

Training for book professionals is provided at various institutions within Ghana, but notably at the Department of Book Industry at Kwame Nkrumah University of Science and Technology, Kumasi. The training is specifically for publishing, printing, book design and illustration, book distribution and marketing at certificate, diploma, degree and post-graduate levels. The Department of Book Industry is working very closely with the industry in Ghana, with the GBPA and APNET, and is currently collaborating with Oxford Brookes University in the UK. The Department has the potential to offer courses to students from other parts of Africa.

Prospects

The approval and subsequent implementation of the Textbook Development and Distribution Policy offers a springboard for strengthening the changing public/private partnership in the book sector. Prospects for bookselling in Ghana are high, and will support the increasing publishing activities. Ultimately, growth of the book industry is contingent upon the new Policy.

Guinea

Guinea imported all textbooks for the school system from France until 1989, when the National Institute of Education, INRAP (Institut Nationale de Recherche d'Action Pédagogique), started developing primary school titles in co-operation with private publishers. The Ministry of Pre-University Education and Civic Education engaged the private booksellers, Sodil, Mabougie and Rivière du Sud to distribute the books. In 1994 the newspaper distributor SOGUIDIP-SA started using its distribution centers in the country for the same purpose. Small traders, who also sell many other kinds of goods, bought books from these depots for sale to the public. The booksellers received a discount on the highly subsidized price of the books, and parents purchased.

According to the booksellers interviewed, the commercial distribution system functioned well and the fact that that parents shared the cost of books was seen as positive: 'Pupils take better care of their books when the family has paid for them.' Booksellers also observed that, 'with totally free textbooks, the government becomes dependent on donors for the financing, which is not sustainable'.

But even with highly subsidized textbooks, the combined costs of school fees, school uniforms and books were high for poor families, and in some rural areas the gross primary school enrolment rate was under 35%; it is around 90% in Conakry. When the World Bank's Education for All programme made funds available in 1996/7, the government began to distribute textbooks and school supplies free of charge directly to schools. The Ministry of Education used haulage contractors for the distribution, and booksellers became redundant. None survived the loss of the textbook market. The booksellers interviewed also mentioned USAID's NFQE/EDC project as another example of one that ignored booksellers. This project has developed and published supplementary readers for the first five grades of primary school, and distributes one million copies every year free of charge, directly to schools without involving booksellers.

Under the centralised single-textbook system, textbooks for the primary schools are bought centrally through international competitive bidding, a system that makes it difficult for small local publishers to win any orders. The ratio of books to students has been brought down to 1:2 in the main subjects. Books are owned by the schools and a rental system has been introduced. According to a World Bank report, the system is successful: 'Teachers are using the books in their teaching; children are taking the books home with minimal loss.' The report estimates that books 'will be maintained over a four to five year period'. If this is correct, it would signify an unparalleled life expectancy for primary books in African climate. Booksellers sell some textbooks to parents and they can also sell supplementary books (which must be approved by the Ministry of Education) to schools.

French is the medium of instruction in Guinea, as in Mali and Senegal. But the introduction of national languages in primary school is being also discussed. Already, when books are bought for school libraries, some books in national languages must be included.

For the next phase of the World Bank project the government will pilot test a multiple-title system in mathematics, French and science for Grade 6 in primary school. Publishers will be invited to develop textbook titles based on curriculum guidelines developed by INRAP. The proposals will be evaluated and approved for use by a national approval commission established for this purpose. Then it will be up to the schools or districts to decide which titles they will use. It is expected that the competition will 'improve quality, add diversity to the system and generally improve service delivery'. It will also allow INRAP to refocus on its pedagogic research. The Ministry will take a cautious approach, but if the pilot testing proves successful, the multi-textbook system will be extended to languages, mathematics, science and social studies throughout primary school. The test will not signify increased business for the booksellers, however, as procurement for schools will continue to be done centrally.

If local publishers print their books in Guinea, they will not be able to compete with the foreign suppliers. The duties on inputs for book production are very high (20–22% on paper and up to 32% on certain other inputs), while finished books are exempt. The fact that Guinea's printers go to the parallel market to find foreign currency for the import of paper makes local printing virtually impossible. Books are printed in Dakar, Abidjan, Benin or Tunisia. Even printing in Mauritius is cheaper than local production, in spite of the long distance.

People in the book trade complained that, in the past, the government had a habit of changing its policies relating to the book sector, without discussing the consequences with the commercial stakeholders. Sudden changes made it risky for publishers and booksellers to invest in their businesses. But publishers have recently noticed an improved climate in their relations with the Ministry of Pre-University Education and Civic Education. Today, representatives of the private sector are invited to meetings at the Ministry from time to time and, for the first time, a textbook for secondary schools published by a private publisher has been put on the approved list, the Liste Officielle.

The USAID book project was criticized for sidelining local publishers and booksellers, but the project was also praised for awarding printing contracts to a local printer, Nouvelle Imprimerie de Kaloum. The printer had used the income for long-awaited investment in new equipment.

A national schoolbook policy is now being developed, and this will hopefully lead to exemption of duties on printing inputs and greater stability in the book sector in the future. A process has started; it is slow, but the local publishers and booksellers are hopeful.

Kenya

Background

The development of textbook publishing in Kenya can be traced through a chequered path that closely mirrors changes in education. There are three distinct phases or 'eras' that are worthy of note:

Independence (1963) to 1984

During this time, the Kenyan education structure consisted of seven years of primary school, four years of secondary school, two years of a preparatory course for university entry, and three years of university education (for most degree courses). This structure is often summarized as 7-4-2-3.

This was a period when the government financed the provision of textbooks to schools with no contribution from parents. Thus the books were procured centrally by the Ministry of Education and distributed freely to schools, and the government set up a unit to facilitate this, at one time called the Kenya School Equipment Scheme.

The books were procured from local branches of British publishers such as Longman, Nelson, Heinemann and Oxford University Press. All Kenyan children in a given class used the same textbook for each subject. It was only at secondary level that some element of choice by teachers was allowed and that there was some variation in the books used from one school to another.

Publishers submitted their books for evaluation by the Kenya Institute of Education (KIE). Once a book was approved, it meant that the Ministry would soon place orders running into hundreds of thousands of copies with the publisher.

1985 to 1997

In 1985, the structure of education was changed to eight years of primary school, four years of secondary school and four years of university education, summarized as 8-4-4. In addition, the curriculum was broadened at primary and secondary level in terms of the subjects covered and the scope within subjects.

These changes created a sudden demand for new textbooks. The government decided to step into the publishing arena to ensure that the required books were made available, as its perception was that the private-sector publishers could not cope. The KIE organised writing panels and the resultant manuscripts were passed on to two government-owned publishers, Jomo Kenyatta Foundation (JKF) and Kenya Literature Bureau (KLB). The KIE-authored books were subsequently designated as the core course books, while those published by private-sector publishers were categorized as supplementary, once they were approved by KIE.

These developments led to a situation in which JKF and KLB had an absolute monopoly in the supply of course books to both primary and secondary schools. The private-sector publishers had to struggle to survive on sales of so-called supplementary books, even though they had developed books that were as good as, if not better than, the recommended course books.

On the publishing front, many new publishing companies were established, mainly because of the opportunities offered by the new education system. The Kenya Publishers Association (KPA), which had been established in 1971, now had the potential to increase its membership considerably. However, it was not until the 1990s that the Association was revitalized and began to command some recognition from the Ministry of Education. By this time, most of the British publishers had left the country, some having sold their companies to Kenyan investors.

The KPA was finally able to establish a secretariat in 1996 and this, coupled with increasing membership, helped to enhance its position as a credible trade-cum-professional association. While in the late 1980s and early 1990s private-sector publishers had been vilified by the government for 'greedy profiteering', the Ministry began to invite KPA officials for consultative meetings. The icy hostility engendered by years of unfair competition was beginning to thaw as both the government and the private-sector publishers became more conciliatory in their stance.

1998 to the Present

In September 1998, the Minister for Education launched the National Textbook Policy for Primary Schools. The policy document acknowledges that:

- There is need to liberalise the book trade in keeping with liberalisation of other sectors of the economy.
- Decisions on the selection of books should be school-based.
- There is need to minimize the financial burden of parents in relation to textbooks. This has arisen as a result of moving from full government supply prior to 1988 to full supply by parents, following the introduction of cost-sharing policies in education.
- The Ministry has the responsibility of ensuring that 'books which go into the market for use in schools are of high quality and relevance for the purpose of meeting the needs of the primary school curriculum'.
- The birth of the policy was closely connected to the piloting of a Dutch government-funded Textbook Procurement Project in 1996/7. Various methods of selection and supply of core textbooks at primary school level were tested and the lessons learnt became part of the policy.

Commercial publishers' involvement

Primary

As mentioned above, the textbook policy for primary schools had as one of its aims the liberalisation of the textbook trade. Consequently, there is now no distinction between the role of commercial publishers and that of state-owned publishers.

In this arrangement, publishers develop the textbooks in accordance with the curricula and syllabuses provided by the Ministry of Education through KIE. They then submit the textbooks to KIE for evaluation and approval. Finally, they are responsible for marketing and promoting their books in the schools as well as ensuring that stocks are available to meet the demand.

Collectively, through the KPA, publishers are also involved in the formulation and implementation of policies relating to textbooks. For example:

- The KPA made a contribution to the development of the textbook policy by participating in the pilot project and providing feedback during the evaluation stage.
- In 1999, the KPA worked with KIE to arrive at mutually acceptable fees for the evaluation of books. The fees were meant to facilitate the evaluation as well as to ensure that KIE gave comprehensive feedback to the publishers so that they would be able to identify areas in which their books needed improvement.
- The KIE consulted closely with the KPA regarding the implementation timetable for the new curriculum (commencing implementation in 2003) as it related to the production and evaluation of textbooks.
- KIE and KPA have formed a joint Technical Committee which advises on technical matters relating to book production and evaluation.
- In April 2002, KPA was invited to become a member of KIE's top decision-making body, the Academic Board. This is of benefit to the publishers because they can keep track of developments in the curriculum area that might impact on their operations, and make contributions in their areas of competence.
- At the beginning of 2003, the newly elected government began implementing its Free Primary Education (FPE) policy. One of the key stakeholders to be involved in the discussions about the implementation has been the publishers. For example, the Ministry has sought and obtained assurance regarding the publishers' ability to supply the large quantities of textbooks required within a limited period of time. The Ministry has, in turn, been able to pass on similar assurance to the development partners who are helping with the funding of the FPE programme.

All this has been done in recognition that the publishers and the Ministry are partners in the provision of education to Kenyan children. Consequently, the two parties need to work in a co-ordinated fashion to ensure effective delivery of this vital service.

Secondary

There is no formal policy for textbook supply at the secondary level. However, a similar situation obtains to that in the primary schools. The publishers still have to develop books and submit them for evaluation and approval by the Ministry, which subsequently issues a list of approved textbooks to schools. Schools then select their preferences from the approved list. The only difference is that, unlike in the primary schools, there is no strict adherence to the approved list, and schools often buy textbooks that are not on that list. They are able to do this because textbooks at this level are financed entirely by parental contribution. This may change when, as is expected, the government resumes the financing of textbook purchases. It will then be possible to restrict such funding to the purchase of duly approved textbooks, as is happening at the primary level.

Tertiary

Virtually all the textbook needs in tertiary institutions in Kenya are met by private-sector publishers. In addition, many of the books are imported. The institutional bookshops order the books directly from publishers or through local agents and distributors. It is likely that the role of the university presses in the provision of textbooks to institutions of higher learning will grow as these institutions are strengthened.

Textkook provision system: the role of major players

It is at the primary level where there is a stipulated textbook policy and a well-developed provision system. The Ministry, publishers, booksellers and school communities all have a role in this system. Below is a summary of how it works:

Ministry of Education

- Develops curriculum through KIE.
- Sets, in consultation with the publishers, the minimum physical production specifications.
- Evaluates and approves textbooks.
- Issues a list of approved textbooks which is sent to all schools.
- Mobilizes funding from local and external sources.
- Provides funding directly to individual school bank accounts.
- Provides training of all the players – Ministry field officials, publishers, booksellers, school committees.
- Monitors the whole process.

- Makes random checks in schools, bookshops and publishers' warehouses to ensure compliance with physical production specifications.
- Ensures effective utilization of the textbooks at school level through the Inspectorate.

Publishers

- Develop textbooks according to the curriculum and syllabuses.
- Submit textbooks (either in finished form or as final proofs) to KIE for evaluation.
- Pay requisite evaluation fees.
- Undertake promotion and marketing of approved textbooks.
- Arrange to hold stocks of the approved textbooks.
- Ensure adherence to physical production specifications.
- Supply school orders through bookshops. There is an understanding between booksellers and publishers that the latter do not sell directly to schools.

Booksellers

- Market themselves to schools so that they may be designated official suppliers.
- Carry stocks (or at least single copies) of all approved textbooks in their shops.
- Receive orders from schools.
- Consolidate school orders according to publishers.
- Obtain textbooks from publishers.
- Deliver textbooks to the respective schools.
- Obtain payment from the schools.
- Pay publishers (if the books had been supplied on credit).

School Communities (teachers, pupils and parents)

- Set up Textbook Selection Committees.
- Open textbook accounts.
- Select textbooks from the approved list.
- Appoint a textbook supplier.
- Place orders.
- Confirm accuracy of delivery.
- Pay supplier.
- Ensure proper storage and care of books.

It is important to note that the whole system is anchored by the following:

- Thorough training of all the players.
- Use of elaborate documentation (handbooks, manuals, order forms, etc.).
- Meticulous record-keeping at school level.
- An audit system for books and funds.

- An undertaking by all players to adhere to the principles of transparency and accountability, and sanctions against those who do not.

Challenges

- Increased competitiveness, especially among publishers, since the number of textbooks to be approved per subject per class is limited to four for secondary and six for primary schools.
- Some schools are still 'stuck' in the days when decisions on which books to use were made for them. They keep buying 'what they know', which are invariably textbooks from government-owned publishing houses.
- Some schools buy a few copies of all the approved textbooks, which means that they do not achieve class sets for any of them. This is ineffective for the teaching/learning process.
- Some booksellers delay payment to publishers; this may have to do with payment delays at the school level. This strains the cash-flow of the publishers and makes them less willing to extend credit subsequently. Since most booksellers do not have adequate operational capital, lack of credit from publishers could adversely affect the success of the supply project.
- Discounts given by booksellers to schools are supposed to be in the form of additional books. However, a few cases of money changing hands have been reported.

A few cases of collusion between a bookseller and a publisher to change a school's choices have been reported.

All these and other challenges are addressed through continuous consultation among the players.

Prospects

The decentralised textbook supply system has been acknowledged as a success by all concerned because of its efficiency and in-built competitiveness. It is therefore expected to be in use for the foreseeable future, and to be similarly applied at the secondary level. It has also been found acceptable by funding partners such Britain's Department for International Development (DfID). Currently, the World Bank is considering waiving its procurement policies in relation to a US$50 million grant that it is extending to Kenya for the purchase of teaching and learning materials in support of FPE. The waiver will mean that the funds will be channelled through the decentralised system. The success of this will no doubt boost the confidence of the sceptics and thus ensure the future of the system not only in Kenya but also elsewhere in Africa.

State of the book sector

As in many other countries in Africa, the Kenyan book sector is dominated by textbooks. However, valiant efforts are being made by most publishers to continue with general publishing, especially of children's books and adult fiction, despite dismal sales.

There are good prospects for the textbook business because of the declaration of FPE and the return of government/donor funding, especially at the primary level.

Mali

For years after independence, Mali, like other French-speaking countries in West Africa, continued to use textbooks published in France. This was made possible by the CONFEMEN project, whereby the former French colonies in Africa would use the same curriculum, developed in co-operation with France. The curriculum co-operation had been initiated by France to strengthen the position of the French language (while creating a large market for French educational publishing).

In 1990, the countries wanted to establish regional textbook co-operation on their own, without France. Under the slogan *'Il faut décoloniser le livre'* ('The book must be de-colonized'), they planned to co-operate with the *Organisation Islamique pour l'Education, la Science et la Culture*, which has a large printing house in Conakry, Guinea. The project failed, as the countries found that, after they became independent, they had developed quite different ideas about the content of education. The young nations were also too nationalistic to be able to use the same textbooks. CONFEMEN still exists, but the publishing has ceased.

The language issue

Many believe that the fact that French has been used in schools from grade one is an important reason for the very low literacy rate in Mali: 39% for men, 23% for women (1995). The former policy of the Ministry of Education, to post teachers in areas where they did not speak the local language, did not make their task any easier. Between 1979 and 1986, the use of local languages as the medium of instruction was tested in the lower grades of primary education in 108 schools. As could be expected, the pupils learned much faster, but changing to French in upper grades was difficult. A system of bilingual education, *classe a pédagogie convergent*, is therefore being tested in a large number of schools and is showing very good results. The system will be introduced gradually in the whole country.

Textbook publishing today

Books for primary education have been published in Mali since 1994/5, when the Ministry of Education took up textbook development. The books are printed in France or Canada after international competitive bidding.

The government of Mali is well aware of the importance of an active commercial book sector for national development (the previous president, Mr. Konaré was once Director of the publishing house Editions Jamana). Different ways of supporting local publishing, e.g. through the reduction of taxes, have also been discussed and a working group within the Ministry of Culture is busy developing a *Politique National du Livre* (national book policy).

The first step towards liberalisation of the textbook market was taken in 2001, when the government invited the four largest publishers in Mali – Editions Jamana, Editions Saheli, Editions Faida and Figuier – to take over the publishing of existing textbook titles. The publishing rights are being transferred to these publishers, grade by grade and subject by subject. The publishers are expected to revise and modernize the titles. The publishers Edicef and Hatier also publish some books for education.

For any new manuscripts from the Ministry of Education, publishers must, however, be selected through international competitive bidding, according to the policy of the financing agency, the World Bank. It will be difficult for the poor and inexperienced local publishers to compete with the French or Canadian companies for contracts if the books are in French. But the titles for *classe à pédagogie convergente* use both French and a local language, and for such publishing the publishers feel that they will have an advantage over the multinational publishers.

The first step towards liberalisation of the textbook market was taken when publishers took over the publishing rights of existing books. Within three years they will recruit authors themselves, according to the publishers' own time schedule. The final goal is that publishers publish their own titles and (after government approval) market and sell them through booksellers.

Book distribution

Marketing will be the most difficult part of the liberalisation. There are practically no bookshops outside Bamako, and the population – largely subsistence farmers – rarely have money. Mali has greater distribution problems than any other West African country because of its size – the size of France and Spain put together. The Ministry of Education distributes textbooks once a year using a 'caravan' of military lorries, which visit all parts of the vast country. Every school it passes gets books for free. In Mali, as in most other African countries, the government cannot finance a textbook–pupil ratio of 1:1. Many parents are interested in buying books for their children but, as textbooks for primary school are government property, booksellers are not allowed to sell them. This has led to the development of a *marché informel* (informal market) for stolen books, as in Tanzania before its liberalisation.

Bookselling

One bookseller explained how he cannot sell books for primary school for obvious reasons, but he sells textbooks for secondary education, which are all imported from France. This market is entirely unregulated and there is no government evaluation or approval of such books. There are 140 private secondary schools in the country. He also sells imported trade books to professional people – in subjects like business administration, IT, medicine, etc. He had a few novels by local authors (in French) on the shelves, but novels are purchased only by foreigners and, occasionally, by nationals living abroad who are visiting their old country or returning. Books are expensive in Mali because the country is landlocked and air transport is expensive. There is also 11% import duty on books, plus sales tax.

Organisations of importance for the book sector

Since 2000 there has been a cultural organisation in Mali called AFLAM (Appui à la Filière du Livre), which has three main objectives:

- Strengthening/creation of public reading centers/libraries (*centers de lecture publique*).
- Strengthening/creation of school libraries.
- Development of human resources in the public and private sector.

AFLAM buys books for public libraries and school libraries from booksellers through local competitive bidding. AFLAM is also one of the organisers of the Bamako book fair SALIBA, *Salon du Livre de Bamako*, which took place for the second time in December 2002. AFLAM has three partners: the Government of Mali (the Ministry of Education and the Ministry of Culture), the Embassy of France (development co-operation department) and the professional organisations in the book sector – there is both a publishers' association and a booksellers' association.

Mali receives support for the education system from a large number of funding agencies: the World Bank, the European Union, UNDP, UNESCO, France, USA, Germany, the Netherlands, Canada, Switzerland and Belgium. Since 2002 it also receives considerable funds from Sweden, through the Embassy of the Netherlands, which has a well-established development co-operation programme in Mali.

COUNTRY STUDIES

Chapter 9

Mauritius

Background

Prior to 1977, primary and secondary school textbooks in Mauritius were being published by Nathan, a French publishing company, and Longman, a British publishing house. This reflects the early settlement of the French and British in Mauritius and their subsequent business interests, even when the small Indian Ocean island has a large Indian population. Nationalism resulted in the setting up in 1977 of a local national publishing company, the Editions de l'Océan Indien (EOI).

EOI is a parastatal, with 60% shareholding held by the State Investment Corporation, (Mauritius), 10% by Nathan (France), 10% by Longman (UK), 10% by Singapore National Printing Corporation (Singapore) and 10% by Macmillan Education (UK).

The privileged monopolistic position of EOI enabled the company to publish textbooks that were developed and written by the National Curriculum Center for Research and Development (NCCRD) of the Ministry of Education and Scientific Research (MESR).

Change in Textbook Publishing

In 1994, when the budget for MESR was reduced, the Ministry began questioning the monopoly of EOI and sought a better offer in textbook prices and service delivery.

This, coupled with growing pressure from other publishers to liberalise the textbook market, resulted in the introduction of open tenders at primary school level, and any winning bidder – printer or publisher – was awarded the job. The print-run is based on the number of schools and pupils.

After the change to an open system, Editions Le Printemps Limited (ELP), a privately owned company that is a publisher, importer and distributor as well as a bookseller, started developing a series of supporting textbooks that were subsequently approved and used in schools.

Textbook Provision Policy

The country has no formal textbook or book policy, neither has the government any formal working structure through a professional book association. MESR collaborates with the two main textbook publishers – EOI and ELP.

EOI, which between 1977 and 1994 used to publish exclusively all primary school textbooks, has since lost Standards 1–3 educational materials because the MESR decided to take the work directly to printers. This essentially affects reprints of previously published and printed textbooks. The experience gained by MESR has created a situation whereby educational materials for upper primary, i.e. Standards 4–6, would easily follow and so be taken away as well.

At primary school level, MESR, through NCCRD has a team of curriculum specialists and trained teachers as well as textbook writers. NCCRD is responsible for developing textbooks, and thereafter for preparing the texts for printing. The Ministry also meets the cost of production and ensures that the textbooks are distributed through regional warehouses. Heads of schools collect their requirements from these warehouses. Books are given to schoolchildren free of charge.

The Ministry, on the other hand, has acknowledged that its involvement in textbook development and printing is a time-wasting process, and that not enough research has been undertaken to establish what should be done in the book sector.

Until 2001, when the government of Mauritius changed the educational policy, getting children who completed upper-primary education into quality junior-secondary schools was competitive. As a way of ensuring a place at a quality junior secondary school, parents arranged extra, private, tuition for their children. Such tuition created an opportunity for enterprising teachers who offer private tuition to get involved in writing textbooks, which they self-published. Some of these titles were sold by the teachers themselves, while, depending on their popularity, some copies were available in bookshops.

At junior secondary school level, covering Forms I and II, the market is, unlike at primary school level, still open for any individual or publisher to develop textbooks for use in schools.

The Textbook Standardization Committee of MESR, comprising heads of subject departments, meets once every two years to review the textbooks on the market, in use or available, in order to recommend those that should be on the official list of prescribed textbooks. The official list is sent to all schools in July, from which they select according to their preference and according to which booksellers they would like to use.

At Forms III–V and Form VI (middle and upper secondary) level students take terminal examinations set by Cambridge School Certificate examining boards of the United Kingdom. It follows therefore that selection of textbooks is influenced by the list of books prescribed by the relevant overseas examining board.

Parents are responsible for buying textbooks from bookshops at secondary school level. The role of publishers is to promote their textbooks by marketing them in various schools.

MESR has a book-loan scheme for needy students. Under the scheme textbooks are issued on loan free of charge to needy students at state and private secondary schools. There are criteria for children to qualify under this scheme, but adequate advertisements in the press are made prior to the start of the school year.

Publishing

EOI and ELP, being the two major textbook publishers, produce 95% of the country's textbook requirement at junior-secondary school level.

The annual output of books published is thirty supporting textbooks. This information is readily available from the national ISBN secretariat, which is located at EOI. The average print-run for textbooks is between 22,000 and 26,000 copies, while between 3,000 and 10,000 copies of supporting textbooks are printed. At tertiary level virtually all textbooks are imported.

Despite having a total population of only 1.2 million, schools teach diverse local languages such as Hindi, Tamil, Marathi, Chinese, Urdu, Arabic and Telugu, for which textbooks are required in addition to those in English and French.

The Mauritius Publishers Association (MPA) is almost moribund, with seven active members – the barest minimum number of members required by law in Mauritius to form an association. The majority, as in the case of EOI and ELP, are involved in other activities such as importing, distribution, bookselling, and publishing materials for the tourist market.

Authorship

Apart from the MPA, the Mauritius Writers' Association brings together more writers of fiction than of textbooks. The Ministry of Arts and Culture provides some funds in its budget for creative writing to support the publishing of deserving works.

Bookselling and Distribution

There are not less than sixty bookshops in Mauritius, catering for the population, whose literacy rate is estimated at 80 per cent. Of these, fifteen are good, well-stocked, 'regular' bookshops. The rest are basically seasonal – operating between October and the end of January, when parents, schools and school managers are busy buying prescribed textbooks for the middle- and upper-secondary school level. It will be recalled that, from primary school level up to Form II, the Ministry of Education and Scientific Research distributes textbooks free of charge.

There are two trade associations – the Booksellers Association (BSA) and the Booksellers and Stationery Owners Association (BSOA). Membership of the two associations is voluntary, but some potential members perceive no benefit in belonging to either. The BSOA is more active than the BSA. Basically there is no co-operation among booksellers as competition is rife – everyone for themselves!

Selling textbooks is the major activity, with some books being exported to Uganda, Zambia, Zimbabwe and Kenya. Mauritius also imports a substantial quantity of books from overseas because of the large number of students sitting for Cambridge School and Higher School Certificate examinations, as well as to cater for the professional and tertiary institutions.

Government Support to the Book Industry

Government support for the publishing and printing sector is channelled through the Development Bank of Mauritius (DBM). There are two categories – the publishing and printing sector and the local newspaper sector. The small and medium enterprise department of the DBM disburses loans of up to three million rupees (US$107,000) to purchase new equipment at 10% interest (instead of the normal 14%), repayable over a period of five years. The large enterprise department of DBM, on the other hand, provides loans of up to twenty-five million rupees (US$890,000) at the same rate, repayable over a period of five years or more, depending on the amount of loan, with a one-year moratorium. An additional loan of up to five million rupees (US$178,570) at 12.5% interest, repayable in five years, is available to purchase IT tools – hardware or software.

The policy of the Government of Mauritius, through the DBM, is guided by the need to encourage local printers to upgrade printing equipment regularly so that they are able to compete favourably on the international market, to support printers to improve quality of production, to encourage local printers to export their printing services, and to enable them to provide quick delivery of printed works. Curiously, although DBM officials emphasized the support given to printers, some of the printers were not aware of this facility.

Incentives to develop the printing industry are further supported by the Mauritius Investment Development Programme, and most government trade delegations outside Mauritius do include printers.

Printing

There are not less than 300 printers in Mauritius, out of whom 15 are engaged in textbook printing. Almost 90 per cent of the printing machines, most of which are the latest models in printing technology, are imported from Germany. Three of the major printers export their printing service as far away as Senegal, Chad, Burkina Faso, Togo, Ghana, Nigeria, Côte d'Ivoire, South Africa, Zambia, Madagascar, Tanzania, and Uganda. Some publishers in England have recently shown interest in getting some of their books printed in Mauritius.

Statistics

MESR publishes and maintains comprehensive accurate educational statistics that are readily available to any interested party. The data contained in the Digest of Educational Statistics cover such subjects as expenditure on education, pre-primary education, primary education, secondary education, technical and vocational education, and post-secondary education, and includes information on numbers of educational institutions, enrolment, and teaching personnel. The Digest clearly helps the work of educational planners, policy-makers and researchers.

Non-Governmental Organisations

No development partners are involved in the book sector of Mauritius. NGOs, however, do play a useful role in the pre-primary school sector, using guidelines prepared by NCCRD.

Partnership

It is evident that there is currently very little public/private partnership in the book sector because the system seems to be self-regulating, save in the area of investment in printing.

There is no structure for any other collaboration except when it comes to tenders. Equally, there is no policy framework to bring the various stakeholders together. The acknowledgement by the Ministry of Education and Scientific Research that its involvement in textbook development and printing is time-wasting may, however, signal a recognition of the need for a change in the roles of the government and book industry through partnership.

Mozambique

In Portugal's Províncias Ultramarinas (overseas provinces), schools were primarily agencies for the spread of the Portuguese language and culture. Textbooks came from Lisbon and pupils studied the history and geography of Portugal. When Mozambique became independent in 1975, the new government took over a country with 76% illiteracy and with very few trained cadres to carry out the necessary reforms.

Textbook monopoly publishing

Mozambique urgently needed a new education system and new textbooks. In 1978, the National Institute of Educational Development (INDE) was established as a UNESCO project under the Ministry of Education, MINED. The Institute was responsible for pedagogic research, curriculum development, textbook development and publishing.

The first textbooks for the National Education System were published in 1983 by the Núcleo Editorial, an editorial department within INDE itself, but soon afterwards a separate publishing house called Editora Escolar was established. Editora Escolar first belonged to INDE but was later incorporated with the government's distribution company for school material, Diname. The well-equipped publishing house was financed by Sida and would continue to receive financial support and technical assistance for more than ten years. All books for schools were based on manuscripts developed by INDE until 1991, when the publisher got permission to recruit writers of its own. Some secondary school titles and children's books were also published, but Editora Escolar/Diname did not succeed in making publishing for the open market profitable.

There was no more publishing for primary schools, as the planned curriculum reform had stalled. Low salaries made it difficult to keep staff, and during the 1990s most of the qualified editors, illustrators and designers left the company.

A monopoly system with decentralised procurement

Diname's textbooks, which cover all grades for primary and secondary school (Grades 1–12), are sold in bookshops at non-subsidized prices, which means that few parents outside the cities can afford to buy them. However, in each of the ten provinces there is a school fund called Caixa Escolar, financed by the government and funding agencies, which provides books for poorer pupils in primary school.

In poor rural areas where the population are subsistence farmers, practically all children receive free books. In other areas where Caixa Escolar finances only some of the books needed, it is up to the head teachers to decide which pupils should get free books. This is a sensitive issue and there is always a risk that families with the right contacts get favours.

The following is broadly how Caixa Escolar normally functions:

- Based on requests from schools (and available funds), the Caixa Escolar in each province orders textbooks from Diname. Each Caixa Escolar also selects distributors (traders or booksellers) to handle the distribution, through local competitive bidding.
- Diname produces the books and sells them at wholesale prices to the traders or booksellers, which have been selected by the respective Caixa Escolar.
- The traders deliver the books to the schools and, after showing proof of delivery, are paid by the province's Education Director for books and distribution services.

Today, however, the system is more complicated. The printing of primary school books takes place in Canada, financed by the Canadian development agency, CIDA. This means that Diname receives printed books from Canada free of charge, but charges the distributors the full price for the books. As CIDA's objective is not to subsidize Diname but the Ministry of Education, Diname has to pay 80 per cent of its receipts to MINED/Caixa Escolar.

Liberalisation

In 1998, the government of Mozambique decided to liberalise textbook publishing, printing and distribution. According to the new policy, both the government-owned printer, CEGRAF, and the publisher Diname were to be privatised and measures would be taken to encourage the development of a national commercial book industry. CEGRAF was soon sold to private investors and Diname was also put up for sale. Many investors were interested in buying Diname, but the privatisation process was never completed.

A new curriculum for primary schools was finally ready in 2001 and, in accordance with the government's new textbook policy, commercial publishers would now compete for contracts to develop the new textbooks. The rules of the funding agency, the World Bank, said that publishers had to be selected through international competitive bidding. Mozambique had only two publishers – the educational publisher, Diname, which was still owned by the government, and Moçambique Editora, a subsidiary of Texto Editora in Lisbon, which has existed in Mozambique for six years and has some Mozambican partners. Moçambique Editora was pre-qualified but Diname was not allowed to participate because it was government-owned. Diname later tried to enter the competition as a partner of the Portuguese publisher Porto Editora, but had to desist after protests from the other publishers.

A total of seven publishers were pre-qualified, but three of them withdrew their proposals when they realised the size of the investment that would be required. Four companies remained: Longman (UK), Macmillan (UK), Moçambique Editora and Porto Editora (Portugal). All of them have offices in Maputo.

The publishers have been required to develop textbook titles and teacher's guides in all subjects for Grades 1–5, which means that more than a hundred titles have been written, edited, typeset and illustrated at the respective publisher's own risk. Most of the development work appears to have been done abroad, but in some cases also Mozambican writers and illustrators have been engaged. The titles will be presented to MINED for evaluation in the form of colour copies and dummies to show the binding style. Although the publishers will not print their books before they have been approved, the development of all these titles signifies a large investment for all participants. It is expected that the new books will be considerably (probably three to four times) more expensive than the existing books from Diname.

A special textbook evaluation board, CALE (Conselho de Avaliação do Livro Escolar), has been established to ensure that all books conform to curriculum requirements and combine quality in content with suitable teaching methodology. Detailed guidelines for the evaluation process have been developed to guarantee objective treatment A secretariat has been established in MINED, and for each subject all titles will be evaluated by a subject panel consisting of a coordinator and three evaluators. All coordinators and evaluators were trained in a three-day programme in Maputo in November 2002.

In the long term, book selection will take place at school level, and in the medium term at provincial level, according to MINED's policy. In the short term, however (as decided in November 2002), the Ministry of Education will decide centrally which books from the approved list will be purchased for the districts. Only one title for each subject/grade (for Grades 1, 3 and 6) will be purchased in 2004. The following year, centrally selected titles (also one per subject/grade) will be purchased for Grades 2, 4 and 7. Publishers whose titles are approved but not selected for central purchase will not be able to market and sell their titles until after the districts have taken over selection and purchase.

The fact that Mozambique already has decentralised textbook procurement makes the transition to a market system easier than in many other countries. Parents will continue to buy books from traders, and Caixa Escolar will provide books for the poorer pupils. The MINED has also decided that all publishers will have to use Diname's distribution system, which is well established with warehouses in eight of the provinces. The decision was a set-back for Moçambique Editora, which had already established a distribution company, DISMOC.

The language issue

The official language of Mozambique is still Portuguese and, from Grade 1, this is also the medium of instruction in schools, but Mozambique has over twenty national languages, and INDE has for many years had a very active research programme in bilingual education. In the new curriculum, which will be introduced in the schools in 2004, 'ability to communicate correctly, both orally and by writing, in Mozambican languages and in Portuguese' is one of the Skills and Basic Competencies.

General publishing

When Mozambique became independent there were some printing houses in the country but no tradition of commercial publishing. The National Institute for Books and Records (INLD), was established in 1978 and given the monopoly position as book publisher (textbooks were excepted). From the beginning, the INLD had a very ambitious policy of publishing Mozambican authors, and when it lost its monopoly status in 1989 it had published more than 700 titles. Its monopoly status had effectively prevented the development of private publishing in Mozambique, but when the monopoly ended, INLDs role was reversed: INLD now works to promote commercial publishing and bookselling, and the Institute functions more like a book council. But with a national literacy rate of 42% and widespread poverty, it is not easy to make commercial publishing profitable. The late Mr Julio Navarro of INLD used the expression 'virtual publishers and booksellers' to signify that they could exist only as long as they were subsidized.

Printing

The primary school textbooks, with their large print-runs, represent a very important market segment for the printers in Maputo. The new owners of CEGRAF have invested heavily in modern equipment for textbook production and there are several other well-equipped printers in Maputo. A UNESCO study of printing capacity was carried out in December 2002 and the preliminary findings confirmed that local production capacity was enough to satisfy the country's textbook needs. Unfortunately, the local printing industry has been barred from this profitable market as the textbooks from Diname have been printed in Canada, financed by CIDA. In December 2002, the three publishers who won the competition to supply new textbooks still did not know whether they would be free to arrange the printing themselves or if Canadian printers would have to be involved.

According to INLD, both paper and other inputs for book production and finished books should be exempt of Customs duties, according to a law from June 1998. But this law seems to be unknown to Mozambique's Customs Department. According to Diname's editorial department, printers in Mozambique do pay import duty on paper for production. A publisher who recently transported a laser-typesetter from Maputo to the manufacturer's agent in South Africa for warranty service had to pay US$1,900 (17% of its value) to the Mozambican Customs, and people importing books from South Africa have to pay more in import duty than they had paid for the books.

Organisations of importance for the book sector

Mozambique's writers have for many years had their own organisation, Associação dos Escritores Moçambicanos. The UNESCO office in Maputo is very active in the book sector. Among other things, it has assisted MINED with the practical preparations for textbook evaluation in co-operation with Danida, and the organisation has also initiated the development of a national book policy, which will include textbooks for schools. The work on this important document is led by the INLD.

Preparations are also under way for the establishment of a joint trade organisation of publishers and booksellers. The Fundo Bibliografico da Lingua Portuguesa (FBLP) has its office in Maputo. It is an EU-funded regional project for the five Portuguese-speaking countries in Africa (PALOP). Although originally conceived to promote publishing in Africa, FBLP is basically focused on the promotion of the Portuguese language, through the distribution of books from Portugal.

Unlike most other countries visited, Mozambique has an art school, Escola de Artes Visuais, which co-operates with the publishers and has trained several good textbook illustrators. Textbooks also need good photo illustrations and the Associação Moçambicana de Fotografia has managed to raise the professional standard of photography in Mozambique through more than twenty years of work with exhibitions, courses and other activities.

Lessons learnt

When Mozambique became independent, one of the government's first priorities was national textbook development and publishing. With financial and technical assistance from Sida and other co-operating partners, a functioning distribution system, Caixa Escolar, was built, and Editora Escolar (later Diname), functioned both as a publisher and a training institution for editors, graphic designers, illustrators, photographers and printers. It was expected that the decision in 1998 to liberalise the book sector, in combination with the introduction of a new curriculum, would lead to a revitalization of Diname and the growth of new local initiatives in publishing – possibly in joint ventures with foreign publishers. Instead, Diname, the publisher of Mozambique's textbooks for twenty years, has been effectively barred from publishing primary school textbooks for the foreseeable future. In the early 1980s, all textbooks for Mozambique were printed in Maputo. Today, they are printed in Canada.

It is difficult to see much positive in recent developments in the book sector in Mozambique. There may be many reasons for this, but the rigid policies of the two funding agencies, CIDA and the World Bank, have not been helpful.

Nigeria

Brief Background of Country Publishing

Early missionaries who settled in Nigeria are credited for opening elementary schools that taught people to read and write, while the publishing that followed essentially supported the educational programme of the colonial government. Oxford University Press initiated visits by its representatives to Nigeria in 1928 that resulted in the introduction of the first Oxford English courses adapted to local educational needs in 1936. Thus Oxford University Press (OUP) became the first commercial publisher to open an office in Ibadan in 1949 and a warehouse in 1959.

The setting up of the OUP office was closely followed by the incorporation of the first indigenous privately owned publishing company, Onibonoje Press and Book Industries in 1958. Evans Brothers, Longman , Thomas Nelson, Macmillan, Heinemann Educational Books and a few other British publishers and indigenous Nigerian publishers also opened offices afterwards because of the opportunities created by the growing enrolment in the educational system.

It is interesting to record that the Midwestern State government of the country also decided to set up in September 1970 the Ethiope Publishing Corporation to publish educational and general books. Though state-owned, Ethiope Publishing Corporation was a purely commercial company that did not enjoy any special advantages or privileges as a result of its relationship with the state government, as was the case with similar state publishing houses in other parts of Africa. The Corporation managed to publish some textbooks and collaborated with Ibadan University Press and OUP in editing and producing scholarly works.

A major break came in 1977 when the government introduced the Nigerian Enterprises Promotion Decree, or the Indigenization Policy, and all foreign publishing companies were forced relinquish 60 per cent of their equity to indigenous Nigerians. Today all former multinational publishing companies are incorporated as Nigerian local companies.

It is this background that has made book publishing and bookselling in Nigeria by and large private-sector led, but the government, at federal or state level, has always played a major role in influencing the status of the book industry through its policies on textbook provision.

In a vast country that has an estimated population of more than 120 million people and more than 60,000 various institutions of learning, including primary schools, secondary schools, colleges of education, polytechnics and universities, with a total enrolment of about 30 million, the challenge to the book industry to supply textbooks is almost unimaginable. In general, there is a clear view that the book industry in Nigeria is still expanding because, in addition to new government schools, private universities, colleges and primary and secondary schools are being opened.

Given a proportion of textbooks to general books of about 70% to 30% in most developing countries, publishers and booksellers have no option but look to the government's educational policy for a conducive environment in which to operate. For instance, the National Policy on Education is to make sure that the medium of instruction in the primary schools is initially the mother-tongue or the language of the immediate community, that the government ensures that all schools are properly equipped to promote sound and effective teaching, and in particular, that suitable textbooks and libraries are provided for schools, and that states set up a National Committee to advise on the production of suitable textbooks and instructional materials for the whole Federation. It is no wonder that the Introduction to the Policy states, 'Education in Nigeria is no more a private enterprise, but a huge government venture that has witnessed a progressive evolution of government's complete and dynamic intervention and active participation.'

Nigeria has had a long experience of trying to find and devise measures to address issues of sustainable educational as well as general book provision, given the massive and growing population. The Fourth National Development Plan (1981–1985), for instance, stipulated 100 per cent local production of all textbooks and equipment at both primary- and secondary school levels and 50 per cent local production of all educational materials at tertiary and professional levels. In essence, the stipulation of the Plan translated into a national requirement of 296 million books. Such a massive requirement created a challenge to the Federal Government and to key providers, such as writers, publishers, printers and booksellers, to find a lasting solution. Government alone could not possibly resolve the issue.

It is perhaps instructive to acknowledge that the country's pursuit for solutions to problems of book scarcity could be considered as the genesis of public/private partnership in Nigeria's book sector. A series of more than ten major workshops, and national and international meetings or conferences were held and specific measures proposed. These included a UNESCO Meeting of Book Experts in Africa, the Ile-Ife International Conference on Publishing and Book Development, the First Nigeria National Congress on Books, the Task Force on the Scarcity of Books and Stationery, the Panel on Book Policy for Nigeria, National Seminars on Reducing Cost of Textbooks in Nigeria, and the

Review Workshop for Solving Problems of the Nigeria Book Industry and Formulation of Implementation Strategies. At each of these gatherings, participation was drawn from a host of active professional book associations or bodies and agencies, all committed to ensuring that in their respective ways they fully participated in the national book industry and positively contributed to national development.

It was at one of the foregoing gatherings that the government was implored not to be involved in the writing of textbooks; instead, it should provide the curricula to be used by private companies in writing the books.

Since the late 1980s every effort has been made to formulate a well-articulated national book policy for Nigeria to guide future national book-development programmes; however, the country does not have an officially approved policy. The prevailing practice and procedures in the country's educational system constitute its 'policy' for textbook provision.

Textbook Provision Policy

Policy on textbook provision in Nigeria has been influenced by the leadership in each state, particularly after the country attained political independence in 1960. In some regions of the country the government supplied books free of charge for certain subjects and grades, while other regions supplied all books free; others required parents to buy the textbooks, or books were supplied free of charge but their ownership was vested in the schools.

Nigeria is made up of 36 states in which private, state and federal tertiary institutions operate. The Federal Government is responsible for the national curriculum, accreditation and monitoring of educational standards, etc. Publishing and distribution of textbooks, on the other hand, has largely remained in the hands of the private, commercial sector. It is at state level that the procedure for developing and evaluating textbooks is effected and exercised.

At state level, publishers periodically submit books for various subjects and levels to the state Ministry of Education for evaluation, and, if approved, the titles are placed on the official list of 'approved' textbooks for use in schools. It is up to schools or parents to select books of their choice from that list for purchase and use. The number of titles approved for each subject varies according to the number of titles submitted by publishers for evaluation: as many as seven titles may be approved. For primary schools, the approval is made once every six years; for junior and senior secondary schools, it is once every three years.

Even though the approval of textbooks is done on state-by-state basis, the subject content should meet requirements of the national curriculum. On this basis, therefore, publishers strive to satisfy this curriculum in the hope that a title approved by one state may also be approved by a number of other states. At secondary school level publishers also make every effort to meet the syllabus of the Anglophone (regional) West African Examination Council (WAEC). In the event that the title is approved for WAEC the market for such a title goes beyond Nigeria.

Authorship: Textbooks and General Books

The initial entry into Nigeria of multinational publishers that saw the country as a market outlet led the same publishers to identify local educationists and teachers to develop publishable materials. The transfer of writing skills from foreign publishers, coupled with strong tradition in fiction and drama, enabled Nigeria to produce a large complement of authors, both for fiction and for textbooks.

At primary school level Nigeria depends wholly on indigenous authorship, while at secondary school level at least 80 per cent of the authors are Nigerian, the balance of the textbooks being published under licence or imported. At tertiary and professional level, 40 per cent of specialist authors are Nigerians. Thus, as far as local authors are concerned, Nigeria boasts of a host of well-established and aspiring authors for both educational and general books and a pool of skilled book professionals to maintain high quality publications.

In spite of the country's massive population, publishing in indigenous language is limited to three major ones – Yoruba, Hausa and Igbo. Publishers tend to commission print-runs not according to the anticipated readership but on specific demand, as population *per se* does not necessarily justify large print-runs as it has proved difficult to sell copies. There is some consolation in this regard as a result of government policy to teach children in the mother tongue for the first three years of formal education.

Bookselling and Distribution

Because publishing in the country originally followed the English tradition of marketing and distribution activities being incorporated within the firm's publishing activity, independent/external bookselling remains the weakest link. For a long time booksellers have been short-changed. Publishers still sell their books directly to government through schools or school libraries. Some publishers have even established bookshops and so compete with booksellers who should be their immediate customers. Where the publishing company has no regional office or warehouse, agents are appointed to cover such areas. As a result booksellers remain deprived of business that would enable them to raise their capital base to expand their operations, including meeting payment schedules.

The sidelining of booksellers was further enhanced by government's procurement of books directly from publishers even under such projects as the World Bank Book Project and the Petroleum Trust Fund Book Purchase Programme. Among reasons advanced for ignoring the booksellers are: failure by publishers to appreciate the long-term benefit to work with booksellers; numerous small bookshops interested in handling textbooks only at the peak 'profitable' time at the beginning of the school year; booksellers abusing credit facilities; the creation of 'expensive' middle parties; and some booksellers being responsible for selling pirated textbooks. The state ministries of education are happier to deal directly with publishers with whom they have very good working relationship rather than with booksellers.

Recognition of Roles: Genesis for Partnership

The enormous potential book population and a thriving Nigerian Publishers Association (NPA) of more than 100 active members has, however, a comparatively small number of notable major publishers of textbooks, who, though originally multinational, were indigenized up to 80 per cent under the Indigenization Decree of 1977.

There is growing acknowledgement that publishers are better off concentrating on publishing and thereby shifting the function of marketing and distribution to booksellers. On the other hand, the Nigerian Booksellers Association (NBA), with a membership of more than 300, also acknowledges that Nigeria is a big country, that communication is difficult, and that the Association is weak. A list of NBA members is not available, meetings are not as well attended as those of other associations, and, because 'old timers' are used to old bookselling methods, the book trade has not improved.

There is a general consensus that the relationship with other book-sector players is symbiotic: the Ministry of Education provides the curriculum and school statistics, schools identify problems, the NPA helps resolve problems, and authors, publishers and booksellers facilitate the generation, development, production and distribution of books. It is in this regard that a national book policy would clearly spell out the roles and the *modus operandi* of the partnership of the stakeholders. For professional associations, a mutually agreed code of conduct or practice would find a place in such a policy and partnership. It should also be noted that some of the stakeholders have multiple roles, i.e. they are publishers as well as printers and booksellers. This multiple role may need to be re-defined.

Efforts by the Nigerian Publishers Association have greatly improved the relationship and interaction with the Nigerian government at both state and federal levels. In fact, the Oyo State Government donated the Book House occupied by the NPA. Dialogue with various key stakeholders has also been enhanced, and even booksellers are invited to address NPA meetings.

Statistics

In general, most states as well as the Federal Ministry of Education maintain accurate and up-to-date statistics on enrolment. These statistics are readily available to interested parties on request. Publishers, however, find it difficult to depend entirely on these statistics in determining print-runs even for approved titles, as there are other, competing titles. Experience has shown that it is more advisable to rely on in-house research and previous sales figures rather than on official enrolment figures that tend to be far in excess of actual book demand.

Copyright and Piracy

The Nigerian Publishers Association and all publishers consider piracy as the major problem adversely affecting publishing in Nigeria. They claim that between 30% and 40% of the textbook market is lost on account of piracy. They claim that some booksellers sell pirated books at cheap prices and, although there are copyright laws in place, enforcement of compliance is rather weak and civil court proceedings take too long (some cases have been going on for more than five years) to deter culprits. In fact there is as long list of court cases still unresolved. Police do not tackle piracy with the same zeal that they use on thieves! The degree of concern is ably demonstrated by the fact that some publishers affected have, in collaboration with the police, carried out physical raids on premises believed to stock pirated publications.

The problem of piracy in Nigeria has also been exacerbated by the massive geographical spread of the country, which publishers and booksellers cannot easily cover and are therefore unable to supply books to. In such cases it also becomes difficult to monitor incidents of piracy.

The Nigerian Publishers Association has continued working closely with the Nigerian Copyright Commission to redress the situation through stricter enforcement of the Copyright Act, and public education through seminars.

Fortunately, the Copyright (Amendment) Decree of 1999 offers some remedies to delays and enforcement. Under this amended Decree, the Copyright Inspector has all the powers, rights and privileges of a police officer, as defined under the Police Act, to investigate and prosecute. Whereas previously a police officer was required to seize incriminating (pirated) materials, arrest and interrogate suspects, and draw up all the documents required to facilitate prosecution, the publishers are now able to prosecute directly. Copyrights Inspectors who are lawyers approved by the Nigerian Copyright Commission can prosecute cases of infringement without going through the Director of Public Prosecutions.

Printing

Nigeria has sufficient local printing capacity. The printing equipment used is quite modern. At present most publishers, by choice, undertake up to 90 per cent of their printing within Nigeria, with the balance sent out to countries in the Far East such as Malaysia. The limiting factor for local printing is the supply of paper, which is normally imported. Local paper mills that have tried to provide an alternative source of supply failed to do so because of high costs.

For the last two years publishers in Nigeria have had to grapple with the problem of a 2.5% levy on imported books imposed by the Federal Government. The Nigerian Publishers Association has made representation to have the levy abolished, as it is affecting the prices of imported books, particularly technical and tertiary level ones.

Nigeria is a signatory to the UNESCO Florence Agreement of 1950, whose spirit and intent is to facilitate the importation of books, *inter alia*, without the imposition of levies. Unless there was proof of abuse of the provision, publishers and booksellers should be able to use this instrument to seek a rebate or abolition of the 2.5% levy on imported books.

Investment

The book industry in Nigeria has been financed mainly by various relevant stakeholders: some of the major publishers have been able to raise investment capital through listing on the stock exchange, while occasional schemes such as the Petroleum Trust Fund and World Bank library contracts have helped to inject money into the sector. Publishers that do not have access to major tenders or income from large orders generally fail to expand their activities or business. This is where an appropriate national book policy framework would facilitate the provision of and access to investment funding.

Non-Governmental Organisations

There are a number of non-governmental organisations involved in one aspect or another of the book sector. Of special note among such NGOs is the Nigerian Book Foundation (NBF). It is an independent, non-governmental, non-sectional and non-profit organisation. It serves as the main forum of interaction for members of associations in the book industry, such as authors, publishers, printers, booksellers and librarians. Included in the membership are representatives of ministries responsible for education and culture, of the national library, representatives of organisations that are relevant to book development, and people appointed for their particular interest in the book industry.

The NBF, which looks after the professional practice of the trades, was established in 1991 and has a seat on the board of the National Educational Research and Development Council. This is an important board that formulates and implements national policy on book development in Nigeria.

With the mission of facilitating the development of a vibrant book industry in Nigeria, the NBF's main objective is 'to encourage the reading habit among Nigerians and promote through books, ideas and ideals that would enhance the socio-cultural development of the country'.

The Foundation as an umbrella organisation endeavours to bring together the key governmental and non-governmental stakeholders in the book industry to ensure that all components of the book chain function to the full and that the state provides a conducive environment for the industry to flourish.

Other relevant NGOs are the Children's Literature Association of Nigeria (CLAN), that encourages reading among children and the provision of suitable reading materials for them; the Young Readers' Club (YRC); the Association of Nigerian Authors (ANA); the Readers Association of Nigeria (RAN); the Network for Promotion of Reading (NEP-READ); Women Writers of Nigeria (WRITA); the West African Association of Book Editors (AWABE); and the Nigerian Association of Researchers and Teachers of Publishing (NARTOP).

The Literacy Enhancement Assistance Programme (LEAP), is another NGO that appears to have made an impression in the book industry; it develops or procures literacy books for supply to selected libraries for Classes 3 and 4.

Prospects

The involvement in textbook publishing and distribution by the government in Nigeria has by and large been occasional and minimal, a situation that has been firmly guided by the private sector. While maintenance of the status quo would be acceptable, it would be useful to refine and enhance the public/private partnerships through a policy that can serve as a guide for all the parties involved. Such a guide would help in facilitating the resolution of problems that continue to adversely affect the production and provision of textbooks in Nigeria.

Senegal

The education system and the language issue

Dakar has a famous university and the country has a highly educated intellectual élite, but the literacy rate in Senegal is very low. The school system has a high dropout rate and only one in three pupils pass the 6th grade examinations. One reason attributed to the poor performance of the education system is the fact that French is used as medium of instruction from first grade. This is a major obstacle to learning, as the absolute majority of the pupils speak only indigenous languages at home. Many children do not attend the state schools but are sent to the informal Koran schools instead. In the Koran schools these children, called *talibs*, study only Arabic and the Koran.

The Quality Education for All Project is designed to establish universal primary education in Senegal. Among the measures now being taken to improve the situation are:

modernizing and formalizing the Koran education, introducing some school subjects from formal education (for example, mathematics and French) and vocational training; and

introducing the national languages – Wolof, Pulaar, Sérère, Joola, Balante and Soninké – and Arabic as mediums of instruction in the lower grades of state schools.

The decision to use national languages for initial literacy training and in the transition to French was taken by President Abdoulaye Wade personally, which indicates the importance of this reform. However, more than twenty languages are spoken in Senegal, and to decide which six of these to use in schools has been a politically sensitive issue. A complication is that the orthography of some languages has not yet been standardized. There will probably also be some problems at school level, as many primary school teachers are not able to speak the language of the region in which they work. The old policy was to send teachers to areas where they would have to teach in French.

Initially, the use of national languages will be pilot tested in fifty primary schools and only for two subjects: mathematics and reading and writing. If the pilot test is successful, the system will be implemented in the entire school system.

Publishing

Senegal imported all books for schools from France until 1987, when the curriculum institute, INEADE, started developing books for primary education. The Institute designed, typeset and illustrated the books, so that they were ready for printing, as well as publishing them. Commercial publishers were sometimes involved, but only as intermediaries between INEADE and the printers. Printers were selected through international competitive bidding. All textbooks after 6th grade are still imported from France.

A new curriculum for primary schools is now on the way, and the government has decided that private publishers should develop and publish the necessary books in local languages. Publishers will be selected through international competitive bidding, according to World Bank rules. The process will begin with publishers submitting proposals in the form of sample lessons, and sample page spreads with illustrations, etc., for evaluation. There will be five stages:

- Proposals will be evaluated and approved centrally.
- Two or three approved titles in each subject will be printed and samples sent out to the districts.
- Titles will be selected at district level.
- The selected books will be centrally purchased.
- The books will then be Delivered to the districts/schools.

Initially, only titles in two subjects – mathematics and reading and writing – will be published in this way. The books will be tested in fifty schools. If the test is successful, the publishers will be invited to develop titles in local languages for the four first grades, in all subjects.

The objective of the new system is said to be to raise the quality of education and to support the development of the national book-publishing industry. A flourishing book industry is seen as critical to ensuring the long-term sustainable supply of textbooks to Senegalese schools. Procurement in international competition would normally favour the French and Canadian publishers, but for books in local languages the indigenous publishers should be competitive.

A project to strengthen the local publishing industry through technical assistance has started. The project, which is financed by the Nordic Development Fund and has its office at INEADE, will offer technical assistance to local publishers during the book development process. Unfortunately, the development of syllabuses for teaching in national languages has been much delayed. As a result, the implementation of the textbook project has also been delayed, and only planning and training activities have started so far.

There are three publishers in Dakar – NEAS, ENAS and XAMAL – with the capacity to take up the publishing of textbooks. Some printers also call themselves publishers, but this is probably a result of the unclear roles of the publisher and printer in the past.

The largest and most prestigious publisher is NEAS (Nouvelles Editions Africains de Sénégal), founded by the President Léopold Sédar Senghor in 1972. Books published by NEAS have won two

Noma Awards for Publishing in Africa and some of its titles are among 'Africa's 100 Best Books', a list developed as a project of the Zimbabwe International Book Fair. NEAS has a backlist of 200 literary titles (all now out of print) and 50 new titles in the pipeline, but lacks funds for their production. The company is anxious to become Senegal's leading textbook publisher under the new policy, but the urgent financial problems must first be solved. A Ministry official noted as a general problem that, because of the financial difficulties of local publishers, schools cannot be sure that books published in Senegal will be available when they are needed.

Bookshops

Dakar has two quite large and well-stocked bookshops, Quatre Vents and Clairafrique, but there are very few bookshops in the rest of the country.

Libraries

A librarian at the Ministry of Education in Dakar is responsible for supervising 400 secondary school libraries in Senegal. There are 120 trained librarians, but although the system is well organised, there is little or no money to buy library books. There are also very ambitious plans for a nationwide network of public libraries, but lack of funds has so far prevented their implementation. The 300 rural communities need libraries with books both in French and the local languages. The library system is important for the development of a reading culture and the indigenous publishers regret that this important public/private partnership in the book sector cannot get financing.

Book Policy

The *Direction du Livre et de la Lecture*, in the Ministry of Culture, is responsible for all issues related to books and reading. It has drawn up a *Loi Sénégalaise sur le Livre* – in practice, a national book policy – which was expected soon to be passed.

Tanzania

Tanzania had a state-monopoly system for textbook provision to primary schools since the beginning of the 1970s. Three ministries shared the responsibility for the development, publishing, printing and distribution, and the Swedish International Development Agency (Sida) was involved as supplier of paper and other inputs for production. Because of the divided responsibilities and the lack of a superior controlling function, planning was difficult, costing was impossible, the pedagogical and technical quality of the books was low and the distribution erratic.

In 1991, it was therefore decided to open the school textbook market for commercial publishing. The goal of the new Textbook Policy was a multi-textbook system in which districts (and eventually schools) could select and buy the books they wanted. Implementation began in 1993, under the Pilot Project for Publishing (PPP), also financed by Sida. Only local publishers were invited to publish the first generation of new books. In this way, not only would the Project provide books but the funding would benefit and reactivate the entire book sector. Capacity-building took place both on the private side (publishers and booksellers) and the public side (the Ministry of Education and Culture and district authorities). The market system was introduced grade-by-grade, beginning in 1993. When the project ended in 2000, the market was wholly open for competition, there were new titles in all subjects (even parallel titles in some) and procurement was done in the districts.

Textbook publishing today

Today, Tanzania has some twenty active publishers, and about half of them can be characterized as educational publishers. Among the more successful of these are Ben&Co, Educational Books Publishers, Mture, and Oxford University Press (Tanzania), but general/trade publishers like Macmillan Aidan, E&D, Mkuki na Nyota Publishers, and Readit Books also publish occasional textbook titles. The only remaining state-owned publisher, Tanzania Publishing House, runs a bookshop, but has not done any publishing for a long time. Some publishers have established joint ventures with overseas companies after the PPP ended. These have positive gains in that Tanzania's publishers obtain access to professional competence and capital for investment, but there are those who believe that joint ventures open the door for take-overs and cultural re-colonization. So far, however, the local publishers seem to be doing very well and to be in full control.

All textbooks are evaluated and approved by the Education Materials Approval Committee (EMAC) at the Ministry of

Education and Culture (MOEC). Tanzania has a long history of mistrust between the MOEC and the private sector; it is therefore especially important that the systems for evaluation and approval are objective and transparent. EMAC's members are all respected citizens of high integrity, the evaluation work is strictly regulated, the criteria used for approval are public, there are three independent evaluators for each title, and, finally, publishers also have the right to appeal against EMAC's decisions.

Textbook procurement

Funds for textbooks, mainly from Tanzania's Sector Development Programme, are devolved to the 113 districts in proportion to the size of their school population. The District Education Officers are responsible for the procurement, but as there are already three to four titles to choose from in most subjects, the officers are supposed to consult a book-selection committee, comprising teachers, before placing the orders. The selection committee system was introduced by the Pilot Project for Publishing, but has so far only been implemented in very few districts. Instead, it is intended that individual schools should take over the procurement of textbooks in Tanzania as soon as possible.

Tanzanian publishers have so far not been very interested in publishing for secondary schools; only 15 per cent of primary school students continue after Grade Seven, which means that the market is small. As English is the medium of instruction at this stage, secondary schools use imported books, but secondary school textbooks should also be approved by EMAC.

Bookselling

The liberalisation of textbook provision has unfortunately not led to the development of bookselling on the same scale as that of publishing. Many booksellers took part in training activities organised by PPP, but they were never engaged in the distribution of the PPP books to districts. The publishers did not want to entrust vast quantities of books on credit to between ten and twenty financially weak booksellers. They also saw booksellers as unnecessary middlemen, and took on the distribution to districts themselves.

Booksellers can sell books to parents however. There should be a market for textbooks, at least in the urban areas, as districts can only afford to buy one book per three pupils. But the booksellers' association, BSAT,[6] is not happy about the situation: it has long argued that the schools should be forced by law to buy books only from booksellers, and is convinced that a countrywide network of bookshops would then soon develop.

Interestingly, the need to integrate booksellers into the supply chain has recently been taken up by the publishers' association (PATA). The publishers are beginning to realise that it is impractical for them to visit 113 districts to market their textbook titles; when procurement is decentralised to the 10,500 schools, it will be impossible. PATA may therefore decide that its members will sell textbooks only through registered booksellers. Hopefully, this will soon become a reality: in a free market, a partnership for mutual benefit is more relevant than a law imposed by the government.

The number of BSAT members actually more than doubled to 55 in 2002. This is, however, mainly the result of the Tusome Vitabu project, a local initiative in co-operation with Care, which gave schools in certain regions funds to buy library books from booksellers. The quick growth supports BSAT's view that booksellers would be mushrooming if they could deliver to districts. The rapid increase has not been entirely positive, however. Most of the newly licensed booksellers have no bookshops, and seem to have entered the business only to grab the funds offered by the Care project. With no fixed costs for shops or warehouses, they have been able to take business from established local booksellers: 80 per cent of those who ordered books from the publisher Macmillan Aidan never appeared again after the first order. BSAT is working on a code of conduct and a new system for the authorization of booksellers in co-operation with PATA.

It has also been found that some of the copies delivered to the Tusome Vitabu project did not originate from the publishers but had been reprinted without permission. Piracy of textbooks is a common problem in Tanzania, and few people seem to be aware that the country has a new Copyright Act, which stipulates very severe penalties for offences. Although publishers have reported several obvious copyright infringements to the police, no offenders have so far been prosecuted. Some sentences are obviously needed to make people realise that the law exists, and this is an area in which PATA needs to work very actively.

The printing industry

During the state-monopoly period, all textbooks were printed on donated paper by the large parastatal printers, National Printing Company and Printpak. These printers do not exist any more, and few other printers can cope with very large print-runs. Printing in Tanzania is expensive as local printers have to pay high import duties on paper and other inputs. Finished books can be imported without duty, however, and most publishers therefore prefer to print outside Tanzania, in South Africa or Mauritius or even India.

The language issue

Kiswahili is the medium of instruction at the primary and inter-mediate levels of education in Tanzania. It is very good for children to be able to learn to read and write in a familiar language. Although the quality of the education system is generally low, almost 70 per cent of the total population aged 15 and over can read and write Kiswahili, English or Arabic.

Which language is to be used in school is nevertheless debated in Tanzania, as it is in Senegal or Mozambique. The main issue is that in all education above Grade Seven, i.e. from secondary educa-tion to university level, the medium of instruction is English. Few primary school leavers are today proficient enough in the language to profit by secondary education in English. English is taught as a subject in primary school, but as the bulk of primary school teachers are themselves primary or secondary school leavers, they are not really capable of teaching the language successfully. The language problem has had an adverse influence on the quality of secondary education, and even university students have difficulty in reading literature in English. An attempt to improve the situa-tion was made in the new curriculum, by introducing English as a subject in Grade One; it used to be in Grade Three. But considering the difficulty in learning an additional language at such an early age and the teachers' lack of training, this will probably have limited effect. Some experts want to change the medium of instruction in secondary school to Kiswahili and combine this with intensive pre-university English courses; a few even want the university to teach in Kiswahili. The other extreme wants to use English as the medium of instruction throughout the school system, starting in Grade One, which sounds like a very poor solution considering the experience of the Portuguese-speaking and francophone countries in Africa.

Organisations in the book sector

Three organisations have existed for many years: The Publishers Association of Tanzania (PATA), the organiser of the annual Book Week, the Booksellers Association of Tanzania (BSAT), and the writers' organisation, UWAVITA. A book development council, BAMVITA, has recently been founded. Resolving the problem of import duties on printing paper will probably be a high priority issue for BAMVITA.

NGOs have contributed immensely to the development of the book sector in Tanzania. A very important – and very long-term – project is the Children's Book Project (CBP), which was initiated by CODE in 1991. The Project, which is still continuing but with other financing, promotes reading among children and for more than ten years has been an important source of income for small publishers. Many publishers owe their very existence and survival during the 'confinement' to the CBP. The CBP has organised training workshops for publishers, writers, booksellers and illustrators, and for some years has even functioned as a de facto 'book council', helping communications and ideas develop in the book industry.

The Children's Book Project has financed the publishing of over 150 children's book titles in half a million copies through its unique buy-back scheme: a certain part of each print-run has been donated by CBP to rural libraries, while the publisher has been free to sell the remaining copies. The fact that the books are in Kiswahili makes them attractive to children as soon as they have learned to read.

The Network of Technical Publications in Africa (TEPUSA) was established in late 1994. It arranges book exhibitions in schools, libraries, cultural centers and markets in Tanzania. It also produces a quarterly newsletter for publishers and booksellers and a catalogue of Tanzanian books. In addition, TEPUSA consolidates orders and distributes books for a number of small publishers.

The Flame Tree Media Trust, a local initiative for training photographers and graphic designers, started in 2001 as a spin-off from a PPP seminar. One of its first activities was to organise the first public exhibition of the work of Tanzanian photographers.

Uganda

History and Background to Current Situation

In the 1960s East Africa had a regional book market dominated from Kenya, and, in the main, textbook provision was in the hands of a number of British multinationals which had active subsidiaries in East Africa during the 1960s and 1970s. Most books were imported. Major UK publishers had offices and agencies in the region. After 1962 the Milton Obote Foundation established a number of subsidiary companies to undertake general publishing, the importation and distribution of school textbooks and printing. In 1972 foreign investors were expelled under the Amin regime. In 1973 the National Curriculum Development Center (NCDC) was established with a mandate to develop the curriculum and originate core primary school textbooks under a monopoly. NCDC-authored books were routinely published by two 'privileged' multinationals with long-term relations with the Ministry, although the Ministry retained copyright. The 1970s were marked by considerable chaos during the Amin era, accompanied by the collapse of the private sector.

There was a period of rehabilitation of the education sector and textbook provision between 1986 and 1992. Books were purchased and printed externally through various aid agreements. In the 1980s there were large-scale World Bank IDA lending programmes (IDA 3 and 4) for textbooks of up to US$18 million in value. These were fulfilled through international competitive bidding, and all the books were purchased overseas and shipped into Uganda. Until the early 1990s Uganda had little or no indigenous commercial publishing capacity, in marked contrast to Kenya.

The 1990s are seen as the effective starting point for the growth in indigenous, commercial publishing. Up to 1992 the government held a monopoly over textbook provision. Books were procured centrally by the Ministry of Education and provided to schools, and as a result there were few commercial publishers.

In 1992 the Uganda Publishers' and Booksellers' Association (UPABA) was founded, giving a voice to emergent publishers and booksellers and opening a new era of dialogue between the private sector and the state. UPABA played a pivotal role in discussions that led to the introduction of new policies (notably a national book policy overview), even to the extent of carrying out a comparative study of book industries in east and southern Africa whose results formed the basis for discussions with the Ministry and funding agencies.

Between 1993 and 1998 around US$20 million was spent under the Support to Ugandan Primary Education Reform programme, whose main funder was USAID. Under this new arrangement, between 1993 and 1995 a new competitive system was introduced as an outcome of the 1992 textbook policy, providing, at policy level, for the participation of local publishers. Book selection was decentralised to schools on the basis of per capita budget. Publishers marketed their books direct to schools. Schools were authorized to select books, within a budget ceiling, on book-selection forms from the Ministry. A list of approved textbooks, with prices, was circulated by the Ministry to all schools as the basis for selection. The procurement exercise was supervised by district textbook-selection committees. Publishers were required by the new procurement system to undertake marketing at school level to some 8,000 government-aided schools. Consolidation and packing of these orders was tendered to the private sector. Orders were placed with the publishers centrally by the Ministry, and delivered to a central warehouse. At this point the orders were broken up according to school and district. Districts were responsible for collection from the central warehouse, and schools were responsible for collection from the district. There was no role for booksellers. Books procured through the system were provided free to schools.

The policy had impressive results in textbook quality, as publishers were competing for a decentralised market. It brought publishers into contact with the end-users of their products and introduced widespread practices of promotional visits and discussions with teachers on textbook usage.

By 1998 each of the four subjects examined in the Primary Leaving Examination (mathematics, English, social studies and science) had a minimum of three core textbooks offered by the ten active commercial educational publishers. Some subjects had in excess of six approved core texts and a similar number of supplementary textbooks. This was described at the time as a tremendous achievement in an industry that five years previously had been in ruins.

It is estimated that new indigenous publishers were supplying around 10 per cent of the textbook market by 1998, with the remainder in the hands of British subsidiaries and some Kenyan suppliers. This has had adverse repercussions for the local Ugandan industry. Most the textbooks published in Uganda were printed in Kenya or South Africa and the print industry did not develop as a result of the massive aid investments into primary education. To a large extent, textbooks from British multinationals were developed outside Uganda, though for the Ugandan market, and the skills of local authors, illustrators, editors and otherswere not developed sufficiently.

By 1998/9 the Ministry began to doubt that it was getting full value for money in terms of textbook provision. It decided to separate the technical (textbook quality) and financial (price) elements of the bids for textbook supply. Thus in 2001 price was included in the evaluation and approval formulas for all textbooks. The result was a 70% reduction in average textbook prices. This development has been received by some of the commercial publishers with mixed feelings. Although the price was driven down by the Ministry's intervention, the publishing sector began to exhibit signs of aggressive competition, which has tended to strengthen the multinational firms.

In 1997 the National Book Trust was formed to undertake book-development activities and provide further impetus to the private–state dialogue. The booksellers' and publishers' trade associations separated in the same year into the Uganda Publishers' Association (UPA) and the Uganda Booksellers' Association (UBA), in itself an outcome of the growing maturity in Uganda's book industry.

Until 2001 there was no limit on the number of textbooks that could be approved per subject and grade in the multiple textbook system, but thereafter it has been limited to three (see below).

The New Primary Curriculum introduced in 1999 expanded the scope of subjects and allowed for the use of local language as the medium of instruction in the first three grades of primary school, as well as making Swahili a compulsory language.

Textbook co-ordination, consolidation and delivery to schools has been carried out under the Instructional Materials Unit (IMU) of the Ministry. IMU administers textbook approvals. Books are exempted from sales and import taxes.

Primary textbook provision situation

Currently (2003), publishers submit tenders for primary school textbooks on a five-year project life-span, in which three titles per grade/subject will be selected. The books are stringently vetted and approved on pedagogical, technical and price considerations. Vetting fees are among the highest in Africa, with publishers paying US$100 on submission of titles and US$500 for each title approved. The price of the book is published with the approved list, and the publisher has to offer 37,5% discount to government on orders of 30,000 or more copies. Selection between the three approved books is decentralised to school level, and publishers receive orders accordingly, print and deliver to a central warehouse as in the previous system. There is still no role in this process for booksellers.

The tenders have been a massive boost to publishing generally – resulting in guaranteed sales. Some publishers have strengthened their position to the detriment of others because of the 'winner takes all' effect of these tenders, which can virtually remove a publisher from business because of the 5-year life-span of title approval/selection. Uganda has moved from a position in which any book could be 'approved' if it met the curriculum requirements (1994–2001), to one in which there is a maximum of three books, and this has proved ruinous for some publishers – some series of books that had been developed previously will have no role for the next five years.

From 2001/2 there has been a pilot 'full decentralisation' scheme, involving booksellers, in four (of the fifty-seven) districts. In this system booksellers receive orders directly from schools for books from a number of publishers and consolidate the orders and deliver to schools. Payment is effected at district level. All orders have to be based on an approved core textbook list.

In the other fifty-three districts, schools make the selection, and these are forwarded to the Ministry of Education, which in turn orders from publishers. Consolidation and delivery is put out to tender as before. The Ministry is considering various options of expanding the full decentralisation of procurement throughout the system, based on the results of the pilot decentralisation.

One major theme in Ugandan publishing circles is the continued dominance of the industry by subsidiaries of British multinationals. Rehabilitation of textbook provision through school-based selection has proved innovative and successful since 1995. However, the market share of indigenous Ugandan publishers has rarely risen above 20 per cent.

Secondary Schools

As booksellers are excluded from the textbook market in all but four districts, they are surviving with purchases by private schools and parents, as well as receiving supplementary orders for school books and orders from secondary schools. There is some confusion surrounding secondary school textbook provision. In principle, the schools receive a per capita grant, and select and purchase directly from booksellers. Most secondary school books are imported, hence booksellers have a role. There are plans to expand the book evaluation and approval system to the secondary school level, but it is not clear when or whether this will be implemented.

Bookshops

While there are said to be 200 booksellers in Uganda, there are clearly big differences in both capacity and competence between the top Kampala bookshops, estimated to number around thirty, and many newly established bookshops in the country. The main network of bookshops in Uganda used to be Uganda Bookshops, run by the Anglican church, but these declined markedly in the 1990s.

In general, Uganda is booming in every direction, with projects too numerous to mention, and money is being spent on book supplies from projects to keep bookshops afloat. Books from India are beginning to be marketed and sold, at significantly lower prices than UK equivalents.

Although foreign currency is simple to acquire and there are no bureaucratic or regulatory problems in importing books, book importers have experienced losses because of delays in payment by government for orders that include imported books. During the delay the local currency will have devalued against foreign currencies – before payment can be made to the overseas supplier.

Printing

Although print quality in Uganda is fair, prices are high since paper is imported and there are taxes on inputs. Virtually all textbooks are printed outside Uganda. Publishers deem production specifications on textbooks tenders to be very high , and local printing cannot offer the required quality, so all publishers tend to import printing.

Curriculum Issues

National Curriculum Development Center (NCDC) is the curriculum authority and it writes the curriculum at pre-primary, primary, and secondary levels, and also undertakes teachers' guides.

Historically, the NCDC has been involved in writing textbooks and instructional materials. At present, books written at the NCDC are not part of the approved textbook list, but a few are nevertheless sold as supplementary school purchases, and to a market comprising private schools, libraries and some parents. Interestingly, the NCDC intends to operate a quasi-commercial publishing wing and to compete with commercial publishers for the textbook market at both primary- and secondary school levels. It has previously done significant joint publishing with Longman and Macmillan. The NCDC has no part in vetting books for approval so there is deemed to be no conflict of interest. Strictly speaking, NCDC staff are not allowed to write textbooks under the new system, so it is not clear how the NCDC will continue to be active in publishing, but they seem confident that they will make a contribution to the publishing landscape.

A new syllabus was introduced 1999. There is, however, minimum contact between the NCDC and commercial publishers about quality, textbook methodology and other issues of mutual concern.

General Book Trade Issues

There is no comprehensive national book policy covering all elements of book provision and libraries in Uganda, though there is a textbook procurement policy. There are about fifteen active publishers and up to 200 bookshops.

Today the situation in textbook provision in Uganda is at a crossroads. While there is growth in the book sector and a high degree of activity by a few UK companies, emergent indigenous publishing is described as 'stagnant', with one or two notable exceptions. There is little general publishing output except from Kampala's Fountain Press and Macmillan (Uganda). There are complaints that the process of liberalisation has been 'donor-driven' and that there has been insufficient dialogue with Ugandan booksellers and publishers.

Significantly there are Kenyan books in Uganda, and Kenyan books are included in the tender process for primary school textbook provision, a situation unique in Africa.

The East African School of Library and Information Sciences (EASLIS), located at Makerere University, offers courses in Bookselling, Marketing and Book Trade, Foundations of Publishing, Book Production, Printing and Binding, and Publishing and Media.

There is a new policy of mother-tongue instruction up to primary Grade 4 level, which promises to be of pivotal importance in years to come in promoting indigenous language publishing.

It is estimated that there is a 55% literacy rate in Uganda. At EASLIS it is emphasized that the real background to 'the book problem' remains that of a society with a weak literary culture, underdeveloped reading habits and poor mother-tongue publishing. Despite Uganda's increasingly vibrant economy, many rural and urban people in the country are deeply affected by poverty issues, including the HIV/AIDS pandemic. There are few or no cheap books available.

Issues of Special Interest that Emerged

Ugandan publishers felt that there should be special programmes for the indigenization of publishing, similar to the training and capacity-building efforts in Tanzania over the past ten years.

Many felt that the tender system has a significant 'winner takes all' effect, closing the door at three approved books per subject/grade, that can be disastrous for publishers who have not managed to get their textbooks into the system. They felt that the market should be unlimited as long as a book meets all the criteria for approval. The costs of manuscript development are very high, and this is a threat to the sustainability of the system – especially if, after a manuscript has been developed, a book is not approved. Publishers also felt that technical specifications for textbooks in the tender system are simply too high. Publishers are concerned about the long-term effects of providing free textbooks, citing what they called the 'free books syndrome', whereby parents and school communities do not attach any value to books when they are provided free by the state.

Zambia

Brief Background of Country Publishing

Book publishing in Zambia has been dominated by the state since 1966, as two years after Zambia attained her political independence, the government established what was known as the Kenneth Kaunda Foundation along with two subsidiary companies, National Educational Company Limited (NECZAM), a publishing company, and the National Education Distribution Company Limited (NEDCOZ), a marketing cum distribution company. The Foundation underwent a major restructuring in 1985, and was renamed Zambia Educational Publishing House (ZEPH) in 1991, when textbook publishing was liberalised; since then it has faced considerable competition.

The arrival of missionaries in the country contributed greatly to setting up schools, the introduction of elementary books brought in from overseas, and basic lessons in reading and writing that facilitated the spread of the Gospel. While the missionary activities, that started with the establishment of the first school at Limulunga in 1883, progressed, the major stimulus for local book publishing was the African Literature Committee that was set up in 1937.

In January 1948, the Committee was transformed into the Northern Rhodesia Publications Bureau, on the lines of the East African Literature Bureau. As a department of the Ministry of Education its main objective was to encourage the publication of works by indigenous people in the local languages. Because of the limited expertise and financial resources available at the time, the Bureau rarely published books on its own: it negotiated and entered into publishing contracts with such publishing companies as Macmillan, Oxford University Press, Longman, the University of London Press, Lutterworth Press, Collins and many others.

The effect of the Bureau on creative writing is indelible in the country's literary history. Numerous Zambian-language works published then remain today as invaluable treasures. Some of them are still used in schools. Writing skills are still being emulated.

In 1966 the government established the Kenneth Kaunda Foundation (KKF) along with two subsidiary companies, National Educational Company Limited (NECZAM), a publishing company, and the National Education Distribution Company Limited (NEDCOZ), a marketing cum distribution company. The government mandated the KKF to produce and distribute all primary school textbooks and other learning materials, while textbooks for secondary schools and tertiary institutions continued to be imported. The Curriculum Development Center of the Ministry of

Education developed and wrote materials for pupils' textbooks and teachers' handbooks and passed them on to the Foundation for publication. NECZAM and NEDCOZ, respectively, undertook the publishing and distribution to schools. This created a regime of one textbook per subject per grade for the whole country, and the procurement and supply of textbooks was centralised.

Two multinational publishing companies opened branch offices in Lusaka, Oxford University Press in 1963 and Longman in 1964. Macmillan Education, on the other hand, was represented by NECZAM, in which the former held 40 per cent shares. Heinemann Educational Books opened a sales office in the early 1970s.

With the Foundation and its subsidiary companies taking away most of the educational textbook market – NECZAM publishing textbooks for the primary school sector, and NEDCOZ importing and distributing secondary school textbooks –there was hardly any role or market for the multinationals. This, coupled with ailing national economy, forced multinational companies to close their Zambian offices between 1972 and 1978. The few local publishing houses that existed at the time made very little contribution to the book sector. The KKF, on the other hand, was also faced with such a myriad of operational problems that it failed to meet the textbook needs of the country's educational system adequately.

The closure of the multinationals' offices reduced the performance of the Foundation in the supply of books, despite local bookshops being 'technically precluded' from selling books to various educational institutions, and the country's ailing economy led to a number of bookshops either diversifying their operations or closing down altogether.

To redress the situation, between 1985 and 1995 the government sought and received financial, material and technical support from development partners such as the Finnish International Development Agency (FINNIDA), the Swedish International Development Co-operation Agency (SIDA) under the Zambia Educational Materials Project (ZEMP). Among the initial objectives of ZEMP in 1985 were development of the quality of locally generated school materials; development of the capacity for local publication of educational materials; rehabilitation of the quality of primary education; and development of self-sufficiency and minimization of costs in the provision of educational materials.

The rehabilitation of the quality of primary education involved large quantities of Zambian primary school textbooks being reprinted in Finland, as a stop-gap measure, for free distribution to primary schools. All the objectives of ZEMP Phase One were undertaken through the Zambia Educational Publishing House (ZEPH).

During the latter phase of ZEMP, attention was paid to building the capacity of Zambia's book industry as a whole.

An attempt was made under ZEMP activities to open more than 400 Zonal Distribution Centers throughout the country to facilitate the distribution of textbooks and other educational materials to various schools. This arrangement, however, was through ZEPH, a statutory organisation. The arrangement thus had the effect, firstly, of entrenching among Zambians the syndrome of dependence on free textbooks from the government and eroding the intrinsic value of the book. Secondly, it fortified the monopolistic role of ZEPH in the book chain, killing off booksellers. Thirdly, the approach did not provide any long-term benefit or strategies for book development in the country. Subsequent experience showed that the Zonal Distribution Centers were not substitutes for sustainable bookshops.

With what seemed to be development in the direction of reviving the book industry, other agencies, such as the World Bank, the African Development Bank, the British Council, the Royal Kingdom of Netherlands, and the Danish International Development Agency (DANIDA), variously funded and supported other textbook or supplementary reading material programmes. These interventions greatly ameliorated the supply of textbooks and supplementary readers in Zambia. Without any long-term plans and strategies by government, however, the problems of the book industry were merely nibbled at; the shortage of textbooks in schools still persisted in spite of the various schemes and interventions.

Up to 1973, when Zambia's economy was relatively buoyant, personal disposable income and foreign reserves for book imports were readily available, people could easily purchase books of their choice – educational or general – from privately owned bookshops that operated mainly in the urban and provincial centers of the country.

Similarly, the country witnessed an interesting period of vibrant creative writing, and publishing houses responded positively to the needs of both aspiring and established writers by publishing creative works.

It is necessary to put into context the fact that after independence in 1964 Zambia experienced three political systems: a multi-party system from 1964 to 1973, a one-party system from 1973 to 1990, and finally back to a multi-party system after 1991. These systems may have had some influence on educational and textbook-publishing policies.

Liberalisation: Genesis of Public/Private Partnership

In November 1991, a significant government policy change resulted in the liberalisation of textbook production and supply. Effectively, the policy change empowered educational authorities to procure their educational materials from any source without channelling their orders through a third party. Similarly, any printer or publisher capable of undertaking the printing and publishing of educational books in sufficient quantities was empowered to offer such services to the Ministry of Education. The geographical location of the supplier, printer or publisher, i.e. within or outside the country, was not a limiting factor in this policy.

Given the status of the book industry in Zambia at the time, implementation of the new policy was not immediately practicable. A number of new indigenous publishing companies emerged, but these lacked both requisite capital and expertise to meet the daunting task of publishing textbooks from scratch. Moreover, the government offered neither incentives nor preferential treatment to indigenous publishers.

The country witnessed the return of Oxford University Press and Longman Zambia, and Macmillan Publishers (Zambia) was locally incorporated.

This development set in motion the need for the Ministry of Education, on the one hand, and the various publishers, on the other, to work together in defining roles, establishing common understanding of issues relating to textbook production and supply, and resolving any problems that arose or were likely to hamper implementation of the policy. This was done through seminars, workshops and open round-table discussions. These provided broad-based representation and in-depth deliberations. It was the genesis of the public/private partnership in the book sector in Zambia.

At the height of the change came the concern by the government to have adequate supplies of textbooks and other educational materials supplied to schools. In the absence of internal resources, outside help was sought. The response and support of co-operating or development partners ushered in the system of open tenders for the publication, production and supply (including delivery) of textbooks. Publishers were first invited to bid for textbook publishing tenders. Publishers were expected to bid to publish and print educational materials developed by the Curriculum Development Center (CDC) of the Ministry of Education. The winner of a tender had to have all the requisite editorial and design facilities in-house. When all the educational materials developed by the Curriculum Development Center had been published, and the CDC gradually withdrew from developing educational materials, publishers were invited to submit bids for educational materials either in the form of camera-ready artwork or as published books.

The criteria for qualifying to bid often precluded the majority of indigenous Zambian publishers. In terms of economies of scale, multinational publishing companies have an edge over indigenous publishing companies. The former are able to draw editorial and financial support from another branch or may even adopt a textbook published elsewhere by an associated company. As a result, the multinationals will dominate the Zambian publishing scene for a long time.

As indigenous publishing companies fail to secure any bids to publish educational textbooks, prospects for their expansion are bleak. It cannot be denied that, with an estimated 90 per cent of the book market being taken up by textbooks, there is very little opportunity left for an indigenous book publisher. The negative effect of the tender system, where one title is chosen for the whole country for a set period of three years, of course, is that the successful bidder will be in the business of supplying textbooks for as long as the title remains on the list of approved textbooks. The losing bidder on the other hand may be out of business until the list is reviewed and revised three years later.

The twelve years since the policy of liberalising the production and supply of educational materials was announced in 1991 is a long time, particularly when the visible signs reflect little or no progress in implementation. It took a UNESCO study of 1993 to stimulate the need for a national book policy for Zambia. The policy that was eventually drafted and finalized in 1998 to a large extent attempted to articulate the practical aspects of implementing the liberalisation policy.

There are a number of possible explanations as to why Zambia has not recorded much progress.

Firstly, the policy of 1991 remains an intention and has not been accompanied by firm practical measures. In the wake of liberalisation, the continued patronage of ZEPH – a statutory organisation falling under the aegis of the Ministry of Education, with the Permanent Secretary, who should ordinarily oversee the entire national book sector, as the Chairperson of ZEPH's Board of Directors – gives the organisation an advantage over other publishing companies when it comes to funding and competitive bidding.

Secondly, the liberalisation of textbook supply when only one title per subject per grade is approved renders such liberalisation restrictive, because it permits a 'winner takes all' situation. One title per subject per grade negates the educational ideal of cross-fertilization required in learning and also negates the high investment incurred in developing textbooks.

Thirdly, tenders, particularly under international competitive bidding and because of restrictive conditions, tend to favour multinational publishers and disadvantage indigenous publishers. This in turn may result in local printing companies losing out on jobs.

Fourthly, funding for textbooks and other educational materials has continued to be centralised at the Ministry of Education. This has effectively discouraged the emergence of booksellers and killed the traditional book-marketing efforts by publishers or their representatives. On the other hand, tendering and central procurement of textbooks has continued because Ministry of Education officials have assumed that the cost of textbooks bought in bulk is lower, oblivious of the hidden costs of distribution and administration. In addition, excessive dependence on funding agencies, with very little, if any, funding coming from the government, has rendered independent implementation of the policy, i.e. by the Ministry of Education, impossible.

Fifthly, booksellers have been marginalized by the Ministry of Education's floating of tenders for textbook production and delivery to schools, which has thereby encouraged a break in the book chain. As a result, it is argued that the system of procurement cannot be decentralised because there are no booksellers to undertake the supply to schools.

Finally, vested professional interests – for instance, from the curriculum specialists who wrote educational materials – engendered the view that the new policy was a threat to their status. They clung to their accustomed role of developing textbooks and getting them published.

It was therefore necessary for all parties to be carefully sensitized about the new policy and the changed roles of each stakeholder. More critical also was a need to understand the implications, challenges and limitations of the draft national book policy. The process of reviewing the draft national book policy, and specifically the involvement of Ministry of Education stakeholders, contributed enormously to the adoption and implementation of liberalised textbook policy.

Changes in the Development and Provision of Textbooks

Defining Roles

The Curriculum Development Center (CDC) of the Ministry of Education maintained its role of developing curricula and syllabuses and concentrated on its quality control function. The Center concerned itself with evaluating and approving educational materials intended for use in schools or textbooks submitted for inclusion in the List of Approved and Recommended Books for Use in Zambian Schools. The CDC therefore gradually relinquished the role that it used to undertake of writing and preparing texts up to pre-press stage for publishing tenders.

Publishers that secured publishing tenders progressed the material further by getting the material printed and delivered to the Ministry of Education. This process essentially involved the Ministry and publishers, thereby marginalizing booksellers as centralised procurement was consolidated. Payment for textbooks supplied was disbursed from the Ministry of Education's headquarters in Lusaka. In character with centralised procurement and supply directly to schools, bookselling remained either overshadowed or undeveloped.

Need for Policy Framework

Practical experience two years after liberalisation showed that centralised procurement and payment and the tender system *per se* were not a panacea to the problems of textbook production and supply: textbooks were not being produced on time and distribution to schools was fraught with problems in spite of development-partner funding being available.

The Ministry of Education approached these problems by fine-tuning the Textbook Provision Policy. This involved:

reviewing the textbook evaluation policy, that resulted in more than one textbook being approved for use per subject per grade;

transferring to the end-users (individual schools) the responsibility of selecting titles from the List of Approved Textbooks; and

recognizing the role of booksellers, not publishers, in the ultimate supply of books to schools.

The approval of more than one textbook per subject per grade widens chances for publishers to participate in the competition for providing textbooks. This measure signified the beginning of decentralisation in the procurement and distribution of textbooks in the country.

In the new Textbook Provision Policy schools would have to form textbook selection committees that would include representatives of the community and parent–teacher associations. The list and quantities of selected textbooks, according to the school's annual per capita budget, would then be submitted to the District Education Officer who would consolidate the requirements or orders for the registered local bookseller. Central tendering would be minimized to special projects or programmes.

At the Ministry of Education a special textbook unit is envisaged that will oversee the smooth implementation of the Policy and redress any relevant issues that hamper progress.

In 1998 a wide ranging draft of a National Book Policy was presented to the Ministry of Education in Zambia. It had been drawn up by a team of stakeholders from the Ministry of Education, commercial interests, and with reference to other interested parties such as NGOs, libraries and printers. It was proposed, and inherent in its drafting, that the Policy be codified in Zambian law as a statutory instrument, which required an Act to be passed by Parliament. Since its drafting, little has transpired and it remains a draft proposed national book policy.

At the center of all the foregoing is the need for the Zambia to put in place a well-co-ordinated system for textbook approval, publishing, production and financial planning, bookselling and distribution. The system should also recognize and accommodate the roles of various stakeholders in the country's book chain and industry. The government, through the Ministry of Education, has been able to gradually evolve an effective public/private partnership. Moreover, in formulating the Textbook Provision Policy and the draft National Book Policy, the Ministry of Education involved the active participation of various relevant stakeholders from both the public and private sectors.

The Zambian education system has, over the years, derived tremendous assistance in the provision of textbooks from co-operating or development partners. Between 1999 and December 2002, the co-operating partners pooled their financial and material resources under the Basic Education Sub-Sector Investment Programme (BESSIP). BESSIP was managed by the Ministry of Education, and as many development partners as were involved in education participated in the Programme. Their participation entailed open consideration of annual plans, review of performance, monitoring the implementation, and funding on the basis of the Ministry's requests. Any remedial action and assistance was taken care of under the provisions of BESSIP. It can be stated with confidence that BESSIP consolidated an effective partnership because the support of funding agencies was mustered and well co-ordinated.

Publishing

ZEPH, that had monopolized textbook publishing at basic educational level now has to compete for the school market against two major publishing companies, Longman Zambia Limited and Macmillan Publishers (Zambia) Limited. At senior secondary school level, these last two companies dominate the market; this supply is supplemented by Oxford University Press and less than five other local publishers. It is true to state that the majority of publishers have concentrated on textbook publishing, which offers better returns on investment. Publishers have to source capital for investment on their own, as there is no special provision for financial assistance from the banks. In any case bank interest rates in the country are prohibitive for loan purposes, while book publishers are a long way from being listed on the Lusaka Stock Exchange.

In the area of trade-book publishing, very few titles have been published since the heyday of ZEPH in the mid-1970s. A generous estimate would be just below twenty titles per year, for a total population of 9.8 million. In fact, some of the general titles published are intended for possible adoption for use in basic and secondary schools.

At tertiary level nearly 99 per cent of the local textbook require-ments is imported, and until such a time as demand for certain titles grows to justify economic local reprints, and adequate provi-sion is made for the externalization of royalties or licence fees, publishing under licence will have to wait.

The Book Publishers Association of Zambia (BPAZ), which by mutual agreement in November 2002 split with booksellers in what was then known as the Booksellers and Publishers Association of Zambia has a registered membership of 15 has worked very closely with other stakeholders promote the book industry in the country.

Bookselling

The Booksellers Association of Zambia (BAZA) was reborn in November 2002. Previously, a Booksellers Association of Zambia, taking over from the Northern Rhodesia Booksellers Association at independence in 1964, had existed until 1975, when it merged with publishers to become the Booksellers and Publishers Association of Zambia. At that time, the bookselling business had begun to decline, and numbers in both trade groups were falling.

Between 1954 and 1975, Zambia had one chain of bookshops named Kingstons that had previously been linked to a similar chain in Southern Rhodesia (later Zimbabwe). This chain had outlets from Livingstone on the southern border of Zambia to Chingola on the Copperbelt. There were other private bookshops along the line of rail and in provincial centers. Partly as a result of educational bookselling being monopolized from 1968 by the KKF and its subsidiary NEDCOZ, and partly because of dwindling foreign currency with which to import books, most private bookshops gradually closed down after 1978.

Printing

With the liberalisation in November 1991, the country witnessed the emergence of new printing companies. The Investment Act of 1993 attracted new investors – local and foreign – to enter the printing business. The number of printing companies increased, although some of the old companies did not upgrade their technology. While there is considerable capacity to print textbooks locally, most of the publishing companies have opted to have their large print-runs printed elsewhere – in South Africa, Mauritius and the Far East, where printing costs are more competitive in spite of the transport required.

Zambia is a signatory to the UNESCO Florence Agreement, but is not a signatory to the Nairobi Protocol. The effect of this is that most raw materials for printing attract Customs duty and VAT, which make local printing costs high, and therefore the retail prices of books. Imported printed books are cheaper because they do not attract any duties or VAT.

The draft national book policy addresses issues of tax and the need to make the book sector a strategic industry, even if this meant a temporary 'tax holiday' being extended to the book sector until pressing shortcomings had been rectified.

Statistics

Reliable data on the country's educational system are critical for planning the financing, production and supply of textbooks; this information is vital to avoid over- and under-supplies. In Zambia, data collection and compilation has been slow. ADEA's Information on Books and Educational Materials (IBEM) and National Educational Statistical Information Systems (NESIS) programmes were initiated, firstly, to develop a monitoring system that tracks the use of books in the classroom, and, secondly, to establish a reliable system for compiling facts and figures that facilitate effective policy formulation and education management. These activities are still in progress, so it is not yet possible to determine the sector's contribution to gross domestic product.

Prospects

Public/private partnership in the book sector in Zambia has evolved out of the desire to redress the unsatisfactory situation in textbook production, supply and distribution. This partnership was triggered by the liberalisation of textbook production and supply in November 1991. Since then, the private sector has been involved in the book sector at one level or another.

Although it has taken a long time for the Zambian government to introduce permanent measures to improve the book sector, this appears to have been a case of *festina lente* [make haste slowly] and a deliberate tactical move. Enough groundwork has been undertaken thoroughly over the years, specific plans are under way to improve the textbook-evaluation process and to allow choice from multiple textbooks. It is to be hoped that, ultimately, the quality of textbooks, and of the educational system itself, will be improved in character with the ideals of liberalisation.

It is clear that the various stakeholders in the book sector will have to be pro-active and respond to the anticipated new challenges of developing and producing suitable textbooks as well as books for general readership. It is evident, too, that Zambia is on the verge of a new era in the book industry.

Zimbabwe

Introduction

Since independence in 1980, Zimbabwe has operated without a documented policy on the provision of textbooks. Lack of an articulated policy, however, has not meant an absence of policy. Innovative 'home-grown' policies were continuously developed and implemented in the 1980s, with impressive results.

There is a history of dialogue and consensus between the Ministry of Education and the book industry that began in the early 1980s, when the country faced a massive growth in textbook needs. Effective communications at senior levels between the well-established Zimbabwe Book Publishers Association (ZBPA), the Booksellers Association of Zimbabwe (BAZ) and the Ministry of Education have laid the foundation for much of Zimbabwe's success.

Zimbabwe has been fortunate in retaining considerable depth and expertise in its book sector. For example, Zimbabwe has hosted Africa's premier book fair, Zimbabwe International Book Fair (ZIBF), since the early 1980s. The ZIBF grew at a tremendous pace in the 1990s, becoming the *de facto* annual meeting point for African publishing, until it began to be overwhelmed by the country's economic problems after 1998.

The success of Zimbabwe's textbook-provision mechanism has been founded on an established commercial publishing industry from independence in 1980, and a country-wide network of booksellers that grew phenomenally between 1980 and 1985. Government-generated funding was sufficient to meet textbook needs in a framework of free, universal primary education during the 1980s. Massive investment in education fuelled growth: over 5,000 new schools were opened in the 1980s. In response to the boom, foreign and local investment poured into the book sector. Textbook publishers recorded fantastic growth. The number of bookselling firms increased from 21 to over 100 by 1987, and peaked at about 140 by the early 1990s, comprising nearly 200 bookshops. About a dozen of these companies operated chains of bookshops, the largest being Kingstons, with 15 outlets, and Textbook Sales, with 12, covering all the main towns.

The Government Contract for Bookselling

From the 1980s the so-called Government Contract was devised whereby booksellers had the sole right sell to government and district council schools on laid-down terms and conditions. These protected schools from unethical practices, regulated procurement and payment, and provided for free delivery from booksellers to schools. The background to this innovation was extensive consultation between the Ministry of Education and the private sector. As a result, bookselling grew, many new booksellers emerged, and booksellers provided an efficient and cost-effective service.

The essential elements of the Government Contract negotiated in the early 1980s were:

- free delivery from publisher to bookseller
- free delivery from bookseller to school
- standard 25% discount across the board from publisher to bookseller
- standard retail price across the country, irrespective of volume of units in an order or location of customer

A vital element with the Government Contract was that only 'approved booksellers' could enter the system. The BAZ itself was the approval authority for applicants. This was a legally binding contract between the Association and the government, was entered into by the Association on behalf of its members, and was therefore binding on its members. Strict criteria for approval was applied, which included the inspection of retail premises. Once approved, booksellers were required to lodge a 'performance deposit' with the BAZ. The interest accrued on these deposits paid for the administration costs of the BAZ over many years. Booksellers that flaunted the system could be removed. This was seldom necessary – the threat of removal of 'approved' status proved a powerful deterrent against abuse. The system remains to all intents self-regulating.

Development of the Textbook Provision System

From independence in 1980 until around 1993, the bulk of textbook needs were met through per capita funding from the Ministry of Education, disbursed direct to the purchasing authorities in a decentralised procurement system. The funds were disbursed initially in a two-tier system – for urban government schools and rural district council schools, respectively. A well-organised network of urban government-owned schools received funds direct and purchased and paid for their textbooks.

Thousands of rural schools were opened between 1980 and 1987. Initially procurement of textbooks for the rural government schools was operated through the District Councils (which became the legal owners of these schools in the mid-1980s). Schools selected their textbooks in line with a budget ceiling provided by the District Council and according to per capita textbook grants from the Ministry of Education. In the first phase, the District Council selected booksellers to supply their schools, though this arrangement was open to some abuse. From around 1987, rural schools selected their own bookseller in addition to their choice of books against their budget ceiling. Both the order and the bookseller had to be approved at district level, but by and large, District Councils did not intervene as long as the bookseller was on the Government Contract. Payment was effected at either district or provincial level on proof of receipt of the textbooks at the school against a previously approved order. This system functioned well for a number of years.

The per capita grant was applied twice annually – 70% in a first tranche during the first term, and 30% in a second tranche, usually during the second term. The planning process of the entire book industry hinged around these dates, which represented the 'textbook sales season'. Many schools supplemented the per capita grant through their own efforts. Church, farm, community and private schools, and many government schools, had sources of funding outside the per capita grant – from benefactors or levies on parents – and would order supplementary books or extra textbooks.

From the early 1990s, inflation began to climb and the purchasing power of the grants provided by the Ministry of Education was significantly eroded. From this period, the ministry began to turn substantially to funding partners. Funding was used to increase the per capita grant, but the co-operating partners and the Ministry were increasingly concerned with problems of poverty and inequity. Schools were graded according to levels of poverty, and to alleviate book shortages the poorer schools were allocated *ad hoc* and special textbook grants from time to time in funded projects.

During the 1990s, the process of decentralisation was deepened considerably. After many years of selecting books, schools were competent to take over direct purchase and payment. Urban government schools were empowered to retain school fees and use these according to their own priorities, including the purchase of textbooks; with the approval of their parent–teachers' association (PTA), they were allowed to enforce levies to meet their financial needs. Having been successfully applied in urban government schools, this method was extended to rural schools.

All rural schools were instructed to open bank accounts, and thereafter the per capita textbook grants were paid direct into the school's bank account. Schools were instructed to form School Development Committees (SDCs), which would check textbook orders. SDCs were given authority to impose extra textbook levies, in agreement with PTAs, to alleviate textbook shortages and to raise funds for library development. As a direct result virtually all secondary schools, and about 40% of primary schools in Zimbabwe had some form of library in the mid-1990s.

However, despite such instances of innovative decision-making and expertise in the textbook system, the instability in Zimbabwe's economy from the late 1990s has put extreme pressure on textbook provision, leading to increased activity from funding partners. The textbook environment today is implemented increasingly in a project-by-project fashion, as a direct outcome of the growing dependency on external aid.

As dependency deepened, funding partners applied various criteria to the approaches of the Ministry of Education, responding to poverty, the needs of specific rural areas, or the need for library books. It is from this point that the integrity of the system, which had been fine-tuned around the disbursement dates of the per capita grant, began to exhibit a patchwork character, although the Ministry of Education, the booksellers and the publishers all agree that the system involving SDCs has proved highly successful.

In 2003 a new phenomenon appeared in the urban centers. Parents were given a list of books to purchase for their children and on the list was a request to purchase a library book as a donation to the school. The response caught publishers by surprise, and stocks of primary school books ran out before they had the 2003 printing in stock.

While this self-reliant spirit on the part of many schools has been the strength of the textbook provision system, it has also led to disparities. In 1998, the Policy and Planning Division of the Ministry of Education took the initiative to develop a policy for textbook provision in an effort to streamline and unify the system. Nothing came of this because the rapidly deteriorating socio-economic conditions undermined efforts at long term planning.

Zimbabwe has been acknowledged as a model of efficiency in textbook provision. Successes have been recorded in the quality and relevance of textbooks, output (both by title and overall volume), choice of textbooks, range of supplementary books, development of publishing capacity, growth of bookselling, and the emergence of an NGO capacity in books and libraries. A few years after independence (by the mid-1980s), Zimbabwe was self-sufficient in textbooks from primary grades 1 to 7 and secondary forms 1 to 4 and provided a choice of up to four textbooks in most core subjects. New titles and editions have continually appeared on the market.

In the early 1980s, all imported textbooks for secondary school, where quantities over 1,000 copies were needed, were required to be licensed to a local publisher and printed locally. The overseas publishers invariably complied or they would lose their market. This made Zimbabwe self-sufficient in previously imported secondary school books. The significance lies in both a transfer of production into Zimbabwe and books priced according to local costs (making the books about one-third the price of the imported equivalents).

These successes reflect the positive circumstances of the 1980s. A robust economy, all components of local printing and publishing in place, international goodwill, and an energetic unity of purpose to correct historical injustices all converged. Zimbabwe continues, even with the collapse of key economic sectors, to have a strong book-chain infrastructure: it remains organised and professional, with all the main players in contact with and supporting one another even in difficult economic and political conditions.

Conditions today are different from those in the formative period of textbook provision in the 1980s. The exchange rate of the currency against US dollar stands, astonishingly, at less than 0.01% of its 1982 value. Per capita incomes in real terms have fallen many-fold. There is an AIDS pandemic in which at least 30 per cent of the 15–45-year age group are estimated to be HIV-positive, with immense social implications (including an estimated one million orphans in a population of twelve million). The financing and provision of social services is strained. The viability of booksellers and publishers is threatened by inflation (600% by the end of 2003). The economy is shrinking, unemployment is about 70 per cent. Systems in the book industry are under severe strain because the conditions in which they emerged no longer exist. Many assumptions that were valid a few years ago no longer apply.

Publishing and Bookselling in the late 1990s

The membership of the ZBPA has fallen from some 25 active publishers in the early 1990s to around a dozen in the early 2000s. A number of new indigenous publishers have been started, but none has developed a significant list.

The book industry grew out of systems of the British book industry in the 1960s and 1970s, its nascent period. This imposed both the strengths and weaknesses of British approaches to educational publishing. The pre-1980 book industry served the book needs of a minority population, in a medium to high income bracket. The industry was small, efficient and emphasized quality. After independence, the it had to expand to serve the needs of a substantial part of the population.

While Zimbabwe has a well-established book infrastructure, it is weak in indigenous and national-language publishing. It has failed to achieve much market growth within deprived communities. Of the five major educational publishers, two are British subsidiaries. These two account for well over 70 per cent of textbook output. The other three include a Zimbabwean company, a church publisher with significant output of general books, and a publisher specializing in licensing secondary texts. The remaining publishers are active in niche markets, fiction, general titles and children's books.

Publishers have responded well in producing culturally relevant textbooks and supplementary books. The approval system of the Curriculum Development Unit (CDU) for core or supplementary books ensured adherence to locally relevant content. By the late 1990s it was felt that publishers had sufficient expertise to develop textbooks of quality and relevance, and less input and guidance was required from the CDU.

In Zimbabwe, textbooks comprise 85%–90% of the book market. Since independence, textbook provision has been carried out in a commercial, free-market system. It has led to a growth in book publishing since there is a direct correlation between returns from textbook publishing and investment in general book publishing. The tendency to solve problem areas of book provision by restrictive controls has been avoided, and dialogue with a private sector has been the major hallmark of textbook provision.

Although Zimbabwe's elevated position has been eroded recently by economic problems, it hosted the secretariat of the African Publishing Network (APNET) and Africa's premier international book fair (the ZIBF) for a number of years, and has a reputation for quality. Zimbabwean books have won awards in the Noma Award for Publishing in Africa and the Commonwealth Writers' Prize a number of times.

The major problem in the industry since the mid-1990s has been the growing financial problems of the Ministry of Education and the consequent late payments to booksellers. As a result, many booksellers defaulted in their payments to publishers. Mistrust grew between publishers and booksellers, even where these had long-standing business relations. There were severe knock-on effects. The rate of net profit fell steadily. Investment, especially by publishers in new books and authors, fell as a result of falling confidence. Experienced people left the industry because of poor prospects. No new publisher of any size has successfully emerged since the 1990s.

The character of bookselling in Zimbabwe has essentially remained intact, although the severe economic problems since 1997 have sharply eroded its capacity. Many bookselling firms have closed and the total membership of the BAZ has fallen to about 70 companies. A number of people have abandoned the industry, reducing skills. Many bookselling companies have changed hands, including the country's largest network, Textbook Sales. Retail stocks of books have been rapidly reduced in bookshops and the volume of imported books has fallen massively. Booksellers have diversified into stationery, photocopying and related services.

Amidst this crisis, interestingly, several new bookshops have opened, featuring imports from India, and otherwise concentrating on educational sales, especially in the area tertiary and commercial studies. Zimbabwe nevertheless retains a national network of booksellers in which virtually every town and city still has a bookshop, despite the downward spiral.

Rural communities have had widespread expectations that the provision of learning materials should cost little or nothing; this perception is less pronounced in urban areas. This is a legacy of the promise, for many years, of free primary education and the provision of textbook funding by the state. Since rural communities were insulated from costs surrounding textbook provision, fewer parents are now prepared for the actual cost of textbooks. This is aggravated by the widespread increase of rural and urban poverty.

Generally, school textbook-selection committees are managing the selection of textbooks, especially in circumstances of insufficient funding, in exemplary fashion: few weaknesses have been seen in selection procedures and criteria. In fact, important innovations have been developed, such as the practice (in certain subjects) of ensuring that the school has at least a few copies of every local textbook.

In a survey of book–pupil ratios conducted in 1997 (Mahere, Moyo and Pfukani, 1997), the average ratios in core primary school subjects, nationally, were:

- English   1 : 1.1
- Shona   1 : 2.1
- Ndebele   1 : 2.8
- Maths   1 : 2.4

By 1999, according to estimates, the comparative average book–pupil was close to 1:4. This implies that there are roughly half the books per pupil in core subjects compared to 1997; similar conclusions obtain for secondary schools. It is also evident that the book-stock in libraries and, indeed, the functioning of school libraries have undergone a similar level of deterioration. One estimate places the number of properly functioning school libraries at half the number there were in 1997.

Changes in the Structure of Poverty

The thinking behind 'disadvantage' in the education system has been based on a framework of historically disadvantaged rural areas. This concept assumes that poverty is 'social' and is expressed in terms of infrastructure, capital stock and investment in the public and private sector, as well as in terms of living standards. Rural dwellers are therefore by definition the poorest social group, the urban working-class are a little better off in towns with more facilities, and the urban élite are well-off. This method worked well because historical disadvantage in specific areas is a continuing reality.

However, the current situation on the ground presents a rather different picture. The biggest single problem, in terms of poverty, is HIV/AIDS. Estimates indicate that:

- 35% of sexually-active Zimbabweans are HIV positive
- the overwhelming majority of those with HIV-positive status fall within the 'economically active' group, between 20 and 45 years of age
- life expectancy in Zimbabwe in 2001 had fallen to about 36 years
- one third of children under 15 are expected to be orphans by the 2010.

The AIDS pandemic is growing exponentially. It uniformly affects rural and urban populations. Practically, it places a high proportion of suffering families in destitution very quickly. The structure of poverty is changing fast. There is hardly a school in Zimbabwe, apart from élite, high-income schools, which does not have destitute pupils, and in which the proportion of destitution is not growing.

Book NGOs

Zimbabwe has three important book NGOs which have remained active. The Zimbabwe Book Development Council (ZBDC) has run annual 'book awareness' campaigns since the 1990s, and has helped to promote the book environment by purchasing and distributing children's books. It has further (much to publishers' consternation) moved into publishing of books fairly cheaply using subsidies from funding agencies.

The Zimbabwe International Book Fair (ZIBF) has remained positive and forward-looking in a harsh economic environment. Even though the number of international exhibitors has fallen dramatically since 1997, the ZIBF has retained its position as the premier book fair in Africa. There have been many significant spin-offs for the Zimbabwe book industry as a whole, especially in raising the profile of books and debates around books.

The Rural Library Resources and Development Project (RLRDP) is the most innovative of Zimbabwe's community rural library campaigns, providing mobile rural library services in several provinces through schools.

Intervention of Donors: Project-by-Project Intervention, some Effects

The seasonal pattern of textbook provision has changed since about 1994 as a result of the gradual shift from government funding to an increasing proportion of funding form external agencies. Accurate forward planning has been an essential feature of Zimbabwe's textbook publishing. Previously, the industry hinged around three dates: the disbursements of the 70% and 30% per capita grants to rural district council schools and the budget allocations to government schools. This pattern of supply was essential in allowing publishers, booksellers and consumers to assess and market new products, look at the impact of price increases, and work out budgets. In recent years, the critical dates have become those of the disbursements of project funds, but these seldom fit into a seasonal pattern.

The 'Patchwork' Character of Policy Formulation since 1980

Since Zimbabwe has never produced a cohesive national strategy for books but has adapted and initiated decisions as needed, Zimbabwe's textbook- provision system has not one but six slightly differing systems of financing and procurement. Although the Ministry of Education has responded in recent years, in partnership with co-operating partners, to the increasing problem of getting textbooks into disadvantaged schools, this has not been achieved through long-term planning. Textbook management decisions have been made as needs arise, on a project-by-project basis.

There are no reliable national data, nor are there data-collection systems, to determine the quantitative elements of textbook procurement. Thus, there are no reliable figures on actual textbook procurement purchases, except on certain donor-funded projects. There is confusion over roles and time-frames within the procurement system, at regional, district and school levels. In short, schools and education officers cannot explain how the procurement system may function next year, or thereafter.

Development of National Language Publishing

Publishing in African languages has proved a difficult area for development. From independence, national-language publishing was championed by the Zimbabwe Literature Bureau within the Ministry of Education. A number of successes were recorded, notably the publication of a standard Shona dictionary. In 1997 the ministry closed the Literature Bureau, anticipating that the private sector would replace its services. This has not happened, and as a result national-language publishing has declined.

REFERENCES

1 Since the ZEPH monopoly was discontinued, its share of the textbook market has been steadily reduced by this competition, despite the large-scale investments of the 1980s, which continued for some years after 1991.

2 The first Ethiopian private textbook publisher of modern times started only in 1975.

3 The Tusome Vitabu project gave schools in certain regions funds to buy library books from booksellers.

4 By 1997, the Booksellers' Association of Uganda had separated from the joint Ugandan Publishers and Booksellers Association (UPABA), founded in 1992.

5 As explained previously, in many African countries finished books enter the country duty-free, while duties are levied on inputs to book manufacturing, such as paper, printing plates, film and inks.

6 The abbreviation for the Booksellers Association of Tanzania has been changed form BATA to BSAT.

BIBLIOGRAPHY

Books, periodical articles and unpublished reports

Adam, Gibrin, *Bookselling in Ghana*, African Publishing Review, 9: 2 (2000), 10–11.

ADEA (Association for the Development of Education in Africa), Working Group on Books and Learning Materials, *Compendium of Successful Reading Projects* (London: ADEA, 2003).

ADEA (Association for the Development of Education in Africa), *Formulating Education Policy: Lessons and Experiences from Sub-Saharan Africa*: Six Case Studies and Reflections from DAE Biennial Meeting (Paris: 1995).

African Publishers' Network, *Register of African Publishing Consultants* (Harare: African Publishers Network, 2nd ed., 2001).

African Publishing Review, 8: 1 (1999), 4–7. *African publishing: Perspectives and prospectives of the millennium*. [Extracted from Lars P. Christensen *et al.*, *Strengthening Publishing in Africa: An Evaluation of APNET* (Stockholm: Swedish International Development Co-operation Agency (Sida), 1998).]

African Publishing Review, 9: 6 (2000), 1–2, *APNET–PABA landmark unity agreement.*

African Publishing Review, 8: 3 (1999), 3–6, *Governments and national book development policies*. [extracted from Lars P. Christensen *et al.*, *Strengthening Publishing in Africa: An Evaluation of APNET* Stockholm: Swedish International Development Co-operation Agency (Sida), 1998.]

African Publishing Review, 10: 1 (2001), 9–11, *Move towards a national book policy in Cameroon.*

African Publishing Review, 7: 5 (1998), 6–9, *National textbook policies in Africa: A sample of current trends from five countries.*

African Publishing Review, 6: 1 (1997), 18–19, *New threat looms in South Africa – state publishing.*

African Publishing Review, 8: 3 (1999), 1–2, *Welcome change in World Bank textbook provision policy.*

African Publishing Review, 8: 1 (1999), 8–9, *World Bank bidding procedures.*

Ahmed, Medani, *In the Sudan: Characteristics and challenges of its book sector,* African Publishing Review, 7: 3 (1998), 3–4.

Ahmed, Medani, *Survey of capacity building of national publishers associations in Africa,* African Publishing Review, 8: 6 (1999), 4–5.

Altbach, Philip G (ed.), *The Challenge of the Market: Privatisation and Publishing in Africa* (Chestnut Hill, MA: Bellagio Publishing Network Research and Information Center 1996; Bellagio Studies in Publishing, 7).

Altbach, Philip G (ed.), *Publishing and Development in the Third World* (London: Hans Zell Publishers, 1992).

Altbach, Philip G. and Teferra, Damtew (eds.), *Publishing and Development: A Book of Readings* (Chestnut Hill, MA: Bellagio Publishing Network Research and Information Center, 1998; Bellagio Studies in Publishing, 9).

Altbach, Philip G. *UNESCO's Interbook Conference focuses on key publishing issues,* Bellagio Publishing Network Newsletter, 17 (1996), 12.

Altbach, Philip G., *Bellagio seminar focuses on trends in privatisation in African publishing,* Bellagio Publishing Network Newsletter, 17 (1996), 3–4.

Altbach, Philip G., *Perspectives on privatisation in African publishing,* Bellagio Publishing Network Newsletter 17 (1996), 16–18.

Altbach, Philip G., *Preparing for multinationals in African publishing: The inevitable impact,* Bellagio Publishing Network Newsletter, 22 (1998), 13–15.

Ambatchew, Michael Daniel, *The invisible Ethiopian publishers,* African Publishing Review, 11: 4 (2002), 13.

Aparicio, Alexandra, *Libraries and the publishing sector in Angola*, African Publishing Review, 6: 2 (1997), 8–9.

APNET, *Strengthening Indigenous Publishing in Africa: APNET's Five Year Strategic Plan 1999–2004* (Harare, 1999).

APNET delegation to World Bank, 8–10 December 1993, *Approaches to Book Provision in Africa: The APNET Perspective: A Synthesis of Major Issues with Recommendations; Submission to the World Bank* (Harare, 1993) [unpublished report].

Askerud, Pernille, *From Plan to Print to Pupils: A Guide to Sustainable Book Provision* (Paris: UNESCO, 1997).

Ayalew, Solomon, *Focus on the Ethiopian publishing industry*, African Publishing Review, 10: 4 (2001), 3–4.

Ayalew, Solomon, *What Ethiopian publishers have done since 1995*, African Publishing Review, 11: 1 (2002), 6–8.

Bamhare, Miriam, *A Study on Textbook Provision in Zimbabwe and Feasibility of Cooperation Amongst SADCC Countries.* Report to UNESCO (Harare, August 1993).

Bgoya, Walter, *The development and future of publishing in Africa: 12 years after Arusha I*, Development Dialogue (1997), 15–38.

Bgoya, Walter *et al* (eds.), *The Economics of Publishing Educational Materials in Africa* (London: Association for the Development of Education in Africa (ADEA), Working Group on Books and Learning Materials, 1997; Perspectives on African Book Development, 2).

Bolze, Louis, *The book publishing scene in Zimbabwe*, African Book Publishing Record, 6 (1980), 229–236.

Book Development Council of Tanzania (BAMVITA), *Preparations for Drafting a Proposal for Formulation of National Book Policy* (Dar es Salaam: 2002).

Bo Sedin Consultants AB; ASG Transport Development AB, *Study on the Distribution of Educational Materials in Tanzania. Final Report. June 1993* (Dar es Salaam: 1993).

Bo Sedin Consultants/Graphium Consult/Opifer, *Streamlining the Transition: The Implementation of Textbook Policy in Tanzania* (Dar es Salaam: 1996).

Brickhill, Paul and Walter, Scott, *Conference on Textbook Provision and Library Development in Africa: Two views*, African Book Publishing Record, 18 (1992), 233–234.

Brickhill, Paul, *Bookselling in Africa: Forgotten, silent and undermined*, Bellagio Publishing Network Newsletter, 19 (1996), 12–15.

Brickhill, Paul, *Support Arrangements to Tanzania Publishers Working with Children's Book Project: An Evaluation* (Dar es Salaam: Children's Book Project, 2001).

Brickhill, Paul et al., *Ministry of Education Sports and Culture: National Textbook and Library Policy and Strategy for Implementation: A Review and Study of Key Issues* (Harare: Ministry of Education, Sports and Culture, 1999).

Brickhill, Paul et al., *Republic of Zambia, Ministry of Education: Procurement and Distribution of Textbooks: A Study Commissioned by Ministry of Education, Zambia. Final Report* (Lusaka, May 2002).

Brickhill, Paul and Lindahl, Bengt, *Towards a National Policy for Educational Materials in Mozambique* (Maputo: Ministry of Education, April 1998).

Brown, A. K., *State publishing in Ghana: Has it benefited Ghana?* in E. Oluwasanmi, E. McLean and H. Zell (eds.), Publishing in Africa in the Seventies (Ile-Ife: University of Ife Press, 1975), 113–127.

Brunswic, Etienne and Valérien, Jean, *Planning the Development of School Textbooks: A Series of Twelve Training Modules for Education Planners and Administrators* (Paris: International Institute of Educational Planning, 1995).

Cassiau-Haurie, Christophe, *Publishing in hard times: DR Congo 1990–2000*, Bellagio Publishing Network Newsletter, 31 (2002), 16–18.

Chakava, Henry, *Wind of change at the World Bank*, African Publishing Review, 6: 5 (1997), 1–3.

Chakava, Henry, *The World Bank and African publishing*, African Publishing Review, 3: 5 (1994), 14–15.

Chakava, Henry, *Publishing in Africa: One Man's Perspective* (Chestnut Hill MA: Bellagio Publishing Network Research and Information Center, 1996; Bellagio Studies in Publishing, 6).

Chirwa, Chris, *Book publishing and liberalisation in Zambia*, Bellagio Publishing Network Newsletter, 26–27 (2000), 27–29.

Christensen, Lars *et al.*, *Strengthening Publishing in Africa: An Evaluation of APNET* (Stockholm: SIDA, 1999).

Crabbe, Richard, *The transition to privatisation in publishing: Ghana's experience*, in Philip G. Altbach (ed.), *The Challenge of the Market: Privatisation and Publishing in Africa* (Chestnut Hill, MA: Bellagio Publishing Network Research and Information Center 1996; Bellagio Studies in Publishing, 7), 29–46.

Da Crux, A. J., *Financing Textbooks and Teacher Training Materials* (London: Association for the Development of Education in Africa (ADEA), Working Group on Books and Learning Materials, 2000; Perspectives on African Book Development, 10).

Darko-Ampem, Kwasi, *Publishing for secondary education in Ghana: A policy review*, Bellagio Publishing Network Newsletter, 31 (2002), 19–23.

Das, Sukumar, *Technological developments in publishing and book distribution*, African Publishing Review, 9: 3 (2000), 5–8.

Davies, Wendy, *The future of indigenous publishing in Africa: A seminar report*, Development Dialogue (1997), 68–91.

De Freitas, Denis, *The Fight Against Piracy* ([n.p.]: International Publishers Copyright Council (IPCC), 1994).

De Souza, Oscar, *The challenge of publishing in Benin*, African Publishing Review, 6: 3 (1997), 8–9.

Dekutsey, Woeli, *The Story of APNET: A Study on the Origins, Structure, Activities and Policy of the African Publishers' Network* (Harare: APNET Secretariat, 1995).

Denning, Carmelle, *Zambia Book Sector Study Printing and Publishing: August 1990* (London: International Book Development, 1990).

Development Dialogue (1997), 92–96, *The future of indigenous publishing in Africa: Summary conclusions.*

Development Dialogue (1984), 73–140, *Developing autonomous publishing capacity in Africa.*

Evans, Matthew, *Some principles of publishing: A British view,* Development Dialogue (1984), 113–122.

Evans, Nicholas and Seeber, Monica, *The Politics of Publishing in South Africa* (Holger Ehling Publishing, 2000)

Faye, Djibril, *Publishing developments in Senegal,* African Publishing Review, 6: 3 (1997), 12.

Garzon, Alvaro, *National Book Policy: A Guide for Users in the Field* (Paris: UNESCO, 1997).

Garzon, Alvaro, *The International Free Flow of Books: A Paper Written for Interbook, UNESCO* (Paris, 1996).

Gibson, Malcolm, *The Complete Guide to Starting and Running a Bookshop* (London: Booksellers Association of Great Britain and Ireland, 1999).

Graham, Gordon, *What Publishers Do* (Paris: International Publishers' Association, 1994).

Graphium Consult and Opifer, *The Pilot Project for Publishing in Tanzania, 1993–2000: Internal Evaluation, December 2000* (Dar es Salaam: Tanzania HB, 2001).

Graphium Consult and Opifer, *Pilot Project for Publishing, PPP, Tanzania: Final Report 1997–2000* (Dar es Salaam: Tanzania HB, 2001).

Hedkvist, Fred, *Final Report on Baseline Study on Teaching Learning Material Availability in Primary Schools in Tanzania* (Umea: SIDA, Department for Democracy and Social Development, Education Division, 1996).

Ifaturoti, Damola, *New blood needed for indigenous African publishing,* Bellagio Publishing Network Newsletter, 25 (1999), 15.

Ike, Chukwuemeka, *Reading promotion in Africa,* African Publishing Review, 7: 6 (1998), 1–3.

International Trade Center UNCTAD/WTO 3rd Buyers–Sellers Meeting African Publishing and Printing Industry, *Statistical Overview of Recent Trade Patterns in Africa for Books and Printed Matter* (Harare: August 1999).

Jaygbay, Jacob, *A glimpse at publishing in Senegal*, Bellagio Publishing Network Newsletter, 19 (1996), 19–21.

Kalinga, Muhwela and Saiwaad, Abdullah, *Towards a Sustainable Book Provision: Report on Symposium held on 7 December 2000 at Tanzania Library Services, Dar es Salaam* (Dar es Salaam: President's Office, Regional Administration and Local Government and Ministry of Education and Culture, 2000).

Katama, Agnes, *Book development in Uganda*, Bellagio Publishing Network Newsletter, 20 (1997), 4–5.

Komarek, Kurt, *Publishing in Africa or African publishing*, African Publishing Review, 6: 6 (1997), 1–2.

Krog, Walter, *The Rhodesian Literature Bureau: Its aims, objects and achievements*, African Research and Documentation, 4 (1974), 1–6.

Kumar, Arvind, *The Indian Experience*, in Murray McCartney (ed.), *National Book Policies for Africa: The Key to Long Term Development: Proceedings of the Zimbabwe International Book Fair Indaba 96 Harare, Zimbabwe, 26–27 July 1996* (Harare: Zimbabwe International Book Fair Trust, 1996), 49–51.

Lawal-Solarin, Yinka, *Publishing in Nigeria*, African Publishing Review, 6: 3 (1997), 10–12.

Lema, Elieshi, *Book publishing in East Africa: A neglected strategic industry*, African Publishing Review, 11: 6 (2002), 3–4.
Lema, Elieshi, *The future of African indigenous publishing*, Bellagio Publishing Network Newsletter, 17 (1996), 4–6.

Lindahl, Bengt, *The Pilot Project for Publishing* (Dar es Salaam, 1997).

Mahere, S. M., Moyo, D., and Pfukani, P. P., *Book Pupil Ratios in Primary and Secondary Schools of Zimbabwe* (Harare: Ministry of Education, Sports and Culture, 1997).

Makotsi, Ruth, *Book trade in Africa: Potential and problems*, African Publishing Review, 7: 4 (1998), 1–3.

Makotsi, Ruth, *Expanding the Book Trade Across Africa: A Study of Current Barriers and Future Potential* (London: Association for the Development of Education in Africa (ADEA), Working Group on Books and Learning Materials, 2000; Perspectives on African Book Development, 7).

Mbilinyi D. and Omari B., *A Study of the Existence of Gender Imbalance and Sex Role Stereotyping in Tanzanian Textbooks* [Unpublished].

McCallum, Kate, *Challenging the threat of state publishing in South Africa*, African Publishing Review, 7: 1 (1998), 15.

McCallum, Kate, *South African Print Industries Cluster*, Bellagio Publishing Network Newsletter, 24 (1998), 9–10.

McCartney, Murray (ed.), *National Book Policies for Africa: The Key to Long Term Development: Proceedings of the Zimbabwe International Book Fair Indaba 96 Harare, Zimbabwe, 26–27 July 1996* (Harare: Zimbabwe International Book Fair Trust, 1996).

McCartney, Murray, *UNESCO/DANIDA: Basic Learning Materials Initiative: Uganda Country Report* (Paris, UNESCO, 1997).

Ministry of Education and Culture of Tanzania, Book Management Unit, *The Textbook Supply System in Zimbabwe: Report from a Study Visit April 1995* (Dar es Salaam: 1995).

Ministry of Education and Culture of Tanzania, *A Strategy for the Implementation of Textbook Policy* (Dar es Salaam, September 1994).

Ministry of Education and Culture of Tanzania, *New Approval System for Educational Books* (Dar es Salaam, Education Circular No. 2 of 1998, 1998).

Ministry of Education and Culture of Tanzania, *Policy on Production and Distribution of School/College Textbooks* (Dar es Salaam: December 1991).

Ministry of Education and Culture of Tanzania, *School Textbook Provision in Tanzania: Policies, Strategies and Implementation*

Issues in the Transition to a Fully Commercialised Textbook Provision System: Working Document, Roundtable Conference on Textbooks, October 3–5, 1994 (Dar es Salaam: 1994).

The Ministry of Education and Culture of Zimbawe, *Towards a National Book Policy and Strategy* (Harare: 1997).

Ministry of Education and Human Resource Development of Kenya, *National Policy on Textbooks Publication, Procurement and Supply for Primary Schools* (Nairobi, July 1998).

Ministry of education of India, Working Group on National Book Policy, National Book Development Council, *Towards a National Book Policy: A Report* (New Delhi: 1986).

The Ministry of Education of Mozambique, *Primary Education: Operational Plan for the School Fund (Caixa Escolar)* (Maputo: 1996).

Ministry of Education of Zambia, *Draft National Implementation Framework: Ministry of Education Strategic Plan, 2003–2007* (Lusaka, 2003).

Ministry of Education of Zambia, *National Book Policy: September 1998* (Lusaka, 1998).

The Ministry of Education of Zambia, *Procurement and Distribution of Textbooks* (Lusaka: 2002).

Ministry of Education of Ethiopia, *Textbook Strategy for Ethiopia* (Addis Ababa: October 1998). [Report from consultants, John Hare and Peter Stoye.]

Ministry of Education Procurement and Supplies Unit of Zambia, *National Seminar on the Educational Book Trade, Distribution and Marketing in Zambia*: Report of a MEPSU/BPAZ seminar (Lusaka, January 1995).

Ministry of Education, Sports and Culture of Zimbabwe, *School Textbooks and Library Policy* (Harare: 1998).

Minzi L. D. T. and Saiwaadand A., *Study on Bookselling in Tanzania* [unpublished]

Momoh, Ansu, *National book policy*, Bellagio Publishing Network Newsletter, 21 (1997), 11–12.

Momoh, Ansu, *Problems of book publishing in Sierra Leone*, Bellagio Publishing Network Newsletter, 19 (1996), 15–19.

Moshoeshoe-Chadzingwa, M. M., *Publishing in Lesotho*, African Publishing Review, 4: 4 (1995), 10–11.

Mosuro, Kolade, *Publishing and bookselling: A bookseller's observations*, African Publishing Review, 10: 1 (2001), 3–5.

Mpanga, Egidio H., *Publishing in Malawi*, African Publishing Review, 6: 6 (1997), 10–11.

Mugiri, Ephantus *et al.*, *Strategy for School Textbook Provision in Zimbabwe* (Harare, 1998) [Report to Ministry of Education, Sport and Culture and SIDA.]

Muhate, Zephanias, *More effective book distribution: The Mozambique experience*, African Publishing Review, 10: 2 (2001), 5–6.

Muita, David N., *Kenya introduces national textbook policy*, Bellagio Publishing Network Newsletter, 23 (1998), 2–3.

Mulokozo, M. M., *Creative literature, language and African identity*, African Publishing Review, 11: 6 (2002), 5–7.

Navarro, Julio, *The book world in Mozambique*, African Publishing Review, 6: 2 (1997), 10–11.

Nwankwo, Victor, *To hell with indigenous publishing in Africa*, Bellagio Publishing Network Newsletter, 19 (1996), 25–27.

Nwankwo, Victor, *The Network is Working: Chairman's Report to the APNET General Council Nairobi, May 1995* (Harare: APNET, 1995).

Nyambura, Gillian, *Capacity building challenges for African publishers*, African Publishing Review, 7: 1 (1998), 3–4.

Nyambura, Gillian, *Research on capital for publishers*, African Publishing Review, 8: 6 (1999), 11.

Nyambura, Gillian, *Strengthening national publishers' associations*, African Publishing Review, 6: 3 (1997), 1–3.

Nyarike, Lily, *Bookselling in Kenya*, African Publishing Review, 9: 2 (2000), 9.

Ofei, Eric, *The state of publishing in Ghana today*, Bellagio Publishing Network Newsletter, 20 (1997), 14–17.

Ofori-Mensah, Akoss, *Book scheme for basic schools in Ghana*, Bellagio Publishing Network Newsletter, 26–27 (2000), 19–21.

Ofori-Mensah, Akoss, *Book scheme programme in Ghana*, African Publishing Review, 9: 3 (2000), 14.

Ojeniyi, Ayo, *The impact of African publishing on world literature*, African Publishing Review, 11: 4 (2002), 3–5.

Okwilagwe, Oshiotse Andrew, *Book Publishing in Nigeria*(Ibadan: Stirling-Horden, 2001).

Oluwasanmi, E., McLean, E., and Zell, H (eds.), *Publishing in Africa in the Seventies* (Ile-Ife: University of Ife Press, 1975).

Pearce, Douglas, *Textbook Production in Developing Countries: Some Problems of Preparation, Production and Distribution* (Paris: UNESCO, 1982; Studies on Books and Reading, 7).

Pehrsson and Grahm, *Textbooks for All*; A. Smart, *A Strategy for Implementing a New Educational Materials Policy in Primary Schools* (London: International Book Development, 2003).

Pehrsson K. and Grahm, Leif, *Textbooks for All: PPP: The First Step on a Long Journey* (Stockholm: Sida, 2004). [Unpublished]

Pontefract, Caroline *et al.*, *Towards a unified textbook system in Kenya*, Bellagio Publishing Network Newsletter, 26–27 (2000), 21–23.

Priestley, Carol (ed.), *Development Directory of Indigenous Publishing 1995* (Harare: African Publishers' Network, 1995).

Priestley, Carol, *Book and Publishing Assistance Programmes* (Chestnut Hill, MA: Bellagio Publishing Network Research and Information Center, rev. edn., 2000; Bellagio Studies in Publishing, 11).

Read, Tony *et al.*, *Upgrading Book Distribution in Africa* (London: Association for the Development of Education in Africa (ADEA),

Working Group on Books and Learning Materials, 2001; Perspectives on African Book Development, 12).

Reece, Jane, *Book development councils in Africa: Part two: The Zimbabwean story*, African Publishing Review, 4: 3 (1995), 12–14.

Reece, Jane, *The Zimbabwean Publishing Scene: A Current View* (Harare: Zimbabwe International Book Fair, 1994).

Rosenberg, Diana (ed.), *Books for Schools: Improving Access to Supplementary Reading Materials in Africa* (London: Association for the Development of Education in Africa (ADEA), Working Group on Books and Learning Materials, 2000; Perspectives on African Book Development, 9).

Ross, Alan, *The impact of technology on the publishing trade*, African Publishing Review, 9: 3 (2000), 2–4.

Rudloff, Biogang Bon, *Bookselling in Botswana*, African Publishing Review, 9: 2 (2000), 9–10.

Saiwaad, Abdullah, *An informal history of publishing in Tanzania*, African Publishing Review, 6: 2 (1997), 15.

Salzano, Carmella, *Making Book Coordination Work!* (London: Association for the Development of Education in Africa (ADEA), Working Group on Books and Learning Materials, 2002; Perspectives on African Book Development, 13).

SIDA, Department for Democracy and Social Development, Education Division, *SIDA Support to Educational Materials Programmes: A Review of Experience and Current Strategies* (Stockholm: January 1997).

SIDA, Department for Democracy and Social Development, Education Division, *Policy for SIDA Cooperation in Basic Education and Education Reform* (Stockholm: January 1996).

SIDA/FINNIDA, *Study on Educational Materials Provision and Utilisation. Final Report. March 1995* (Zambia, Lusaka, Ministry of Education, 1995). [Report.]

Smart, A. *A Strategy for Implementing a New Educational Materials Policy in Primary Schools* (London: IBD, 2003).

Sosale, Shobana, *Educational Publishing in Global Perspective – Capacity Building and Trends*, The World Bank (1999)

Sow, Mamadou Aliou, *A Guinean perspective: Book publishing and distribution*. Bellagio Publishing Network Newsletter, 23 (1998), 11–12.

Sow, Mamadou Aliou, *Publishing in national languages: Some key issues in Guinea*, African Publishing Review, 6: 6 (1997), 3.

Stebbing, Lyle, *Report on the Bellagio Publishing Network Roundtable on Book Marketing and Distribution in Africa*. Supplement to African Publishing Review, 4: 3 (1995).

Stringer, Roger, *Publishing in Zimbabwe*, in Hector Blackhurst (ed.), *Africa Bibliography 1986* (Manchester: Manchester University Press, 1987), xvi–xxvi.

Stringer, Roger (ed.), *The Book Chain in Anglophone Africa* (Oxford: International Network for the Availability of Scientific Publications (INASP), 2002).

The British Council, *Conference on Textbook Provision and Library Development in Africa* (Manchester, 1992).

Tsekpo, Seth, *Publishing in local languages in Ghana*, African Publishing Review, 6: 1 (1997), 17.

Tshimanga, Freddie Ngandu and Tita, Julius Che, *Cameroon publishers against monopoly*, African Publishing Review, 8: 1 (1999), 1–3.

Tugaineyo, Catherine, *Current Priorities in Book Policy in Uganda*. Paper presented at ADEA Steering Committee Meeting, London, 13–14 March 2003.

Tumusiime, James, *The state of publishing in Uganda*, in Carol Priestley (ed.), *Development Directory of Indigenous Publishing 1995* (Harare: African Publishers' Network, 1995), 88–89.

Tumusiime, James, *Book procurement: Will the World Bank change strategy?*, Bellagio Publishing Network Newsletter, 21 (1997), 2–3.

Tumusiime, James, *Uganda's book industry: Flourishing without roots*, Bellagio Publishing Network Newsletter, 22 (1998), 12–13.

Tumusiime, James, *World Bank changes textbook provision policy*, Bellagio Publishing Network Newsletter, 25 (1999), 2–3.

UNESCO. *Importation of Educational, Scientific and Cultural Materials: A Guide to the Operation of the Florence Agreement and its Protocol* (Paris: UNESCO, 4th edn., 1978).

Van der Werk, Jan Kees, *The Right to One's Own Publishing Firm: Publishing in Africa*. Excerpts of a Paper Presented at the Seminar on Communication, Cultures and Development, Harare, May 1990.

Waddington, Jenny, *Nigeria: Education and books in crisis*, African Publishing Review, 3: 5 (1994), 18–19.

Walter, Scott *et al.*, *National Book Sector Outlines: Discussion Paper prepared for Interbook, UNESCO* (Paris, 1996).

Wassie, Atnafu, *Ethiopia: A new beginning in publishing*, Bellagio Publishing Network Newsletter, 16 (1996), 9–11.

Wong Chee, Harold, *Zimbabwe International Book Fair (ZIBF): Strategic Planning Workshop: 3–5 June 1997* (Harare: Zimbabwe International Book Fair, 1997).

World Bank, *World Bank Support for Provision of Textbooks in Sub-Saharan Africa 1985–2000* (Washington: World Bank, 2002; Africa Region Human Development Working Papers Series).

Zell, Hans, *The Book Trade of the World: Vol. IV – Africa: Introduction* (Munich: K.G. Saur, 1984).

Zimbabwe Book Publishers Association, *Full Proposals for World Bank Assistance to the Publishing Industry* (Harare: April 1991).

Zimbabwe International Book Fair, 2000, *Pan-African Booksellers Association. Workshop on Publishers–Booksellers Interface.* (Harare). [Workshop facilitator's report.]

NOTES

NOTES

NOTES

NOTES

NOTES

NOTES